TH
BERMONDSEY
MURDER

To To

Nick Kaaven

For Warren, Ella and Ethan,
whose ancestors lived nearby

THE
BERMONDSEY
MURDER

SCOTLAND YARD'S FIRST GREAT
CHALLENGE & DICKENS' INSPIRATION

ANGELA BUCKLEY

PEN & SWORD
TRUE CRIME

First published in Great Britain in 2024 by
PEN AND SWORD TRUE CRIME
An imprint of
Pen & Sword Books Ltd
Yorkshire – Philadelphia

ISBN 978 1 39904 420 2

A CIP catalogue record for this book is available from the British Library.

Typeset in Times New Roman 11.5/14 by SJmagic DESIGN SERVICES, India.
Printed and bound in the UK by CPI Group (UK) Ltd, Croydon, CR0 4YY.

Pen & Sword Books Limited incorporates the imprints of Atlas, Archaeology,
Aviation, Discovery, Family History, Fiction, History, Maritime, Military,
Military Classics, Politics, Select, Transport, True Crime, Air World, Frontline
Publishing, Leo Cooper, Remember When, Seaforth Publishing, The Praetorian
Press, Wharncliffe Local History, Wharncliffe Transport, Wharncliffe True Crime
and White Owl.

For a complete list of Pen & Sword titles please contact
PEN & SWORD BOOKS LIMITED
George House, Units 12 & 13, Beevor Street, Off Pontefract Road,
Barnsley, South Yorkshire, S71 1HN, England
E-mail: enquiries@pen-and-sword.co.uk
Website: www.pen-and-sword.co.uk

or
PEN AND SWORD BOOKS
1950 Lawrence Rd, Havertown, PA 19083, USA
E-mail: uspen-and-sword@casematepublishers.com
Website: www.penandswordbooks.com

Contents

Preface

Bermondsey is one of my favourite parts of London. Steeped in history, it is a lively and culturally rich district. It was also the home to a branch of our family's history. My husband's 3 x great-grandparents lived in Bermondsey for a century, and they were there when Charles Dickens was exploring the dark streets of its seedy underworld.

By the time of the cholera epidemic in 1849, the Corderoys had been living in Bermondsey for eighteen years. William and Eleanor had moved south of the river from Shoreditch in 1831, with their family of four sons: William junior, aged 6; Thomas, 4; James, 2; and 1-year-old George. William found work as a hoop bender for a local cooper. However, they did not fare well in their new home, as baby George died soon after their arrival and was buried in the graveyard of St Mary Magdalen's church. Over the next almost two decades, they had nine more children, four of whom died in infancy.

William and Eleanor's thirteenth child, Joseph, was born in April 1849. He only survived for three weeks, and his death certificate revealed that he had died of 'want of breast milk': the Corderoys were living in one of the poorest and most unsanitary districts of London. When Joseph died, they were lodging in George Row, close to the infamous Jacob's Island, which shortly after became known as 'the capital of cholera'. Journalist Henry Mayhew described the squalid, cramped lodgings along the street and the devastating effects of the disease on the residents. That summer, at the height of the epidemic, the Corderoys lost yet another son. This time, their eldest child, William, aged 24, died at Guy's Hospital of fluid on the brain, which may have been caused by a tumour.

Shortly after these tragic events took place, PC Barnes and PC Burton walked past the same hospital towards Minver Place, where they would find the body of missing customs officer, Patrick O'Connor. The Corderoys lived just 15 minutes' walk away. Despite their own tragedies, they most certainly would have heard about the 'Bermondsey Horror' – perhaps they stopped to listen to the ballads sung in the neighbourhood (they were illiterate) and discussed this infamous case with their neighbours. Maybe they visited the crime scene, as was customary, to get a glimpse of the action, or they might even have attended the execution of the convicted murderers. It was through my investigation into the family's past that I came across this brutal murder.

Today, although the area has been redeveloped, if you follow in the footsteps of the two police officers on their way to make their gruesome discovery, you can still see vestiges of the past. When you step out of London Bridge tube station beneath the dazzling tower of the Shard, it doesn't take long to be back in the small, labyrinthine streets of old Bermondsey. Passing Guy's Hospital and then walking down Weston Street, you soon come to the Leather Exchange building with its stonework friezes depicting the processes of leather-tanning. Built in 1878, this replaced the old leather market, which had first opened in 1833. Maria and Frederick Manning, who were hanged for the murder of Patrick O'Connor in 1849, lived opposite, in Minver Place, which has now disappeared.

When I wandered round these streets for the first time, on a wet summer's day, it brought this dramatic and shocking crime case back to life. Using original documents, such as the police reports and trial records, I have pieced together this legendary true crime story in an attempt to verify the facts. Where sources have differed, I have selected the information which I consider to be the most accurate. It is a tale of passion, greed and self-interest, with a brutal murder and a desperate race to catch the killers. It also sheds a fascinating light on aspects of mid-nineteenth century society, including the impact of the cholera epidemic, the emerging role of police detectives, and the development of new technologies, such as the telegraph.

The case was sensationalised at the time as the prime suspects were a married couple and, due to Victorian stereotypes and opinions towards women, Maria Manning instantly became a 'femme fatale'. Almost two centuries later, this historical homicide is still well known, especially as two of the protagonists in this real-life drama were immortalised by Charles Dickens.

Angela Buckley
Bermondsey, 2023

Chapter 1

'A frightful murder'

Shortly before 1 pm on Friday 17 August 1849, two police constables met at the corner of St Thomas Street and Weston Street in Bermondsey, on the south side of the Thames. Although the day was overcast with a strong breeze, the officers would have been hot in their regulation uniform of tightly buttoned thick blue tunics with stiff collars, and top hats. PC Barnes from K Division in Stepney, who was stationed at Arbour Square police station, had crossed the river at London Bridge and then walked past Guy's Hospital to join his colleague PC Burton from Stones End police station in M Division, which served Southwark. Together, the officers made their way through the crowded tenements, warehouses, builders' yards and tanneries of Weston Street towards Minver Place on New Weston Street, where they were about to make a gruesome discovery.

In the early decades of the nineteenth century, Bermondsey, together with its neighbouring district of Rotherhithe, in the borough of Southwark, was one of the most important industrial centres of Victorian England. In the eighteenth century, Bermondsey had been a spa town but by the early 1800s, the ancient river stairs and waterways of Shad Thames, the historic street that gives its name to the surrounding area, had been transformed into one of the busiest cargo ports in Great Britain. Ships bearing exotic goods from all over the British empire came to dock in the River Thames. Merchandise was unloaded onto the wharves at Bermondsey, where it was stored and processed in the warehouses and manufactories along the river and in its vicinity. In 1853, when Charles Dickens accompanied the Thames River Police on a nocturnal excursion, he described passing through the rows of ships moored on the river: 'the tiers were so like houses, in the dark, that I could almost have believed myself in the narrower byways of Venice' ('Down with the Tide', *Household Words*, 5 February 1853). Many household brands, such as Peek Freans biscuits, Jacobs cream crackers, Courage beer, Hartley's jam and Sarson's malt vinegar have their origins in Bermondsey, which became known as 'London's Larder'.

In 1849, Bermondsey was the centre of the leather trade. Animal skins had been processed and traded in the district since medieval times because of its freshwater tidal streams and proximity to the city of London. Easy access to water from the river; oak tree bark, which was used in the tanning process; and cattle hides from the capital's butchers made this the ideal location for the industry; by the end of the 1700s, it produced a third of the leather in the United Kingdom. Tanneries and processing plants populated the area, with their characteristic stink of rotting flesh and noxious chemicals, which made the air reek with 'evil smells' as described by Charles Dickens junior in his *Dictionary of London*. The process of leather dressing involved soaking the hides in urine and lime, which loosened the hairs and flesh to aid removal. Next, the skins were pounded with dog faeces (known as 'pure') to soften them. Following this, the leather was oiled and prepared by immersing the skins in a pit filled with chemicals. The tanned hide was then rolled and dried ready for trading in the leather market at the heart of Bermondsey.

Amid the stench of the tan pits, a few minutes' walk from Guy's Hospital and London Bridge railway station, Police Constables Henry Barnes and James Burton passed by the rows of soot-blackened back-to-back houses, with listless children gazing out from dank doorways. The officers walked through the bustle and clamour of narrow streets lined with hop warehouses, breweries and rope works as they made their way past the tanneries in the leather-making district, towards the Bermondsey Leather Market, where tens of thousands of skins were processed and sold. The leather market had opened in 1833, after being relocated from Leadenhall Market and the building was replaced in 1878.

The constables were investigating a missing person from PC Barnes' patch in Stepney. Patrick O'Connor, a customs gauger at the London Docks, had not been seen for just over a week. He had left his lodgings in Mile End Road, Stepney, at 7.30 am on Thursday 9 August. Later that day, at about 4.45 pm after finishing work, he bumped into two colleagues, William Patrick Keating and David Graham, on the south side of London Bridge, to whom he mentioned that he was heading to Frederick Manning's house in New Weston Street, Bermondsey. His acquaintances were not surprised by this, as it was O'Connor's usual practice; he was a frequent visitor to Manning's home, being particularly friendly with his wife Maria. However, when Patrick failed to turn up for work the following day, his colleagues became suspicious.

On Friday, as there was still no sign of him, his friends took action. Keating went to O'Connor's lodgings in Mile End to look for him, but he was not there. Another colleague, William Flynn, who was also Patrick's relative, reported him missing to PC John Wright at Stones End police station, the headquarters of M Division, Southwark, where he shared his suspicions that 'foul play had been directed towards him [O'Connor]'. The following day, William Keating tried O'Connor's lodgings again, but there was no sign of the customs officer having returned there. On Sunday, Patrick's friends paid a visit to his landlady, Ann Armes, who told them that he hadn't been home since Thursday. She suggested they try Maria Manning who 'was a great friend of his'. Keating and Graham went straight to Minver Place to see if Mrs Manning had any news of him.

When they arrived at the house about midday, Maria opened the door and invited the two men in. Keating asked her if Patrick had come to the house for dinner on the previous Thursday, as he had planned. She replied that he had not turned up. Keating commented that it was strange, as Patrick had been seen coming over London Bridge that evening and was clearly heading in her direction. Mrs Manning had nothing to say to this, except to accuse O'Connor of being 'ungentlemanly' in missing their dinner date. When Keating questioned her about her visit to O'Connor's lodgings on the night he disappeared, she explained that she had gone to inquire about his health, as he had been at her house the night before and had been unwell. She recounted how he had laid on the sofa and she had rubbed eau de cologne on his face. Keating then asked if he could see her husband, but she said that he was out at church. William suggested coming back later, but she put them off by saying that she and Frederick were going out to tea. He later described Mrs Manning's demeanour as 'nervous'.

Later that Sunday, William Flynn also paid a visit to Minver Place, but there was no one in. Afterwards, he met up with Keating and Graham, and they went to Stones End police station to ask the police if they could put a watch on the Mannings' house and if PC Wright could visit Minver Place with them the following day. With still no word from the missing man by the end of the weekend, his friends issued handbills for information. Funded and organised by William Flynn, they were circulated to all the police stations in London and to the press:

£10 REWARD! MISSING, Mr. Patrick O'Connor, who left his residence, 21, Greenwood-street, Mile End Road, on

THURSDAY, the 9th Inst., at half-past Seven o'Clock; was last seen at London Bridge, about 5 o'Clock the same day. DESCRIPTION – About 50 Years of Age, 5ft. 11in. high, Fair Complexion, Light Hair, Sandy Whiskers, Aquiline Nose, Stout made, Stoops a little when walking, wears a Set of False Teeth, Dressed in a Black Dress Coat, Light Plaid Trousers, Black Silk Stock, and Albert Boots. Any Person giving such Information as will lead to his discovery, shall receive the above Reward, by applying as above, or at the Arbour Square Police Station.

On Monday 13 August, PC Henry Barnes and PC James Burton were instructed by their respective superiors to look for the customs officer and they set out to get to the bottom of this pressing and worrying matter.

The row of four 'respectable' houses of Minver Place (also written as 'Miniver' and 'Minerva') was in the middle of New Weston Street, on the corner of Guy Street. They were approached at the front by a flight of several stone steps from the street, with iron railings on either side. The façades were stuccoed to the first-floor windows, above which was a broad cornice. The roofs were flat with chimneys. Each house had a small garden at the rear, overlooked by a kitchen window and accessed by a back door. Inside, there were six rooms over three floors; with two parlours on the ground floor, two bedrooms above and two kitchens in the basement below. The two-storey houses were built by James Coleman, who lived at number one. He ran the construction business with his brother, and they had sixty employees. He had named the row of new houses after their home town of St Minver in Cornwall. Coleman was the landlord of number three, which was next door but one to his house. He had sublet it for six months to Frederick and Maria Manning. The builder later revealed that he had not let the house directly to the couple, but that a previous tenant had wanted to leave and had found them to replace him. Maria Manning had given Patrick O'Connor's name and work address to the landlord's brother. James visited the London dockyard where he saw O'Connor, who had provided a reference for his prospective tenants. After paying the half quarter's rent in advance, Mr and Mrs Manning took on the tenancy on 25 March.

At 10 am on Monday 13 August, PC Barnes, who was in uniform, Patrick's cousin William Flynn and PC John Wright, who was wearing plain clothes, visited Minver Place. Mrs Manning answered the door. Flynn described her as 'a handsome well-dressed 30-year-old with a slight French accent'.

She was home alone and invited them into the front parlour, where PC Wright asked her if she had seen O'Connor. Manning said she had not seen him since the previous Wednesday when he had been 'very tipsy', and his friend Pierce Walsh had had to escort him home. Flynn commented on how strange it all was. Maria agreed and explained his continued absence by saying that he was a 'very fickle-minded man', and he often visited their house but left again after a few minutes. She added that he might be at Walsh's house in Vauxhall. Mrs Manning then sighed, saying, 'Poor Mr O'Connor! He was the best friend I had in London!' At this, her face paled and Flynn noticed that she was shaking; when he inquired after her health, she told him that she had been ill some six weeks earlier and had not yet recovered. He asked her if she had visited O'Connor's lodgings on Thursday 9 August, to which she replied that she had. As the party left, Mrs Manning remarked, 'You gentlemen are very susceptible,' but offered no further comments. During the informal interview, which lasted about 20 minutes, Maria had responded to their questions 'with coolness and composure' and, according to *The Morning Post*, 'her coolness quite threw the police off their guard.' They did not press her any further.

That evening, about 8 pm, PC Barnes, William Keating, William Flynn and a Mr Pervis went to O'Connor's lodgings at 21 Greenwood Street, Mile End Road. In the presence of his landlady, Ann Armes, the police officer searched O'Connor's room. He forced open a trunk in which they found an unlocked cash box. Inside were a few IOUs and memoranda but no shares or money. As well as working for the customs, Patrick O'Connor was a moneylender, and it was believed that he had as much as £4,000 (about £400,000 in today's value) in railway shares, all of which were missing. His landlady confirmed that no one had been into Patrick's room since the previous Friday evening, when Maria Manning had visited for a second time since the lodger's disappearance. This new piece of information aroused PC Barnes' suspicions even further.

By the next morning, Patrick's friends had become extremely concerned for his safety and 'sinister apprehensions began to be entertained respecting his fate' (*The Morning Post*, 20 August 1849). They returned once again to Minver Place with Constables Barnes and Burton. Acquiring a key from a neighbour, they entered the property but found it empty; no one was at home. They searched both the front and back kitchens but, despite the house being suspiciously 'disordered', found no evidence to suggest that O'Connor had been there. Despite this, the police removed several personal items including twenty-eight or thirty pieces of recently washed linen, which was piled up on the shelves of a cupboard in the front kitchen, and two pencil portraits of the recent inhabitants. PC Burton found a coal shovel, which he also took away. His colleague PC Barnes noticed that the flagstones in the back kitchen looked as if they had recently been paved and scrubbed. However, they left the premises without taking any further action.

A few days later, there was no new information on the whereabouts of the missing man. However, when PC Barnes received reports of threats made to O'Connor by Frederick Manning, he proceeded straight back to Bermondsey with Constable Burton. On Friday 17 August, they arrived at 3 Minver Place just after 1 pm and the landlord gave them a key to the property.

The two officers began by searching the garden, which was small with a few shrubs and some scarlet-runners, a type of runner bean. Finding no obvious signs of disturbance, they returned to the front of the building, and PC Burton opened the door to let his colleague in. As the police constables entered from the street, they stepped straight into the front parlour on the ground floor. This substantial room ran the width of the house and had a large fireplace on the right-hand wall. They passed through the room to the back parlour, which was directly behind. To the left was a small passage with stairs leading down to the basement and up to the first floor. Constables Barnes and Burton descended the stairs to the kitchens, which were directly below the parlours. Both kitchens had a fireplace, and the front room was larger with a cupboard. The police officers walked through the front kitchen into the back one, which had a window with iron bars that looked out into the garden.

As they inspected the flagstones of the back kitchen in the dim light, 'sharp-sighted' PC Barnes spotted a damp patch between the edges of two of the flagstones on the floor. He further observed that the cement between the slabs was of a slightly different colour to the others and that, although the flagstones in both kitchens had been cleaned, it looked as if dust had been swept onto these two and the surrounding ones, perhaps to cover up recent scrubbing. Barnes tested the mortar between the joints with his penknife and found that it was soft. Suspecting that the floor had been disturbed, he called his colleague who, after borrowing a crowbar from a neighbour, helped him to lever up the flagstones. Made of Yorkshire stone, a type of sandstone known for its durability, the flags were thick and heavy; one measured 3 feet by 2 feet and the other was 2 feet square. PC Burton lifted one stone with a boat hook, while PC Barnes raised the other with the crowbar. Underneath was a layer of wet mortar and then earth, which was composed of limestone, hardcore and clay, as would have been used in the house's construction. The earth was damp and loose. After calling for further assistance, they began to dig.

The officers started by removing the loose soil with a shovel and, after a foot of digging, they came across a piece of rag (some newspapers speculated that it was, in fact, a brand-new woman's stocking). They continued to dig, and PC Barnes uncovered a human toe 'protruding through the mould'. Another few inches revealed the rest of the body. The naked man was lying on his front, with his legs doubled up behind him and tied around his thighs with a rope resembling a clothes line. The man's head was buried slightly lower in the ground, embedded in slack lime, which 'had commenced its work of destruction … the flesh in several places being eaten away' (*Lloyd's Weekly*, 19 August 1849).

While they had been carrying out their excavation, Samuel Meggitt Lockwood arrived at the house. The surgeon, who lived nearby in Newington, had heard about the discovery and rushed to the address, closely followed by a newspaper reporter. Lockwood entered the back kitchen just as the body was being uncovered. The dead man's head was battered and there was a bulge in his temple above the right eye, which suggested that a bullet might have lodged there. As he watched the officers uncovering the body, the surgeon reached down and removed a set of false teeth from the victim's mouth.

The hole in which the body had been buried was 5 feet long and 2 feet wide. The officers had dug to a depth of between 2 and 3 feet. Once the body had been completely exposed, they removed it from its shallow grave and carried it into the front kitchen, where Lockwood immediately undertook an initial examination. He was assisted by another surgeon George Odling who had, by this time, joined him.

The surgeons began by examining the head. The small lump over the right eye was hard but moveable. Lockwood cut into the flesh and removed a bullet, as suspected. There was a hole in the skull under the site of the bullet, directly over the eye, but it had not pierced the skin and extensive fractures at the back of the head prevented them from tracing the bullet's trajectory. The brain had decomposed so much that it was almost in liquid form.

On discovery of the body, the police had sent messages to the missing man's colleagues. William Flynn and Pierce Walsh arrived at the house first, as the body was being removed from the hole. From the shape of the chin and the set of false teeth, they identified the victim as their friend, Patrick O'Connor.

Chapter 2

'The ill-fated gentleman'

The inquest into Patrick O'Connor's death took place on Saturday 18 August in the New Leather Market Tavern (also known as the Skinmarket Tavern) on New Weston Street, close to the Bermondsey Leather Market and to Minver Place where his remains were discovered. The current inn, the Leather Exchange, dates from 1878.

It was customary for inquests to be held in public houses, as they required a large room for the proceedings. As described by Charles Dickens in *Bleak House*: 'The coroner frequents more public-houses than any man alive. The smell of sawdust, beer, tobacco-smoke, and spirits is inseparable in his vocation from death in its most awful shapes.' Even though the coroner would have been used to this, it would have been a major event for landlord Henry Bailey, who had only taken over the licence for the tavern the previous month.

The proceedings began at 2 pm presided over by William Carter, the coroner for Surrey. The large room was crammed full of spectators and the overcrowding caused such noise and confusion that, according to the press, it was difficult for the members of the coroner's court to make themselves heard. Most of those present were friends and relatives of the deceased, with the notable absence of his brother, the Reverend Dr Thomas O'Connor, who had arrived in London the previous evening from Ireland but did not appear at the inquest. The jury of fourteen men were described in *The Morning Post* as 'the most respectable tradesmen in the neighbourhood'. After the jurors were sworn in, the coroner explained that, as he had received news of the event late the previous evening and did not know the important details of the case, he had instructed that the body should stay in situ at 3 Minver Place overnight. He requested that the jury view the body, so that they might give their agreement for the necessary medical examination to take place. Following this, they would seek to identify the body formally through the witness testimonies so that the family could arrange the burial as soon as possible. As the jury prepared to leave the room for the viewing, one member raised an objection to the presence of another.

Mr Meade, who was a friend of the deceased, objected that James Coleman, the builder of the houses at Minver Place and the Mannings' landlord, was on the jury, as he might be later required as a witness. The coroner granted the objection and Coleman was removed from the list. The remaining thirteen jurors then proceeded to Minver Place to view the body. As the house was still teeming with people anxious to glean any titbits of information about the crime, the police had to work hard to keep the thoroughfare clear so that the coroner and members of the jury could enter the property.

As instructed by the coroner, Patrick O'Connor's body was still lying naked in the front kitchen. The legs had been re-tied to the thighs with a new piece of rope so that the jury could get a good impression of how it had appeared when it had been excavated from the hole in the back kitchen floor. Although the body had been washed, it was still partly covered with quicklime, and decomposition was quite advanced; there was extensive discoloration of the face, neck and chest. *The Morning Post* reported that his 'remarkably thin and projecting' chin was visible, as was the mouth, which was toothless now that the false teeth had been removed. Having performed this unpleasant duty, the jury returned to the tavern ready for the start of the formal proceedings.

The first witness was Patrick's friend Pierce Walsh, a former grocer's clerk from Islington. Walsh confirmed the identity of the body, which he had seen at 3 Minver Place on the day of its discovery: 'I have not the slightest reasonable doubt as to the identity of that body. I recognised it by its features.' He explained that he had met O'Connor in April. Although they had not been acquainted for long, Walsh had known Patrick's friends for many years in Ireland and they had given letters of introduction to the customs officer. Calling him 'my personal friend', he described to the jury how they were connected through the marriage of Patrick's sister to his cousin. Walsh confirmed that O'Connor lived at 21 Greenwood Street, Mile End Road, and that he was single. He went on to recall the last time he had seen the deceased alive.

Pierce and Patrick had spent the evening together on Wednesday 8 August in the company of the Mannings. The friends had met at 6 pm at Patrick's lodgings in Mile End Road. Walsh remembered how, when he had arrived, he found O'Connor lying on the sofa and he 'seemed as if he had been drinking'. At this point in the testimony, Mr Meade interjected saying that the witness must have made a mistake as the deceased had been a teetotaller for some 13 years. Walsh did not respond and continued his account. Later that evening, Walsh and O'Connor left for Bermondsey, arriving at Minver Place at about 9.45 pm. Mrs Manning opened the door to them, and the two men went into the front parlour. They sat down and, after a while, Maria remarked to Patrick: 'Mr O'Connor, why did you not come to dinner today? We kept dinner waiting an hour for you.' Before he had time to answer, she asked, 'Did you not get my note?' When O'Connor replied 'No', she explained that she had sent a letter to him at the docks inviting him to dinner earlier that evening. Walsh suggested to her that she had posted the note too late and that it had arrived after O'Connor had left work for the day. She replied, 'It was two o'clock, and he will receive it tomorrow,' and the matter was not discussed any further. In court Mr Meade confirmed that the jury had possession of the note, but he did not produce it as evidence. However, it was reported in *Clark's Edition* to have stated: 'Dear O'Connor: We shall be happy to see you to dine with us today at half-past five o'clock. Yours affection [*sic*], Maria Manning.'

The witness continued his account of the evening, telling the coroner that O'Connor had mentioned to Mrs Manning that he had received the balance of a bill that day. The bill, which was to the value of £5 and 6 pence, had been owed to him by a Mr Pitts, a grocer from Bethnal Green Road. Walsh had executed it on O'Connor's behalf, receiving the cash as four sovereigns, two half sovereigns and 6 pence. Walsh was rather surprised that Mrs Manning seemed to know so much about O'Connor's transactions, and intimated that he must have discussed such matters with her previously. She mentioned three other bills, saying, 'I suppose you will take proceedings against him [Mr Pitts] for their recovery.' Patrick replied that he would.

After this, the conversation at 3 Minver Place fell silent while O'Connor and Frederick Manning smoked a pipe. Soon after, Patrick began to feel faint, although he had not been drinking, and he lay down on the sofa. The Mannings brought him some brandy and water, and Maria poured a liquid out of a bottle to rub on his temples; Walsh thought it was eau de cologne and stated that it had been ineffective in reviving O'Connor. When he eventually came to, Patrick refused the brandy and after he had drunk some water, he resumed smoking. While O'Connor was recovering, Frederick engaged Walsh in conversation. Walsh told the court that he thought that his friend had remained in the room the whole time, but he conceded that he might have gone into the yard for a minute for some fresh air. The two men left the Mannings' house at about 11.20 pm. They passed through St Thomas Street and by Guy's Hospital, before crossing London Bridge and continuing into Whitechapel. At the corner of Leman Street and Commercial Street, they said goodnight. When they parted company at midnight, Walsh said that the deceased was 'in a good state of health'. As they had walked so far, he had no reason to think that O'Connor was planning to return to Bermondsey that evening.

The coroner asked Walsh if he knew of any specific reason for visiting the Mannings that evening. Walsh answered: 'I had no object to come there, but he (the deceased) had, though I did not understand from him his object.' He continued by saying that he had visited the couple with O'Connor at least four times previously, and that his friend and Mrs Manning 'were very intimate'. Pierce Walsh concluded his testimony by saying that O'Connor had told him that he had known Mr and Mrs Manning for some time, having met Maria when she had been living with the Duchess of Sutherland, for whom she worked as a lady's maid. Before her marriage to Frederick Manning, O'Connor used to call on her at the duchess's mansion. A juror then asked, 'Did you think there was any improper connection going on between them?' to which Walsh replied, 'I do not think it. I have no knowledge of the fact.' Nor did he know anything about any financial transactions between the Mannings and O'Connor.

Mr Carter asked Walsh whether he had any doubts as to the deceased's identity, to which he replied that he had not. According to the *London Evening Standard*, it was stated that there were other people present in court who had seen O'Connor at 4 pm on the day after Walsh had left him in Whitechapel. The coroner responded: 'Oh, then, let them come forward. I have been examining this witness, believing him to be the last person who saw the deceased alive.' No witnesses appeared to substantiate this claim. However, another person interjected with an accusation that the police had prevented O'Connor's brother-in-law from identifying his body after its discovery, but the man in question, Mr Ryan, denied it, claiming, 'I did not wish to see him.' When questioned further by a juror as to his reasons, he said: 'I do not think I should know him, I only saw him once or twice since I became related to him, now seven or eight years.'

The question of whether anyone had seen Patrick O'Connor on the day after he visited the Mannings' house on 9 August was not pursued. William Carter concluded: 'It is useless to attempt going further with the case at the present moment. We cannot properly go on without the medical testimony.' He suggested that the jury would wish to 'have the body opened' by the first doctor on the scene, Samuel Lockwood. However, it was then discovered that Lockwood was no longer in practice, so the coroner ordered the second doctor, George Odling, who was present in court, to conduct the post-mortem examination.

Still not completely satisfied with the identification of the body, Carter then called a second witness, William Flynn, the customs officer who had worked with the deceased. Flynn stated that he had seen the body at 3 Minver Place, and he had no hesitation in confirming that it was Patrick O'Connor: 'I know him by his chin, which was very long. He wore false teeth. He told me so; and I saw them taken from his mouth yesterday, and they were a perfect set.' Next, the coroner turned to the summoning officer, Charles Slow, and asked him about the police officers engaged on the case. Police Constables Henry Barnes and James Burton stepped forward and said that they had the matter in hand and requested an adjournment for a week so that they could 'procure most important evidence, to some of which they already had a clue' (*The Morning Post*, 20 August 1849). Carter agreed as it would allow time for the post-mortem examination to take place. After a brief consultation with the jury, he adjourned the inquest until Friday 24 August at 11 am. The first stage was complete, and Patrick O'Connor had been formally identified as the victim.

Patrick O'Connor was born in 1798 in County Tipperary, Ireland. The customs records cite his birthplace as Clonkelly, whereas the press noted that he was from Fethard, which is 30 kilometres to the south east of Clonkelly. The newspapers also stated that he had several brothers and sisters, but the only one who rose to prominence was his older brother Thomas, who entered the priesthood and became principal of St Patrick's Roman Catholic College in Thurles. The Reverend Dr Thomas O'Connor oversaw its construction and assumed the role of president on its opening for boarders and day pupils in 1837. He held the post until 1847.

According to *The Morning Post*, Patrick O'Connor was educated at Abbey School. As a boy, he was 'large for his age' and 'somewhat pompous'. Apparently, when he was young, he had offended his elder brother Thomas, who was a parish priest at the time, by disarming a police constable. The paper also asserted that Patrick too had been intended for the priesthood, but he 'had no relish for the tonsure', and left Ireland for England, settling in the capital.

After his arrival, Patrick found employment as a tide waiter at the London Docks in August 1831. He had acquired this post following a recommendation to the excise authorities from the bishop of Llandaff, to whom he had been introduced by an associate of his brother. Patrick's job was to inspect the cargo onboard ships, while the tide turned, to make sure that there were no goods being smuggled in and that the correct levy was being paid. However, as Patrick began to establish himself among the middle-class Irish community in London, he was able to secure a promotion through the patronage of the Right Honourable Richard Lalor Sheil, master of the mint, who had been the MP for Tipperary in the late 1830s. Sheil knew Thomas O'Connor through their membership of the Tipperary Society. It also seems that he was linked indirectly to the family by marriage.

Patrick was further supported by his friend Thomas Parker, a builder also from Ireland, who provided a substantial amount of money in security, as required, for his new position as a customs gauger in 1836. In his elevated role, O'Connor inspected goods for duty. The importance of this work was reflected in his annual salary, which increased immediately from £40 to £150. He progressed through the classes of gauger to reach the pay of £175 per annum in 1844. (In relation to average incomes at the time, this would be the equivalent of about £150,000 today). On the custom officers' return, he is described as 'competent and attentive but heavy', which might allude to his being serious and cheerless. Although his earnings were inflated in the contemporary press, it was generally accepted that Patrick was expecting it to increase further.

With his new-found wealth, Patrick was able to move lodgings. In 1845, he relocated from Sidney Square in Whitechapel to his new home above the Armes sisters' pastry shop at 21 Greenwood Street, Mile End Road. Originally from Norfolk, Ann was a baker. Her younger sister Emily was her assistant. Both were single and lived in the Mile End Road with their elderly parents and a third sister, Martha, who also helped out in the bakery. Patrick occupied two furnished rooms, a drawing room and a bedroom, on the first floor. His considerable increase in cash also enabled him to run a moneylending business on the side.

Patrick O'Connor became known as 'the Customs' moneylender' and he would regularly supply cash to his friends and acquaintances for a high return. After his death, his brother visited the Bank of England and discovered that he had between £3,000 and £4,000 in his account in overseas railway shares and bonds, along with other securities. He also kept a large sum of money and shares at his lodgings. However, his usurious activities often landed him in court. In 1845, he had testified in the trial of an acquaintance, Michael Lee, at the Old Bailey who, he had alleged, had tried to obtain money from him with threats. At an earlier hearing Lee, who was a private nightwatchman, claimed that he had given O'Connor £5 to procure him employment at the docks and, when the job had fallen through, the customs officer had not returned his money. Lee threatened O'Connor with exposure should he continue to withhold his cash. The latter arranged to return the sum at a meeting at his lodging house but when Lee arrived, there was a police constable waiting for him and he was promptly arrested for threatening behaviour. O'Connor gave a slightly different version of events under oath at the Old Bailey. He stated that Lee was an informer for the London Dock Company, and he had threatened to tell the authorities that O'Connor had accepted a bribe of 5 shillings to procure him a position. Patrick told the court that Lee had said that he would expose him unless he paid him £5: 'If I would not give him £5, he would prefer a charge against me.' When Lee was apprehended, he was found to have a five-pound note in his possession bearing Patrick O'Connor's name. He was subsequently convicted and served 12 months in prison. This time, O'Connor's story was believed but, according to the newspapers, he had been suspended from the customs several times on charges of malpractice but had always somehow managed to restore his position and reputation.

After his murder, Patrick's financial dealings were highlighted in the press as a clear example of his avarice. *The Morning Post* carried a rather scathing sketch of his character:

> Of sordid habits, and silly to excess, he was not at all liked by his brother officers who indeed seldom held any intercourse with him except upon business and when on duty, while his vanity contributed not a little to keep him in continual hot water on the subject of women, with some of whom he was always improperly entangled. He likewise followed the obnoxious occupation of a small money lender, or usurer, and, like men of his class, was the reverse of merciful to his debtors. It would appear that his propensity to intrigue cost him his life.

The journalist conceded that although he was 'excessive fond of money', he had paid for the education of a niece at a convent in Thurles. His generosity was further indicated by a letter to the editor of the *Tipperary Free Press*, in which the anonymous writer, who claimed to have known Patrick for many years, sought to vindicate his friend's memory by stating that, despite his shady moneylending practices, he was a regular attendee at church in London and contributed to many charities, as well as assisting members of his family with financial support. According to the correspondent, he was a vigilant and disciplined customs officer, who was exonerated of any wrongdoing at work. Patrick was a teetotaller, and his only known habit was that he was a heavy smoker.

However, the English press was unabating in their character assassination, and *Lloyd's Weekly* summed up his life as seeming 'to have been divided between the indulgence of the most sordid avarice and the most depraved licentiousness', although it also described him as being regarded in the Irish community as 'a pleasant companion'. Other newspapers, such as *The Morning Post*, speculated about his personal life, describing him as 'exceedingly fond of the society of ladies'. Moreover, the publication suggested that he had refused offers of marriage from women 'of the highest respectability'. Despite the alleged attention, Patrick O'Connor remained single and, in 1846, at the age of 48, he met Maria de Roux.

It is not known where Patrick met Maria, but the general consensus of opinion was that it was during a boat crossing to Boulogne. O'Connor had obtained a fortnight's leave and decided to travel to France. He left from London Bridge wharf on a boat, on which Maria was also a passenger with her employer. It is not clear whether the pair enjoyed an intimate relationship, but they became close friends which was, according to *John Bull* newspaper, 'a connection which has terminated so fatally'.

Chapter 3

'This most disagreeable duty'

When Patrick O'Connor's body was discovered under the floor of Minver Place, there were no standardised procedures for crime scene examination and management. The first instructions for crime scene investigation for police officers were issued in Sir Howard Vincent's *Police Code and Manual of the Criminal Law*, the first edition of which was not published until 1881. According to the late Victorian guidance, the first officers at the scene, along with the police surgeon, were required to make note of any footprints, the position of the body, any obvious wounds and the condition of the clothing. In addition, they were to check for evidence of the victim's name, such as papers found in their pockets, for any weapons and for clues to the perpetrator's identity. Before the victim's body was removed, the most senior police officer had to note its exact position.

In 1849, the only publication available to those investigating the Bermondsey murder would have been *Principles of Forensic Medicine*, published for the first time in 1844, by Professor of Forensic Medicine, William Augustus Guy of King's College, London. However, this practical handbook was written for medical practitioners, who might have to give expert evidence in court, rather than for police officers managing and examining a crime scene, so it is unlikely that any of the officers involved in this case would have read it. The second section of Guy's book was devoted to the finding of dead bodies, which included guidance on observing the location in which the deceased person was discovered:

> the medical man must needs observe many things connected with the body itself, such as the position in which it is placed and the objects that surround it, which might be observed and stated in evidence.

Guy's detailed instructions cover the observation and analysis of the position of the body in relation to surrounding objects, such as the soil or surface on which the body lies, and the inspection of the deceased's clothing. There is no indication that either of the first doctors on the scene, Samuel Lockwood or George Odling, followed this advice. Neither is there any evidence to suggest that Constables Barnes and Burton carried out careful observations and analysis of the crime scene, as they both left the house soon after the excavation of the body.

At the time, it was usual practice for any incriminating items recovered from the crime scene to be removed by individual officers and kept either at home or at the police station in case they were needed in the event of a trial. These would later be produced in court, often still bearing dried blood stains. Sometimes key evidence was cleaned, or even broken, as there was no procedure for its recovery, transportation or preservation at this time.

In this case, Patrick's body was washed to remove the quicklime prior to the examination by the surgeons Lockwood and Odling. Soon after, the summoning officer from the coroner's court, Charles Slow, arrived at the house and, after taking the set of false teeth for safekeeping, he gave the instructions that the body was to remain in the front kitchen of 3 Minver Place until after the inquest and post-mortem.

Straight after the inquest on Saturday 18 August, George Odling conducted the post-mortem examination in the front kitchen of 3 Minver Place, as was customary at the time. Aged 53, Odling was an experienced physician, being medical officer for St Saviour's Union Workhouse and divisional surgeon for the Southwark police. The doctor who had examined Patrick O'Connor's body at the scene, Samuel Meggitt Lockwood, assisted him.

As ascertained at the time of the discovery of his body, the victim had sustained a gunshot wound to the back of the head. Mr Lockwood had removed a one-inch bullet from his right temple prior to the post-mortem. The shot had entered the victim's head through his crown and bore down through the skull in a slanting direction, until it had become lodged in the frontal bone, just above his eye. It did not penetrate the skin, nor pass through any organs that would cause death. The report in *The Globe* newspaper speculated that if the ball had measured an inch in diameter, then a large rifle must have been used, such as was usually employed for 'shooting tigers'. Other possibilities included an airgun. During the post-mortem, after removing a large portion of the hair, Odling examined O'Connor's head and extracted three further pieces of lead from under the right temple. The back of Patrick's skull had also been smashed and the doctors counted eighteen incised and contused wounds at the back and top of the head on the right side, some of which were more severe and deeper than others. Odling surmised that they had been inflicted with a hammer or a crowbar, which had a sharp end like a 'chopper', such as that used by a plasterer. He removed sixteen bone splinters, which he kept ready for exhibition at the adjourned inquest.

The doctors concluded that Patrick O'Connor was shot in the head first but, the wound not being fatal, he had then struggled violently to preserve his life as he was struck repeatedly with a heavy instrument. The violence of the successive blows, which forced the splinters of his fractured skull into his brain, killed him instantly. 'Fracture of skull' was recorded on his death certificate as the cause of his death. Odling further suspected that O'Connor might have been drugged with a narcotic before he was attacked, as he deduced from the position of the bullet that he had been lying down at the time of the assault. In the final stage of the post-mortem, Odling opened the abdomen and removed the stomach contents to be sent to expert toxicologist Alfred Swaine Taylor at Guy's Hospital for analysis. He also examined the intestines and organs, which were healthy.

The police wasted no time in investigating Patrick O'Connor's death; initial inquiries, as soon as his body was discovered, were undertaken by the divisional police. Information had been sent immediately to Superintendent Evans, who was in charge of Southwark Division. He circulated a route form (a written report passed by officers meeting on foot or by horse) with a description of the alleged perpetrators to all police stations in London. He also instructed his officers to make inquiries at second-hand clothes dealers in the area to find out whether they had bought any of the clothes worn by the deceased when he was last seen by his friends. They were instructed to look for a black dresscoat, light plaid trousers, a black silk neckcloth and Albert boots, which was a type of walking boot designed for the Prince Consort.

Meanwhile, at Minver Place, M Division officers had begun searching the premises. Sergeant Baker found Patrick's umbrella stuffed up the chimney breast. After they had examined the house, they moved out into the garden where Baker uncovered a cheque for £800 belonging to O'Connor in a dust-hole, which was used as a repository for household waste. The police also found his belt, which had been cut into pieces, and some vomit which they preserved for analysis as, according to *Lloyd's Weekly*, 'there is every reason to believe that the deceased was drugged previously to the perpetration of the cruel and diabolical deed.'

At the same time, PC Barnes returned to Patrick's lodgings in Mile End Road with William Flynn to take another look around. The officer checked the box which had been forced open by Flynn the previous Monday, while they were still searching for O'Connor, and then resealed. Barnes searched the compartments and found some more papers underneath, but still no money or share documents.

On Saturday afternoon, while the doctors were carrying out their medical examination in the front kitchen, the police returned to 3 Minver Place to look for further evidence, especially Patrick O'Connor's clothes, as his body had been naked when it was discovered. They continued searching the rest of the house and garden, beginning with digging up the garden at the rear of the house. According to the press, a waistcoat was discovered, which was badly torn but was alleged to have been worn by the victim on the night he was murdered. In addition, some women's underclothing, which was quite new, was also found, and one garment was completely saturated with blood, which the press surmised was 'most probably from the deceased's wounds'. According to the newspapers, three buttons were uncovered in the fireplace in the back bedroom, which were likely to have been from O'Connor's topcoat. Also in the back bedroom, there were marks on the walls, which appeared to have been recently washed with soap and water, and there was even a bullet mark on the ceiling. The papers speculated that Patrick had been shot and died in the bedroom, his clothes were then removed and burned, and his body was taken downstairs to the basement, where it was buried in the previously dug pit.

Later that day when the police examined the 'grave' in which O'Connor's body was found more closely, they uncovered some more crucial evidence. There were traces of blood where his head had lain, and the impression of his upper body was clearly visible. When the officers removed the layer of lime that had been under his body, they discovered a small cut glass bottle, probably from a medicine chest. The one-ounce laudanum bottle was half empty, and the missing amount would have been sufficient to drug, and maybe kill, someone. This, together with a scent bottle smeared with lime on the sideboard, suggested that the victim may have been drugged prior to his murder, as surgeon George Odling had suspected.

The discovery of Patrick O'Connor's body at 3 Minver Place had continued to arouse great excitement in the neighbourhood of Bermondsey and news of the murder travelled fast. By nightfall on the first evening, hundreds of people had gathered in front of the house. The crowd was so intense and excited that extra police were drafted in to keep order.

The day after, reports of the murder appeared in the London newspapers and throughout the country, spreading like wildfire through the home counties to the north of England and to Scotland, and across the Irish Sea to Dublin. Drawn by the shocking headlines, more spectators flocked to the scene and, as Saturday's police investigation drew to a close, there were thousands of onlookers still blocking the road outside the house at 11 pm, while the police struggled to keep the throng under control.

The crowds watched as the victim's body was finally removed from the premises in a temporary coffin and taken to a mortuary to await burial. The newspapers were clear that he had been murdered, such as was reported in *The Morning Post*: 'That Patrick O'Connor was foully slain there can be no question.' Furthermore, they were convinced of the Mannings' guilt, not only in the absence of any other suspects but also because, on the day that O'Connor disappeared, Maria Manning had been seen at his lodgings in Mile End, and it was alleged that she had stolen all the valuables from his room. As soon as the police had begun to make enquiries, the couple had sold all their furniture and, according to *The Globe*, had 'exhibited a great desire to leave the neighbourhood'. Details were also coming to light suggesting that the act had been premeditated, as the grave had been dug some time before O'Connor's death, and lime had been procured to hasten the disintegration of the corpse (later scientific evidence confirmed that this was a myth). *The Morning Post* further concluded that O'Connor's body had been deposited 'by the woman with whom he is believed to have been criminally intimate, and by her husband, who is understood to have had a full knowledge of their adulterous connection.'

However, there was still much speculation as to how the murder had been committed, and by whom exactly. It seemed doubtful that Patrick O'Connor was killed in a fair fight with Frederick Manning, as the former was of a much greater stature than his alleged opponent. Nor was it probable that the victim had been drunk, as it was generally agreed that he was a teetotaller and drank only water at the Mannings' home. The most likely scenario, according to the newspapers, was that tobacco infused with laudanum was used to stupefy him before the attack. However, despite the uncertainty about the nature of the murder, it was agreed that he was killed in an atrocious manner. After a day of frantic coverage, *The Morning Post* issued a final warning that 'if his

[Patrick O'Connor's] murderers shall pass unpunished it will be a disgrace to civilisation,' adding 'that they will be detected there is, however, every reason to suppose.'

As there was still no trace of the prime suspects, Maria and Frederick Manning, Inspector Perkins and PC Barnes, both of Southwark Division, appeared at Southwark police court, just before the magistrate was about to leave the bench. They gave statements on oath about the murder and Mr Isaac Secker instantly granted them a special warrant to arrest the couple. It was now time to call in the detectives, and the officers passed on the licence to their colleagues at Scotland Yard.

Chapter 4

Catching Monsters

When the sensational news of the body discovered in Bermondsey hit the headlines, *The Morning Chronicle*, where Charles Dickens had been a reporter in the mid-1830s, stated:

> One of the most appalling and cold-blooded murders that has probably been heard of since that perpetrated by the notorious Daniel Good was discovered yesterday afternoon.

In 1842, the investigation into this grisly homicide, known as the Roehampton Murder, had revealed inadequacies in the uniformed ranks of the Metropolitan police and led to the formation of the new detective department at Scotland Yard.

On Wednesday 6 April, PC William Gardiner had been walking his regular beat on Wandsworth High Street, when a pawnbroker reported the theft of a pair of black trousers. The thief was Daniel Good, who worked as a coachman for Queely (also written as 'Quelaz') Shiell, a wealthy plantation owner from Montserrat, who lived nearby. At around 8.30 pm, Good had bought one pair of black knee breeches and helped himself to another on the way out. The pawnbroker's two young assistants led PC Gardiner to Shiell's large house in Roehampton to confront Good, who had a reputation for violence. By the time the three men had walked the two miles to Putney Park Lane, it was about 9.30 pm and the estate buildings were locked up for the night. After making enquiries at the house about Daniel Good's whereabouts, the police officer crossed the yard to the stable where he slept. He knocked on the door and, when it opened, found himself face-to-face with his prime suspect.

Forty-four-year-old Daniel Good was originally from Ireland and had been working for Mr Shiell for just over two years – he looked after the ponies that pulled the four-wheeled chaise. Good was five feet six inches tall, with a very dark complexion and long features. He had black hair and was balding at the crown of his head. That night he was wearing a dark frock coat, drab breeches and gaiters, and a black hat. On being confronted by PC Gardiner, the coachman admitted to the theft and offered to return to the pawnbroker to pay for the trousers. 'Let us go to Wandsworth and have it settled', he said as he stood in the dark doorway of the stable. But PC Gardiner insisted on searching the premises to look for the evidence. As he entered the building, he noted the presence of an 11-year-old boy running around the stable yard, whom he presumed to be Good's son.

Once inside, holding his lamp aloft, the police officer cast his flickering light over the shadowy stalls of the harness room and stables. Good became increasingly agitated and suggested once again that they depart for Wandsworth, but PC Gardiner refused, determined to search every corner for the stolen trousers. He soon noticed, however, a 'very bad, fulsome, sickly smell … like a rind of bacon' pervading the outbuilding. As Gardiner moved methodically through the stalls, he saw Good shift a truss of hay from one side of the fourth stall to the other. The police officer went over to investigate and, pulling back the hay, he spotted what looked like a dead goose. On closer inspection, the weak light from his lantern revealed a woman's mutilated torso.

As the horrified constable struggled to comprehend the scene, Good fled into the night, locking the stable door behind him. PC Gardiner responded quickly and, after prising the door open with a pitchfork, he despatched one of the pawnbroker's lads to Wandsworth police station to inform his colleagues. The first officers to arrive at the scene were Constables Samuel Palmer and Josiah Tye, and Inspector John Busain. Together they made a more meticulous search of the stable, finding a mattress and two urine-stained blankets tied up with cord. Pieces of charred bone were discovered under the ashes in the fireplace, as well as torn female apparel and a silk handkerchief spotted with blood. More bones were uncovered in the cinders, as well as a bloodstained knife in a drawer and an axe. A tiny chunk of flesh, about the size of half a pea, was found on the outside of the carriage.

PC Gardiner and his colleagues removed the evidence from the scene, including pieces of bone, the axe, the knife and a hand saw. The Wandsworth police officers were used to dealing mostly with theft and assault, and the Good case was their first high-profile murder investigation. Therefore, they had no real idea of how to respond to a murder. A rent book found at the scene identified the victim as Jane Jones, a laundress living in Manchester Square, Marylebone. A mole on what remained of her neck was conclusive evidence of her identity, confirmed by her neighbour. The young boy in the stable yard told the police that the victim was his mother, Good's estranged wife. She had been in a relationship with Good for about three years and may have been pregnant when she died. Although the couple did not live together nor were they married, Jane began using Good's name about six months after they had met. Jane Good was of medium build and quite plump, with fair skin and dark hair. She was in her early thirties and her 'son' may have been her deceased sister's child, whom she had adopted. Jane was last seen alive on Sunday 3 April by a police officer on his beat. She had been wearing a blue bonnet, a cotton dress and a black shawl with a pattern of coloured flowers. Following an argument with Daniel, she had left the boy in the care of a friend, but Good had taken him away the following day. According to Jane's neighbours, 30-year-old Lydia Susannah Butcher, a single woman living with her parents in Woolwich, had recently attracted Good's attention, and this had caused friction between the couple. Lydia had visited Good several times at the stable, even staying the night. On Wednesday 6 April, Good had brought her gifts, including a fur tippet and gown, a pair of boots, a handkerchief and a blue bonnet, which he said had belonged to his 'deceased' wife.

Jane's remains were left in the stables for a further two days, while they were examined by a number of medical experts called by the coroner. Putney surgeon Benjamin Ridge complained later in court that he had been prevented from making his examination for 24 hours by the police, until they had washed the corpse, 'on account of the body being so dirty'. Ridge concluded that the woman had been healthy, and that her head and limbs had been severed after death. When he had completed his assessment, the coroner took the unusual measure of instructing PC Tye to transport the victim to his own house in Roehampton, as the spectacle was attracting crowds of onlookers. Tye later returned the body to the stall. Ridge had also examined the knife found in the stables and discovered a piece of blood-soaked flannel in the handle, which he produced in court. He asserted that, in the absence of any kind of scientific test, the blood was unmistakably human due to its 'strong animal smell, very much like our dissecting knives'.

Within a week, the news of the 'Roehampton Murder' hit the headlines across the country, terrifying the Victorian public who were becoming increasingly anxious about their safety and the inability of the police to protect them. The idea of 'evil' infiltrating a respectable, secure home through the actions of a servant exacerbated their fears. As days passed with no news of an arrest, the public followed the unfolding events with morbid fascination and mounting anxiety. At first, the newspapers were confident of a swift resolution: 'The police, it is almost needless to state, are exerting themselves to the utmost to catch the monster' (*The Times*, 8 April 1842). But Daniel Good was proving difficult to track down. Despite the officers at Wandsworth police station having circulated a route paper with details of the crime and a description of Good to neighbouring divisions, it took almost 24 hours before the information was fully disseminated to the police stations throughout the capital, leaving Good with a head start. His first port of call, after his escape, was apparently Jane Jones's lodgings, but as the route paper had not reached the Marylebone police by this time, they were not on the alert for him and Good passed by the address unnoticed. A cabman later confirmed his presence there and told the police that he had taken the fugitive to Whitcomb Street, near Trafalgar Square, and then to the Spotted Dog public house in the Strand, before dropping him in the East End.

Handbills and placards, with notices of Good's particulars and the charge levied against him, as well as a £100 reward for information leading to his arrest, were issued and, over the following days, there were sightings of Good all over the capital, even by a constable on his beat whom Good had asked directions to a local livery stable. The police questioned several individuals known to Good, including Lydia Susannah Butcher's mother and Good's estranged first wife, Molly – Good had been using Molly's address in Spitalfields, even though they were no longer living together. Molly had last seen her former husband the week before the crime, when he had left her waiting in a coffee shop in Whitechapel, saying he was going to buy her an egg. He never returned. As the officers continued their search, they kept missing Good, who even had enough time to pawn some of Jane's belongings. Always on his tail but never quite close enough, by the time the items were discovered in the local pawnbroker's, Good had escaped the net once again and left London for Kent.

Daniel Good was finally arrested after ten days on the run. Former Wandsworth police officer, Thomas Rose, had been working as a labourer on the new railway line at Tonbridge, when he recognised Good from a notice in a copy of *Hue and Cry* (an early version of the *Police Gazette*) which he had seen in his lodgings. A woman's apron spotted with blood was found in the prisoner's possession and Good was taken into custody at Maidenhead Gaol. He appeared before the magistrates at Bow Street police court shortly after. On 13 May 1842, he was tried at the Old Bailey. The court was packed with spectators who watched as he 'leaned upon the bar in a most unconcerned manner', according to *The London Standard*. Good pleaded not guilty to all charges. The police officers produced the evidence they had removed from the crime scene, including bones which had been tied with string, and the bloodstained knife and axe. The jury took just 35 minutes to return a guilty verdict and Daniel Good was executed in Newgate Prison in front of a large crowd on 23 May 1842.

Although he had been brought to justice, the Good case revealed endemic flaws in the fledgling Metropolitan police force, created just thirteen years earlier, and the public continued to rail against their ineffectiveness, stating vociferously that they expected better from a force of 3,800 men spread over a 15-mile circuit of the city. The newspapers were quick to criticise the lack of communication between police districts and even hinted at poor governance, leading *The Times* to wonder 'whether or not the metropolitan police force are at all effective as a detective police'. This accusation was, in many ways, justified, as Sir Robert Peel's original objective had been to prevent crime by establishing a more organised and centralised body. However, little thought seemed to have been given to the procedures once a crime had been committed.

Since the creation of the new police in 1829, there had been twenty-two homicides in London and, in the weeks following the Roehampton Murder, the press dredged up other similar recent outrages as proof that the police were indeed failing to protect the public. Just five years earlier, in 1837, 15-year-old John Brill had been murdered in Uxbridge. Three suspects were detained but there was insufficient evidence to press charges. A few months later, barmaid Eliza Davies was found with her throat cut in a public house in Camden where she worked. The perpetrator was never identified. The murders of prostitute Eliza Grimwood in 1838, who lived near Waterloo Bridge, and, in the following year, of Soho watchmaker, Richard Westwood, also remained unsolved.

Two years later, when Lord William Russell, uncle of the foreign secretary, was murdered while sleeping, the skills of individual prototype detectives started to come to the fore. On 6 May 1840, the police were called to a grand house near Mayfair, where the elderly widower had been killed in his bed. To all appearances, a burglar had entered the house and cut Lord Russell's throat after accidentally waking him. He had then departed with several valuable items. Former Bow Street Runner, Inspector Nicholas Pearce, now working in A Division (Whitehall), brought his superior detective skills to bear on the case later that day. By the time Pearce arrived, the first officer on the scene had already matched tools found at the property to marks on the back door leading to the pantry. He had also experimented with rushlights, which were candles created by soaking the dried pith of rushes in fat or grease.

It had been Lord Russell's nightly habit to leave a rushlight in a shade by his bed, which usually burned out by morning. On this evening, as only a third of the candle had been used, the police deduced that it must have been extinguished at the time of his death: approximately an hour and a half after he had retired for the night. When questioned about this, Lord Russell's Swiss valet, François Courvoisier, claimed that he had left his employer reading in bed. This was a blatant lie as, confirmed by the rest of the staff, Lord Russell never read in bed. Courvoisier became the prime suspect, but there was no evidence that he was the killer. Inspector Pearce conducted a thorough search of the premises, during which he spotted a key detail; the plaster on the skirting board near the fireplace in the pantry had been disturbed, leaving behind a scattering of lime. The officer wasted no time in pulling apart the skirting, behind which he found the missing items: a purse containing five gold coins and several rings, as well as a beribboned medal from the Battle of Waterloo. This was definitely an inside job and only Inspector Pearce had been observant enough to locate the incriminating evidence. 'I generally make a search with every degree of minuteness,' he later explained in court.

Determined to prove his case against Courvoisier, Inspector Pearce next examined the marks on the pantry door, which had supposedly been forced open to admit the intruder. He matched the household tools to the various marks on the frame and, with the assistance of an expert carpenter, concluded that the door had remained open all the time with the damage caused afterwards to stage the burglary. The tenacious detective even brought a section of the door into the trial at the Old Bailey to demonstrate to the jury that the forced entry into the house had been faked. Courvoisier was found guilty and executed.

The murder of Lord William Russell caused panic within the upper middle classes and highlighted the ineffectiveness of a preventive police force. When Daniel Good butchered his common-law wife, Jane, two years later, it was obvious to all that the need for a detective force was more urgent than ever. It was suggested that the botched investigation that had allowed Daniel Good to evade justice for so long was the latest example in a long list of failures. *The Times* opined:

> but the want of that tact and ability as a detective police displayed on all occasions by the old Bow-street officers has been more fully demonstrated in the present case of Daniel Good, the Roehampton murderer.

The police authorities responded to the criticisms by suspending several inspectors for neglect of duty. But this was not enough for the press, which considered them merely scapegoats, and journalists continued to campaign for the appointment of a detective police force. The pressure mounted even further when, just six days after the execution of Daniel Good, John Francis pointed a pistol at young Queen Victoria's carriage as it passed along the Mall. The only action taken to find the culprit by the police was to repeat the journey the following day, in an attempt to flush out the would-be assassin. As the queen passed for a second time, Francis fired again, fortunately missing his target. The monarch's lucky escape immediately led to more clamours in the press for a detective force.

Three months later, in August 1842, the Detective Branch of the Metropolitan police was established at Scotland Yard, with the following understated announcement in the press:

> It was stated a few weeks since that it was the intention of the Commissioners of Police to form, out of the present police force a new company, to be called the 'Detective Force.' The arrangements for carrying out the same are now completed and will come into operation this day. (*The Morning Post*, 8 August 1842)

Five years later, the Bermondsey murder was an opportunity for the Metropolitan police to prove that their investigative strategies had finally improved.

In 1849, the detective department was led by Inspector Charles Frederick Field. An innkeeper's son from Chelsea, he had joined the Metropolitan police at the age of 24, at its foundation in 1829. He was assigned as a sergeant to E Division (Holborn) and, in 1833, was promoted to inspector and transferred to L Division (Lambeth). Shortly after, he was moved to R Division (Greenwich), where he worked first in Deptford Dockyard and then in Woolwich. A keen actor in his youth, he was known for wearing disguises when on undercover operations. In 1848, on the retirement of the incumbent head of the detectives at Scotland Yard, Field took his place at the helm.

Alongside Field were five other detective officers who worked with him on the Mannings case, four of whom belonged to the original eight detectives appointed by Police Commissioner Richard Mayne when he created the detective department seven years earlier. One of the most experienced was Inspector John Haynes, who had been the deputy to Nicholas Pearce when he had led Scotland Yard. Born in 1806 in the village of Peasmarsh near Guildford in Surrey, John had moved with his family to Southwark and, according to one of his later police colleagues, he worked as a chemist before joining the Metropolitan police in 1833, aged 27. He spent nine years serving in P Division (Camberwell) before being promoted into the newly-formed detective department in 1842. Haynes had a reputation for catching horse thieves and often undertook special missions for Commissioner Mayne.

Stephen Thornton was also one of the first Scotland Yard detectives. He was born in Epsom, Surrey, in 1803 and his father was a carpenter. At the age of 29, Thornton joined Holborn Division of the Metropolitan police, where he worked with Inspector Field. Known for working undercover at race meetings, where he was said to inspire fear in pickpockets, he was soon promoted to sergeant. After his involvement in the search for murderer Daniel Good in 1842, he was selected to join the elite detective unit at Scotland Yard soon after.

Another long-standing colleague of Detectives Field and Thornton was Frederick Shaw, who also joined the detective department in 1842. Born in 1809, Shaw was from Richmond, Surrey. He joined the police in 1830, serving in E Division for nine years, after which he followed Inspector Field to Greenwich Division. Promoted to sergeant, he collaborated with Inspector Nicholas Pearce on the investigation into the murder of Lord William Russell in Mayfair in 1840, and this high-profile case would have brought him to the attention of the police commissioners when they were making their choices for the first detective department.

The fifth detective engaged on the hunt for the Mannings was Jonathan Whicher, who was known as 'Jack'. He had also worked with the others throughout his police career. After joining the Metropolitan police in 1837, he was assigned to Holborn Division where Detectives Thornton and Shaw were still operating at that time. With a reputation for being observant and for following his instincts, Whicher soon became involved in detective work, most notably on the Daniel Good case in 1842, after which he was chosen to join Scotland Yard as a detective sergeant. The final member of the group was Edward Langley. He was from the village of Stock in Essex where he was born in 1805. He joined the force in 1830 and served as a constable in L Division (Lambeth). After his promotion to sergeant, he moved into the detective department at A Division (Whitehall) in 1845.

When Charles Dickens met the Scotland Yard officers in 1850 for a 'social conference' at his editorial offices, four of the detectives engaged on the Mannings murder case were present. He later described them in an article for *Household Words*:

> They are, one and all, respectable-looking men; of perfectly good deportment and unusual intelligence; with nothing lounging or slinking in their manners; with an air of keen observation and quick perception when addressed; and generally presenting in their faces, traces more or less of habitually leading lives of strong mental excitement. They have all good eyes; and they all can, and they all do, look full at whomsoever they speak to.

In 1849, when the Scotland Yard officers received the special licence to arrest Frederick and Maria Manning for the murder of Patrick O'Connor, they would need all their powers of observation and perception to track down this elusive couple, especially after their still-remembered failure to find Daniel Good. They began their search by circulating posters with details of the fugitives.

Chapter 5

Ménage-à-trois

The special arrest warrant for the Mannings was passed immediately to Detective Sergeants Langley and Thornton, both of whom were already acquainted with Frederick Manning due to his alleged involvement in railway robberies in Exeter. A telegraph was sent immediately to Home Secretary Sir George Grey, who gave instructions to the police commissioners to offer a reward of £100 for the apprehension of the couple, or of £50 for either of them. As reported in *Lloyd's Weekly*, he also offered a pardon from the queen for 'any accomplice not being the actual person who fired the shot, or inflicted the mortal wound, who shall give such information and evidence as shall lead to the discovery and conviction of the murderer or murderers.' All information was to be communicated to Inspector Field of Scotland Yard, or to any of the Metropolitan police stations. Handbills with the details were posted throughout the city. In the meantime, Superintendent Evans of M Division in Southwark had circulated descriptions of the suspects to all police stations in London and in other cities and towns, as well as in the press. Their full physical description and details about their personal history were printed in the newspapers with the announcement of the reward. Maria Manning was described as:

> a native of Geneva, 30 years old, 5 feet 7 inches high, stout, fresh complexion, with long dark hair, good looking, scar on the right side of chin, extending towards the neck, dresses very smartly, and speaks broken English. Has been a Lady's Maid and a Dressmaker.

It further stated that she had left Bermondsey at 4.30 pm on Tuesday 14 August in a cab. Nothing more had been seen of her since.

Maria's family history remains unknown. However, press reports generally agree that she was from Lausanne, near Geneva, in Switzerland. Her later marriage certificate confirms that her birth name was de Roux, and her father is recorded as David de Roux, a postmaster in Geneva. The newspapers also claimed that, by 1849, both her parents had died, and she had inherited a small sum of money with which she came to England in about 1840. References to her age vary, but the criminal records state that she was 28 years old at the time of her trial. There was also some speculation that Maria was related to François Courvoisier, the Swiss valet who was convicted of the murder of Lord William Russell in 1840, but these rumours proved to be unfounded.

In 1841, Maria (she had anglicised her name from 'Marie') was working as a servant in the household of the Dowager Lady Arden at St James's Place, near Green Park in central London, close to St James's Palace and the Mall. The 72-year-old widowed dowager was living in splendour with her daughter, the Honourable Helena Trench, and her two granddaughters, who were aged 21 and 19. Lady Arden's late husband, Baronet Charles George Perceval, was MP for Launceston and then Warwick, master of the mint and lord lieutenant of Surrey. He had died the previous year. This grand household had twelve servants, including Maria. Next door to the dowager's home was Spencer House. This was the eighteenth-century townhouse of the Spencer family. In 1841, it was home to the 4th Earl Spencer, Frederick, his wife Elizabeth and their three young children. Similarly to Lady Arden, they had thirteen servants working in their household. Maria Manning's first place of work no longer exists, but it was likely to have been similar to Spencer House in its grandeur.

Within five years Maria had found a new position, this time in the home of Lady Anna Palk, daughter of Sir Bourchier Wrey, who was married to Sir Lawrence Vaughan Palk, 3rd baronet and MP for Devonshire. They lived at Haldon House, near Exeter, in Devon. Built in the style of Buckingham Palace, Haldon House was bought by the baronet's grandfather, who had been in the service of the East India Company and had returned from his role as governor in Madras with a great fortune. Haldon was considered to be one of the finest houses in the county. Maria's role was upgraded to lady's maid and her duties would have included taking care of her mistress's wardrobe, dressing her hair and helping her with her make-up. She was also required to accompany Lady Palk on visits and journeys, and it is generally believed that it was while Maria was travelling with her employer by train that she met her future husband, Frederick George Manning, who worked for the Great Western Railway. After Lady Palk's death in 1846, Maria used her experience to gain an even more elevated position.

Moving back to her earlier location in London, she took up a place as lady's maid to Lady Evelyn Blantyre, daughter of the Duke and Duchess of Sutherland, the latter being the granddaughter of Georgiana, Duchess of Devonshire. Lady Evelyn was married to the 12th Lord Blantyre, Charles Stuart, a Scottish politician and landowner. She spent her time between London and Scotland, often visiting her sister and her brother-in-law, the Duke of Argyll. This was a family of the highest society with connections to the Crown, as the Duchess of Sutherland was Queen Victoria's mistress of the robes, which was the most senior female position in the Royal Household. The Sutherland family was based at Stafford House (now Lancaster House and home to the Foreign and Commonwealth Office), five minutes' walk from Maria's first place of employment at St James's Place. The duke and duchess regularly hosted receptions for the royal couple and prominent politicians. An engraving from 1845 shows the Duchess of Sutherland in the company of the Duke and Duchess of St Albans, Lady Peel, and Viscounts Villiers and Castlereagh, all enjoying Queen Victoria's fancy dress ball. Apparently, Maria used to boast that she had seen the queen several times.

Maria joined this illustrious household in July 1846 and accompanied Lady Blantyre to Scotland in the autumn of that year, after Evelyn had given birth to her second daughter at Stafford House; they then travelled north for the child's baptism. Between her arrival and the trip to Scotland, it is possible that Maria accompanied her mistress on a journey to the continent where she made the acquaintance of Patrick O'Connor on a crossing to Boulogne. It was alleged in the newspapers that he began corresponding with her while she was in Scotland. In early 1847, Maria returned to Stafford House where she was visited frequently by both Frederick Manning and Patrick O'Connor. In August, she left the opulent residence temporarily to marry Frederick, receiving handsome gifts from members of the family who held her in high esteem. Lord Blantyre also used his influence to procure a position for one of Frederick's brothers as a messenger for the Board of Trade. However, Maria regained her position for a brief time after her marriage, during which she once again accompanied Lady Blantyre abroad, perhaps to put her own affairs in order before settling down to married life.

Maria de Roux and Frederick George Manning were married on 27 May 1847 in St James's church, Westminster, near Piccadilly Circus. Her husband's occupation was noted as 'clerk in railway', even though in reality he held the lowlier position of guard. His father was recorded as Joseph Manning, gentleman. The two witnesses were (Jean) Étienne Beauvais, a valet who had arrived in England from France in 1840, and Louisa Salanson, also French, who worked as a court milliner. Presumably Maria had met Louisa during her time at Stafford House.

Frederick George Manning came from much humbler roots than suggested by his marriage certificate. He was born on 22 March 1821 in Taunton, Somerset, and his parents were Joseph and Blanch (née Ellis) Manning; they had married in 1799 in the village of Madron in Cornwall. At the time of Frederick's baptism on 12 April at St Mary Magdalene's church, also known as Taunton Minster, they were living at Magdalene Lane, a two-minute walk away. His father, Joseph, was a sergeant in the 1st Somerset Militia. According to *Lloyd's Weekly*, he was a respectable man who ran the Bear Inn and rented turnpike tolls in Taunton. He also collected the tolls from Taunton market, as well as being an agent in letting property for which he collected rents for the owners. Frederick was the youngest of nine children, with four sisters and four brothers. His eldest sister Elizabeth was born in 1800, followed by Susanna in 1803. His brother Charles was born in 1806, then Joseph Henry in 1808 and Ann in 1810. His fifth sibling was Edmund Ellis born in 1815, then James in 1816 and finally Harriet, who was born in 1817. In 1841, the Mannings were living in North Town, less than a mile from their previous residence on the other side of the River Tone. Frederick, aged 20, was a painter's apprentice. His brother James was working as a gilder, and his sister Harriet as a milliner. On 18 September 1845, Joseph Manning senior died of typhus fever and an obstruction of the bowels at the age of 69 which, according to the newspapers, resulted in Frederick inheriting some property. However, by this time, he had joined the Great Western Railway as a porter working on the line between Bristol and London, after the opening of Taunton station in 1842. He had then worked his way up to the position of guard.

After their marriage, the Mannings spent over a week in Devonshire before Maria returned to her employer in Stafford House for one more stint, which included the final trip to the continent. Meanwhile, Frederick continued his work as a railway guard for the Great Western Railway. On her return to England, Maria joined her new husband at 2 Church Street, Paddington. During the following twelve months, gold bullion worth £4,000 (almost £500,000 today) went missing from the train on which Manning worked as a guard. He was never charged with this alleged offence but was dismissed from the company in 1848. It was later considered to have been the work of a gang, which may have included Frederick. In January 1849, when

Edward Nightingale and former GWR guard Henry Poole were arrested for a mail robbery on the Great Western Railway line, Scotland Yard officers Charles Field and Edward Langley investigated possible links with Frederick Manning. Disguised as passengers so that Poole would not be recognised by any former colleagues, the suspects had boarded the train at Bristol and moved through the carriages to the mail van to which they gained access. By candlelight, they ransacked the mailbags and parcels for money and valuables, and then resumed their seats in the passenger carriage. They were dressed identically so as to provide an alibi for each other.

Poole had also been dismissed by the Great Western Railway prior to this event for misconduct, possibly on suspicion of robbery. The detectives discovered that the robberies had been planned at the White Hart Inn in Taunton some months earlier, the landlord of which was Frederick Manning. Following a quarrel with her husband, Maria had informed the brewer and other members of the local community of the plans for the robbery, after which the group disappeared. The couple fled too. After weeks of searching, Field and Langley finally arrested the Mannings at a lodging house in Mile End, near to where Patrick O'Connor lived. However, when they searched the premises, they could not find any evidence of a robbery. Maria denied having any knowledge of the incident and Frederick offered to give information about his former acquaintances implicated in it. The pair were eventually discharged, but Henry Poole and Edward Nightingale were both convicted and sentenced to 15 years' transportation.

Although the Mannings were absolved of any involvement in the GWR robberies, it was enough to ruin their reputations and adversely alter their fortunes. *Lloyd's Weekly* speculated that the Mannings were no longer welcome in Taunton due to the hostelry's dubious nature, which was considered to be 'a regular rendezvous and reception house for a desperate gang of criminals, putters up of bank and railway robberies, and receivers of stolen goods'. Landlady Maria Manning was criticised by local inhabitants for her coarse language and displays of violence. Before the GWR robbery had taken place, Frederick had signed over the lease to another party and left. His wife, who was away at the time of the transaction, returned to discover that he had gone. She followed him to London where he was living in Newington with one of his brothers.

Prior to this, in October 1848, Frederick and Maria had opened the Old King John's Head beerhouse at 90 Mansfield Street in Kingsland Road near Hackney. A few weeks later, Maria left the marital home for a brief spell and

Frederick was forced to relinquish the business after the railway thefts in January 1849. Now unemployed and with dwindling funds, the Mannings rented an apartment for a while, during which time Frederick travelled to the Channel Islands for three weeks. They moved into 3 Minver Place on 25 March, five months before Patrick O'Connor's body was discovered under the kitchen floor.

On 18 August 1849, the police issued a handbill stating that Frederick George Manning was wanted for 'murder and robbery'. He was described as:

> Frederick George Manning, 35 years old, 5 feet 8 or 9 inches high, stout, very fair and florid complexion, full bloated face, light hair, small sandy whiskers, light blue eyes, and a peculiar fall of the eyelids at the corners and large mouth. Was dressed in an invisible [this relates to the colour] green overcoat, brown trousers, black hat, and wore a small, plaited linen shirt front.

His less attractive characteristics were emphasised in the press, as well as his alleged connections with the criminal fraternity and likely involvement in railway robberies. The general opinion of him was summarised in *Famous Crimes Past and Present*:

> There must have been something peculiar in Manning which attracted the florid beauty, for it is not often that a woman marries a man so singularly like herself in all his characteristics. With the sole exception that Manning had thin lips, he was the male counterpart of his partner for life. He was not gifted, however, with the same intellect, and it can be readily understood that his training as porter and guard had done little to develop any brain that he might have had.

By contrast, Maria was portrayed as good-looking, accomplished and well connected, although *The Morning Post* could not resist adding that she was 'of almost masculine stature'. A later report in *Lloyd's Weekly* stated that she was 'a woman of very violent passions'. The newspaper claimed that Frederick's brother (they did not state which one) said that Maria had attempted to stab him with a knife more than once during family quarrels in Taunton.

Not surprisingly, there was much speculation in the press about the relationship between Frederick and Maria Manning, especially regarding the apparent differences in their physical attractiveness, with journalists making assumptions about what motivated each of them to marry the other. It was generally believed that Frederick had sought Maria's hand in marriage due to her associations with the higher echelons of society. Apparently, Secretary of State for War and the Colonies Lord John Russell (nephew of the politician murdered by Courvoisier) offered him a post as a messenger, but he declined. It would seem that Maria too was looking for a fortune, perhaps to cement her own position in London society as a married woman rather than a servant. It is certainly true that she was upwardly mobile and ambitious, as each of her positions had been more elevated than the last. According to *Clark's Edition*, Frederick had told his future wife that he was due to inherit about £650 from his mother's estate on her death (Blanch Manning died in 1848). He even drew up a fake will leaving his fortune to his wife, making her co-executor with the convicted railway robber, Henry Poole.

If the newspapers and the general public were interested in the relationship between Maria and Frederick, then they were almost obsessed with that between Maria and Patrick, and these complex connections were more often than not presented as a *ménage-à-trois*. During her time at Stafford House in the employment of Lady Blantyre, Maria had received visits from both men, with O'Connor being seen as her suitor. When Maria finally chose Frederick as her husband, perhaps because her hope of marrying her alternative suitor was fading, *Lloyd's Weekly* described Patrick's reaction in the most dramatic terms: 'he manifested the greatest distress of mind, tore the hair from his head, and conducted himself in a most extraordinary manner.' Despite his seemingly emotional response, the same newspaper stated that he had attended their wedding.

After her marriage, Maria continued to visit Patrick and she even moved in with him briefly when she left Frederick after the railway robbery in early 1849. After a short while, the abandoned husband managed to trace her through a cab driver, and she returned to the marital home shortly before they rented the property in Minver Place.

It is not known whether the relationship between Maria and Patrick was a sexual one, although the press mostly assumed they had intimate relations, which Frederick was aware of and which caused violent quarrels to break out between the married couple, with Maria sometimes threatening Frederick with a knife. However, those who actually knew the threesome were less sure as to the nature of their friendship. Patrick's colleague at the customs, William Patrick Keating, described how he had regularly seen his friend in the company of Maria: 'I have met them alone together a good many times, I have met them late of an evening walking in the street together. I have been to O'Connor's lodgings and have seen Mrs Manning there.' He also stated that the relationship between Patrick and Frederick was not particularly warm: 'They appeared to know each other; they were not unfriendly.' By contrast, Pierce Walsh claimed that Frederick was 'as friendly with him [Patrick] as brothers could be.' David Graham, who also worked with Patrick, said that he did not know whether he had been intimate with Maria, but he too had seen the pair out walking together and at O'Connor's lodgings. Patrick's landlady, Ann Armes, told the court later that Maria had visited him frequently during a 12-month period but, as far as she was aware, she never stayed longer than two or three hours. Sometimes, her husband accompanied her, and his visits became more frequent during the month before her tenant's death.

Whatever the nature of the trio's relationships, the newspapers all agreed that Patrick O'Connor had died at the hands of the Mannings. But Maria was painted as the principal culprit motivated by a desire to obtain the victim's money and property to enhance her own wealth and status. *The Morning Post* concluded:

> There is not a shadow of a doubt that Patrick O'Connor had a strong predilection towards her, of which she was fully aware, and in consequence of that knowledge she had for some time past used every means in her power to increase her influence over him by continually visiting him privately at his own lodgings, to which she had access at all times by his direction.

The newspaper even pointed out to its readers Maria's barefaced audacity: 'To show the extraordinary nerve of the Mannings, particularly the female, she on Sunday prepared her dinner in the back kitchen, where she roasted a goose over the spot where her murdered paramour was lying.' There is no evidence that this was true.

Despite the intense speculation about the alleged murderers, by the end of Saturday 18 August, the day after the discovery of Patrick O'Connor's remains, there was still no trace of the Mannings. However, the detective officers at Scotland Yard were following every lead to track down the killer couple.

Chapter 6

A Desperate Flight

Charles Dickens described the four Scotland Yard detectives who had been involved in the investigation into the Bermondsey murder in his weekly publication, *Household Words*, in an article entitled 'Detective Police', published in 1850. He portrayed Stephen Thornton (using the moniker 'Dornton') as:

> About fifty years of age, with a ruddy face and a high sun-burnt forehead, has the air of one who has been a Sergeant in the army … He is famous for steadily pursuing the inductive process, and, from small beginnings, working on from clue to clue until he bags his man.

In comparison, Sergeant Jonathan Whicher (whom he referred to as 'Witchem') was:

> Shorter, and thicker-set, and marked with the small-pox, has something of a reserved and thoughtful air; as if he were engaged in deep arithmetical calculations. He is renowned for his acquaintance with the swell mob.

Whereas Detective Frederick Shaw (renamed 'Straw') was 'a little wiry Sergeant of meek demeanour and strong sense, [who] would knock at a door and ask a series of questions in any mild character you choose to prescribe to him'.

However, the writer's 'favourite' seems to have been Charley Field (or 'Wield'), whom he described as:

> A middle-aged man of a portly presence, with a large, moist, knowing eye, a husky voice, and a habit of emphasising his

conversation by the aid of a corpulent fore-finger, which is constantly in juxtaposition with his eyes or nose.

This meeting took place the year after their search for the Mannings but, by the end of the first two days since the discovery of Patrick O'Connor's body under the floor of 3 Minver Place, it was still uncertain whether they would succeed in catching his killers at all.

The uniformed police officers who had been sent out initially with the messages about the murder had returned with no new information about the fleeing couple. It was time for the Scotland Yard detectives to take the lead and, after circulating the poster with the details of the prime suspects on Saturday 18 August, the detective officers proceeded to follow several lines of inquiry proactively.

Detectives Langley and Thornton were intending to travel to France, where they would be 'readily assisted by the French authorities, who have been informed of the horrible tragedy by telegraphic communication.' As the officers were already acquainted with Frederick Manning from his suspected involvement in the railway robberies in Exeter, they would be able to recognise him. At the same time, Inspector Field and Sergeant Whicher set out for Germany, as they surmised that Maria might have taken this route due to her familiarity with it from her previous travels as a lady's maid.

Meanwhile, back in London, other detective officers were tirelessly conducting inquiries and following up leads. One of their first actions was to contact second-hand clothes dealers in the capital in a search for Patrick O'Connor's distinctive clothing, which the Mannings might have pawned before they fled. The list of missing items included a black dress coat, light plaid trousers, a black silk stock (a necktie), and Albert boots. Throughout the weekend, several detective police officers, including Constables Burton and Barnes, who discovered the body, were deployed in surveillance at the railway stations watching the departing trains to see if they could catch sight of the fugitives.

As the detectives and their uniformed colleagues continued their investigation, personal testimonies began to appear in the press which offered insights into the Mannings' characters and their actions in the run-up to, and around, Patrick O'Connor's murder, with reports such as the one in *The Morning Post*, which claimed that 'scarcely had they been a week in the house than suspicion was excited amongst the inhabitants of the neighbourhood by their extraordinary conduct.'

An unnamed neighbour informed the same publication that the Mannings appeared 'to be up all night', as there was always a light burning and 'there always appeared to be something mysterious going on.' Patrick O'Connor was seen frequently at the house and the neighbours on both sides remarked on his 'jocularity' with Mrs Manning. He was often spotted through the back parlour window smoking in Maria's company or in the back garden, which was where he was last seen with Frederick Manning on 9 August, the evening before he went missing. The newspaper further speculated that a liaison between Patrick O'Connor and Maria Manning had existed for some time, and that Frederick Manning had been aware of the fact. The reporter added that the deceased was frequently cautioned by his friends to discontinue his visits to Mrs Manning, to which he always replied that he did not fear any harm from her husband, as they were on the best of terms, and he did not like to abandon a long-standing companion. This was corroborated by a Mrs Parker, whose husband was one of O'Connor's friends; Thomas Parker was a frequent visitor to Minver Place and was well acquainted with Mrs Manning. His wife told a journalist from *The Morning Post* that she had never liked Maria Manning and that she was suspicious of 'improper intimacy' between her and the deceased. She had even forbidden them from coming to their home in Museum Street, Bloomsbury. Moreover, Mrs Parker had a sense that 'something fatal would occur' and she confirmed that his friends had indeed warned him repeatedly that he would suffer 'at the hands of Manning and his wife'.

In relation to the murder, a neighbour of the Mannings, James Hitchcock, who was a potato salesman, told *Lloyd's Weekly* that on the evening of Patrick O'Connor's disappearance, 'not the least disturbance was heard in Manning's house, neither was there anything resembling the discharge of fire-arms.' As Hitchcock had four young children under the age of 5, it is likely that if a gun had been fired, one of them would have been woken by the noise. This led to speculation that O'Connor had been lured into the back kitchen in the basement by the couple, where he was shot with an airgun, the sound being muffled by its underground location. Hitchcock later told *The Globe* newspaper that the Mannings had stayed up all night on Sunday 12 August. He had got up at 4.30 am to get ready for a trip to Margate and, hearing noise from next door, had assumed that the Mannings were going on the same excursion. The publication linked this to O'Connor's murder: 'there is no doubt the parties were busily engaged in finishing the deceased's grave.' Hitchcock further stated that he believed that the Mannings had not slept a full night in the house since Patrick's disappearance.

A Mr Truck, who lived at 4 Minver Place, reported that he had heard a noise around midnight on Thursday 9 August, and that it had woken him up. Thinking that they were being burgled, Mr Truck roused his wife, who dismissed his concerns as 'nonsense'. Unable to return to sleep, her husband had got out of bed and looked out of the window, where he saw the shadow of a man in a stooping position on the wall opposite the window of the room where Patrick O'Connor's body was later found.

Despite the contradictory evidence, *Lloyd's Weekly* concluded that, contrary to other reports, the murder must have been perpetrated in the front kitchen as, if it had taken place in any other room, the neighbours would have heard the gunshot due to the houses being separated by thin partition walls 'through which the slightest sound can be heard'. However, the truth would not be known until the police had tracked the Mannings down.

Throughout the day of Saturday 18 August, Superintendent Evans of Southwark Division had worked with his colleagues, Inspectors Yates, Froud and Cowler, and in collaboration with Detective Inspector Field, to glean as much information about the Mannings' recent activities as they could. A major breakthrough was the discovery that on 13 July, Frederick had called at an ironmonger's shop on King William Street, on the other side of the Thames not far from London Bridge. He gave instructions for a special crowbar to be made; it had to be about 11 pounds in weight for lifting heavy objects such as stones. Manning drew his required design on the counter in chalk. After paying the bill of 4 shillings, he gave his name and address and ordered for it to be delivered the next day to Minver Place. As the ironmonger did not have any instruments with these precise requirements, he sent messages to other businesses in the city in an attempt to procure one. He was unsuccessful so he sent the money back to Manning, who responded by saying, 'Never mind, I shall be able to do it without it.' Later, the shop clerk who took the booking happened to be passing Minver Place as news of the murder broke. He went straight to the local police station and informed them of Manning's rather unusual request.

Sergeant Kelly of M Division sent an officer to the ironmonger's, Messrs Dray, Dean and Dean, in King William Street to check the books, which confirmed that Manning had indeed ordered the crowbar. *Lloyd's Weekly* commented: 'There is not the least doubt that this instrument, if procured, was for the purpose of assisting in the disposal of the body.' *The Morning Post* noted: 'It is pretty clear, from the appearance of the place where the body was concealed, that it had been some time before prepared, and an instrument of the kind would be necessary to raise up the stones.' The police had also started to piece together Frederick and Maria's actions around the time of Patrick's disappearance.

The Mannings' neighbours Joseph and Sophia Payne, who lived at 2 Minver Place, told the police that they had seen Frederick on 9 August. Joseph, 38, was a lithographic printer and he ran the family business from his home, which he shared with his wife and their two sons, Joseph junior, aged 9, and Frederick, who was 5. The boys were lively children and spent time in the back garden, from where their mother spotted Manning on the Thursday evening. Sophia said that she had seen Frederick sitting on his garden wall at 6.45 pm. He was smoking a pipe. As she was also outside, they had chatted for 15 or 20 minutes, after which Manning jumped down from the wall. Saying that he had to get dressed for an appointment, he then left, and she saw no more of him until the following Monday. At 6 pm on 13 August, Frederick Manning knocked at the Paynes' door. He told Sophia that his wife was out and asked if she could let him through her house into the garden so that he could gain access to his own, which she promptly did.

Another neighbour, Mary Ann Schofield, who lived opposite 3 Minver Place, at 12 New Weston Street, saw Mrs Manning leave the property in a cab on the afternoon of Monday 13 August at about 3.15 pm. Frederick appeared at the house at about 5.30 pm. He knocked at the door twice and then tapped at the window. As there was no answer, he crossed the road and knocked at the Schofields' door. When Mary Ann opened it, he asked, 'Have you seen my wife?' She told him that she had seen Mrs Manning leave in a cab. He then asked, 'Had she any luggage with her?' Mary Ann replied, 'Yes, a great deal.' She informed him that his wife had departed at about 3.30 pm. He thanked her and crossed back over the road to no. 2 Minver Place, where he asked for access to his own house. Soon a fresh lead came to light about further events of early that week, which finally gave the police a clearer idea of where the Mannings might have gone.

Information was received at Scotland Yard, in response to the posters about the Mannings which had been circulated throughout the capital, which confirmed that Frederick Manning had left Minver Place on Monday 13 August. He had arranged with Charles Bainbridge, who was a furniture dealer, to sell all the furniture at the property for £13 10s (the police estimated it to have been worth £40). Manning had then stayed at the Bainbridges' house for two nights. Charles and Mary Ann Bainbridge lived at 14 Bermondsey Square, which was a seven-minute walk from Minver Place. Bainbridge had known the Mannings for about two months and the sale of their furniture had been first discussed on 20 July, about three weeks before they moved out of the house, with Maria initially asking for £16. After that, Charles had visited the property several times and, as he told *The Morning Post*, he had had several discussions with Frederick Manning about the removal of the furniture, with the latter constantly changing his mind. They finally agreed that Bainbridge would remove the items on Tuesday 14 August.

Manning and Bainbridge arrived at Minver Place together in the morning and when Bainbridge offered for Frederick to come into the property to wait while he cleared it, he refused saying, 'No, I would not come into the house for £20.' He opted to wait in the nearby Leather Market Tavern instead. Bainbridge sent the goods to Bermondsey Square by cab. The inn's potman later told *The Globe* that Bainbridge left a trunk and a carpet bag at Minver Place, saying that he would collect them another time. The trunk was small with two handles. According to the glass collector, someone else took them away.

When they were settled at Bermondsey Square, Frederick asked Bainbridge if he had any apartments to let for a fortnight. The furniture dealer said that he had, and it was agreed that the Mannings would lodge with them for 10 shillings a week. Frederick then sent a message to his wife for her to come to Bermondsey Square to inspect the accommodation, but Maria never appeared. Presumably it was at this point that he went back to Minver Place to look for her. *The London Evening Standard* claimed that after he had arrived at Bainbridge's house, Frederick had sent out for a shilling's worth of brandy, which he drank as soon as it came. While he was drinking, he asked Mrs Bainbridge to say to anyone who might come looking for him that she had not seen him for a fortnight, as he had defaulted on a bill worth £200.

During the evening, whenever anyone came to the door, Frederick became agitated and asked anxiously if the police were coming for him. The newspaper also revealed that Manning asked the dealer if he knew anyone in the City who would buy French railway shares. Bainbridge apparently recommended one of his contacts. The same newspaper speculated that the Mannings had procured the house at Minver Place for the purpose of killing O'Connor, after which they had got rid of almost all their property. The report concluded that 'through their extravagance and dissipation', their situation had become critical.

The following morning, despite a night of heavy drinking, Frederick was out of bed and packed by the time the Bainbridges had got up. After resisting their attempts to persuade him to have breakfast with them, he left Bermondsey Square in a cab at 8 am, after which the trail ran cold. His destination was a mystery, and the Metropolitan police were baffled about where he might have gone. However, there was soon a breakthrough in the investigation due to the assistance of another constabulary.

After receiving information about the missing couple, Superintendent Hodgsale, of the City of London police, instructed his officers to find out if any cab drivers had taken a fare from Bermondsey Square around the time that Frederick had disappeared. An Inspector Perkins discovered that John Marshall had collected Manning in his cab from 14 Bermondsey Square at 7.50 am. Manning had instructed the driver to take him through the back streets to Waterloo station, from where he had caught a parliamentary train on the South Western Railway to an unknown destination at 8.20 am. Bainbridge informed the police that Manning had a carpet bag and a leather trunk with him, containing three new suits. By 10 am, assuming that Frederick was making for the coast to flee overseas, the Scotland Yard detectives had already sent telegraphs to Southampton, Gosport and Portsmouth to warn the authorities to be on the lookout for the fugitive.

The Morning Post speculated that Manning had taken a parliamentary train due to a lack of funds (this was basic rail travel provided at low cost by the government), as he had spent money on wine and more brandy after leaving Bermondsey Square, as well as settling a bill, which had left him with only £11 for his onward journey. The report also stated that he had separated from his wife, but rather due to their incompatibility than in connection with the murder of Patrick O'Connor: 'Upon her side her love was not of a very ardent character; they were frequently in the habit of fighting.'

However, despite all the efforts of the police and the new leads they had uncovered, up to late on Saturday evening, there was still no news of the whereabouts of Maria and Frederick Manning.

Chapter 7

An Exciting Chase

Patrick O'Connor's funeral took place on Sunday 19 August, just two days after his remains had been found under the floor of 3 Minver Place. His body was interred in the Roman Catholic cemetery on Commercial Road East 'in the presence of a vast concourse of people, who followed the corpse from Bermondsey', according to *The Morning Post*. The funeral was attended by Patrick's brother, Reverend Dr Thomas O'Connor. It is not known which of Patrick's friends were in attendance, but it was reported in the press that they complained bitterly to Constables Burton and Barnes, who were present, that the police had not implemented surveillance on the Mannings' house after Patrick had gone missing.

While the burial service was taking place, the murder scene was still being visited by thousands of people, who were attracted to Minver Place by the lengthy and detailed accounts of the crime published in the newspapers. Although several police officers were on duty at the house and in the street, under the direction of Inspectors Perkins and Cowlan of the Southwark police, it was extremely difficult to keep the crowd from entering the premises, as the sightseers were anxious to see the exact spot where the murder was committed. The situation was so disruptive that the landlord, James Coleman, made a formal request at Stones End police station for the officers to withdraw from his rental property, as their presence only encouraged more interest; he was keen to fill the hole in the basement and so remove the cause of so much unwelcome curiosity. Coleman received £6 and 10 shillings from the Metropolitan police for the damage and disruption.

While Patrick's friends and family were laying him to rest, the police continued to search for his killers. Although the Mannings had left Minver Place on different days, the detectives assumed that they had planned to meet at a port on the south coast, from where they might have taken a passage overseas, especially as Maria had strong links with the continent, and experience of journeying around it. With that in mind, the police sent a message to Superintendent Rutt of the neighbouring division of Lambeth, who happened to be in Southampton for his health. They asked him to look for the suspects in the coastal city, but he was unable to find any trace of them.

The Scotland Yard officers also learnt, via a communication from Whitehall, that on the day Patrick's body was found, a police constable had travelled to Portsmouth with a man whose wife had run away. While searching a vessel for some possessions that the eloping woman had taken with her, he spotted a man matching Frederick Manning's description, who was securing a berth on a passage to New York. Once again, the search led to a dead end. Despite these setbacks, however, the police soon gained some new information, which would help them build their case against the couple.

It transpired that Frederick Manning had acquired the quicklime, which was allegedly used for O'Connor's grave, from a Mr Wells, who was a bricklayer and plasterer in Russell Street (now Tanner Street), about five minutes' walk from Minver Place. On 23 July, ten days after he attempted to buy the crowbar, Manning went to Wells' house and asked to buy 6 pence worth of lime for killing slugs in the garden. When the bricklayer's daughter, Mary, asked him whether he would like grey or white lime, Frederick replied that he wanted that which burned the quickest. Mary responded that the white would be best, but that they did not have any. Frederick agreed to take the grey, and he wrote the delivery address on a piece of paper and left.

Two days later, the builder's young assistant, Richard Welsh, took the bushel of lime to Minver Place as directed. On arrival, Manning instructed him to take it down into the kitchen, which he did. Frederick followed him down the stairs to the back kitchen and showed him where to empty it. Welsh put the lime into a basket, after which Manning told him to return the next day for a tip. The following day, the boy received three halfpennies from Mrs Manning for his trouble. Richard Welsh later remembered Frederick Manning because 'he behaved so rude'.

The police also received information from the furniture dealer, Charles Bainbridge, that the Mannings had had a lodger called William Massey, aged 19, who was a medical student at Guy's Hospital. Originally from the hamlet of Ingleby near Swarkestone in Derbyshire, the farmer's son had been educated at a private academy in Mackworth and was later admitted to London University to read medicine. He had moved in with the Mannings on 26 May and stayed with them for two months until 28 July, after which he lodged with the Bainbridges. Charles recounted an incident to PC Burton that occurred between Massey and Manning, which offered further evidence of the latter's guilt.

One evening, while they were having a drink and smoking a pipe together, Manning said to Massey, 'You know that old fellow, O'Connor, who comes here?' After William had replied in the affirmative, Frederick said, 'Well, you can get some stuff to drug him, and if you will do so, I'll give it to him, and then we can make him sign his name to a bill for two or three hundred.' 'It will be all right,' he reassured the younger man, 'we'll halve it.' Massey responded by saying, 'I am a gentleman. I'll do nothing of the sort.' According to Bainbridge, it was after this altercation that the medical student left Minver Place. This was confirmed by a report in *Bell's Weekly Messenger*, in which it was stated that a cabman named Reed had taken William and his luggage to 14 Bermondsey Square, which was the Bainbridges' home. (They had gained this information from a Sergeant Henhinick.) The newspaper speculated that the Mannings had given their lodger notice 'to accomplish their diabolical intention'. At the time of Patrick O'Connor's death, Massey was away in the countryside, where he was visiting some friends. PC Burton wrote to him requesting him to return to London so that he could give a testimony at the next sitting of the adjourned inquest.

As the investigation was taking place, a number of reports of sightings of the culprits were forwarded to the police. Frederick Manning had apparently been seen at Paddington railway station, where he had been drinking beer with a porter. The witness added that when the fugitive had caught sight of a newspaper, he had fled. He was also spotted in Liverpool. The police dismissed these accounts as 'absurd'. At this stage, they believed that Frederick was in France and the Metropolitan police commissioners had sent information about him to Constantine Phipps, 1st Marquess of Normanby, who was the British ambassador in Paris, and had given him the authority to make an arrest. In the meantime, they turned their attention to Mrs Manning.

It was soon discovered that Maria had visited Patrick O'Connor's lodgings in Mile End on the day he was murdered, but it had not been considered suspicious as she was a regular visitor, and his death was unknown at the time. She arrived at Greenwood Street at 5.45 pm, entered through the private door and went up the stairs to Patrick's rooms, where she stayed for an hour and a half. She went in alone and no one joined her. When Maria visited again at the same time the following day, the landlady's sister let her in. On her way out, Maria bought a biscuit from the shop and when she took the change, Ann Armes noticed that her hands were shaking. It was later found that Maria had rummaged through the drawers in Patrick's accommodation and taken some watches, several items of jewellery, a considerable sum of money and some railway shares.

On the afternoon of Monday 20 August, in the company of Patrick's brother Thomas and their cousin William Flynn, PC Burton went to the gaugers' office at the London Docks where the deceased had worked, to see if they could find anything of interest. After breaking into his desk, they undertook a thorough search and came across several letters written to O'Connor by Maria Manning, while she was still single. They were, as cited in *Lloyd's Weekly*, 'couched in the most endearing terms'. Many of the letters contained references to financial transactions with third parties. The searchers also found correspondence from Patrick to Mrs Manning, in which he addressed her as his 'dear Maria'. The newspaper reported that: 'The clerks in the office have generally been much amused by his [O'Connor's] gallantry with the female sex, as he generally exhibited all letters received from ladies of his acquaintance and felt very vain of them.' In the office, they also found a letter from the Mannings' lodger, William Massey, inviting him to dine at Minver Place as 'Mrs M wishes to see you particularly.' The letter was undated, but the postmark revealed that it had been sent to Patrick at the docks on Tuesday 7 August, two days before he went missing.

The police further discovered that Mrs Manning had called at a stockbrokers three weeks before Patrick's body was found. Apparently, she had inquired as to where she could dispose of overseas railway shares, which were likely to be those she had taken from the deceased's lodgings. According to *Lloyd's Weekly*, Maria had also written to a hotel owner in Geneva about selling railway stock. The report stated that a detective was sent to Switzerland to investigate.

The detectives knew that Mrs Manning had left Minver Place for the last time during the afternoon of Monday 13 August in a cab. She had loaded three boxes and a carpet bag into the vehicle, put her head out of the window and shouted, 'Be quick, drive fast!' Detective Sergeant Shaw of Scotland Yard tracked down the driver, William Kirk. He revealed that Maria had hailed him at his stand on Joiner Street, Southwark, between 3.30 pm and 4 pm. Kirk had picked up his fare at Minver Place and driven her to London Bridge station. En route, Mrs Manning pulled the cord in the cab for the driver to stop at Mr Ash's stationer's shop, so that she could buy six plain white cards to make labels for her luggage. Borrowing a pen from the stationer, she wrote on four of the tags, 'Mrs Smith, passenger to Paris. To be left till called for'. On arrival at London Bridge station, she enlisted the help of a porter from whom she acquired some tacks, which she used to attach the labels to her luggage. She then deposited two boxes, one large and one small, in the left luggage office, after which Kirk took her to Euston station with her remaining baggage. He dropped her there at 5.45 pm. It seemed that Maria Manning was heading north and not joining her husband as assumed. However, before the police could investigate further, an exciting potential lead materialised.

During the day on Monday 20 August, more information had come into the capital's police stations about the possible escape route of the missing couple. Firstly, that Frederick Manning had cashed a cheque drawn by O'Connor for £50 at the Bank of England, on the morning of Saturday 11 August. In light of this intelligence, the detectives printed a new handbill which included the numbers of the five £10 notes that he had withdrawn from the bank. They were all dated 11 June 1849. It further cautioned anyone who had received the notes against changing them, requesting that they be presented at Scotland Yard. *The Globe* commented that: 'The deceased generally carried cheques about him, and there is no doubt this is one taken from him after the murder.' Also, the newspaper reporters had uncovered significant evidence which might finally lead to Frederick Manning's arrest.

During a visit to Minver Place, a journalist found two cards in a fireplace at the house, one of which was a list of the departure times of a line of packet ships sailing between London and New York. The other was a plain card with, 'Mr Wright, passenger to New York' written on it. The reporter handed these to the police who were guarding the house, one of whom tore them up, remarking 'it was not very likely that, if they had intended to go to New York, they would have left the cards behind.' The reporter tried again to speak to the police about the matter on Sunday 19 August, but they too dismissed it and, despite the journalist's persistence, did not act on the information.

The following day, the rather determined reporter contacted the vessel's brokers, Messrs Phillips, Shaw and Lowther, who instructed a clerk to accompany him to the London Docks to check the passenger list of anyone who had paid for a passage to New York on the *Victoria,* which was due to sail. The list only contained the names of those booked into steerage. However, they discovered that six packages in the name of 'Manning' were listed on the emigrant ship, but it was not possible initially to tell whether this was a man or a woman. It was later ascertained that a Mrs Manning had taken four packages on board, and her supposed husband had transferred the other two.

It was presumed therefore that the Mannings were travelling together. There was also a box directed to a Mr Wright in New York, as had been written on the card, which had been transported down to the docks but, due to an error, had not been placed on board.

Unfortunately, by this time, the *Victoria* had already sailed and had left the London Docks on Friday 17 August. She was expected in Portsmouth on Monday. The information was sent to the lord mayor, Thomas Farncombe, who transmitted it to Metropolitan Police Commissioner Richard Mayne. He, in turn, passed it on to Detective Inspector Haynes. The Scotland Yard detective telegraphed the authorities in Portsmouth, requesting them to send officers on board the vessel and apprehend the Mannings, should they be there. Detectives Thornton and Langley, who would be able to identify Frederick due to his alleged involvement in the railway robberies, were granted a special warrant by the Southwark magistrate for the couple's arrest.

As soon as the detectives arrived in Portsmouth, they contacted the head of the borough police, Superintendent William Leggatt. They soon discovered that the *Victoria*, which had more than 270 emigrants on board, had already set out on its journey across the Atlantic and was scheduled to pass Portland Bill. The police officers signalled to the vessel to stop but it carried on its way. Frustrated, the detectives returned to the telegraph office, where they transmitted the news back to London. However, while they were waiting for further instructions, one of the local magistrates advised them to apply to the commander of the Royal Navy, who was based in Portsmouth, for one of Her Majesty's steamships, with which they could give chase to the *Victoria*. Thornton and Langley went straight to the dockyard with Superintendent Leggatt, and Admiral Thomas Bladen Capel, the commander-in-chief, immediately placed HMS *Fire Queen* at their disposal. The vessel was an iron paddle steamer with two masts, which had been built on the Clyde in Scotland. She was launched in 1844 and, by 1847, had been placed at the disposal of the Admiralty.

The Scotland Yard officers boarded the vessel at Gosport at 8 pm and, an hour later, she was ready to set out under the command of a Captain Allen. They passed several ships in the night, including a Prussian man-of-war, which they initially thought was the emigrant ship, before finally catching up with the *Victoria* at a quarter to two in the early hours of Tuesday morning. The captain signalled to the vessel, and it hove to. The Scotland Yard detectives went aboard with Superintendent Leggatt. The captain of the *Victoria* confirmed that there were indeed two passengers on the ship with the name of 'Manning'. After an hour and a half of searching, the police officers finally located them.

Detective Thornton later disclosed to Charles Dickens that they had not informed the travellers on the emigrant ship that they were looking for the Mannings. He described how he went down below decks into steerage with the captain. He was holding his lamp in his hand as it was dark, and all the passengers were in bed. After a search, the officer located Mrs Manning, who raised her head and turned towards the light. He questioned her about her luggage and concluded that she was not the woman who was wanted for the murder of Patrick O'Connor. Rebecca Manning was a 39-year-old emigrant who was travelling to America with her young daughter. The six parcels listed on the ship belonged to them.

Despite the police's disappointing failure, the press maintained optimism that Frederick and Maria Manning would still be caught:

> In the meantime, patience must be practised, and the public at large is entreated as well as enjoined, in the interests of the society at large, to afford every facility for the arrest of the individuals charged with this dreadful murder, and for bringing them to a speedy punishment for this awful crime. (*The Morning Post*, 20 August 1849)

Chapter 8

The Electric Constable

Shortly after the discovery of Patrick O'Connor's body on Friday 17 August, the message bearing the description of the alleged perpetrators had been sent to all the police stations in the capital. At the same time, police officers had been despatched to the railway stations and steamboat piers in and around London, requesting information about anyone who might fit the fugitives' description. The detectives of Scotland Yard had also sent a 'telegraphic communication' along the railway lines to reach every large town and city in the country where, by Saturday, posters with the Mannings' particulars had also been circulated.

In 1849, the telegraph had only been in existence on the railway lines for just over a decade, and about a third of the network had been connected, covering some 1,800 miles of track. Four years earlier, the police had used this new technology to catch a killer for the first time.

On New Year's Day 1845, Mary Ann Ashley of Salt Hill, a suburb of Slough, spotted a man visiting her next-door neighbour, Sarah Hart. Two hours later, Mrs Ashley was sitting by the fire in her home when she heard a scream. Grabbing a candle, she made her way into the garden and saw that the man was leaving. Thinking she could hear moans, she then entered her neighbour's property and found Sarah Hart lying on the floor. Her clothes were dishevelled, and she was foaming at the mouth. Despite Mary Ann's efforts to revive her, Sarah died.

The man visiting Sarah that afternoon was her lover and former employer, John Tawell. Aged 61, he was a respectable merchant. A married man, John was a member of the Society of Friends. Sarah had been nursemaid to his children after the death of his first wife and had had two children with him. When he married again, Sarah was dismissed, but Tawell continued to pay for his illegitimate family. The two young children, Frederick, aged 5, and Sarah, 4, were both in the house when their mother died. The post-mortem revealed that she had been poisoned with prussic acid.

When John Tawell left the house on the evening of 1 January, he was seen by several witnesses, as well as the neighbour. These included the post boy, who recognised the frequent visitor, and the local vicar. Tawell was particularly conspicuous as he was dressed in the typical garb of a Quaker, wearing a broad-brimmed hat, a white cravat and a loose brown greatcoat. After spotting him, the vicar went straight to Slough railway station and informed the superintendent of his suspicions. However, by this time, Tawell had already left on the 7.42 pm train to Paddington.

The line from London Paddington, which had been extended to Slough two years earlier, carried an electric telegraph system. Developed in the 1830s, the telegraph was first used on the railway between Euston Square terminus and Camden in 1837, initially for warnings about oncoming trains. The following year, inventor William Fothergill Cooke and scientist Charles Wheatstone established the world's first telegraph network on the Great Western Railway. In 1845, Superintendent Howell used this groundbreaking innovation to his advantage. He sent a message via the stationmaster to his colleagues at Paddington station, who were waiting for the prime suspect when he alighted the train. Two constables tailed him into the city and John Tawell was arrested the following day in one of his favourite haunts, the Jerusalem Coffee House near Cornhill. He was later convicted of Sarah Hart's murder and executed. Citing the Tawell case, an editorial in *The Illustrated London News* praised the efficiency of this new invention, particularly in relation to offenders who fled the scene of a crime by train:

> detection is sure to dog the footsteps of crime – that the guilty wretch, flying on the wings of steam thirty miles an hour, is tracked by a swifter messenger – and that the lightning itself, by the wondrous agency of the electric telegraph, conveys to the remotest parts of the kingdom an account of his crime, a description of his person, and an incentive to the officers of justice, in the shape of a promised reward, for his capture and conviction.

The telegraphic system that facilitated John Tawell's swift capture in 1845 became known as 'the electric constable'. It would be used to great effect in the hunt for the Mannings in contrast to the slow communication by paper and on foot that had so badly impeded the capture of Daniel Good just three years before the new technology's inception.

On the morning of Tuesday 21 August, four days after the discovery of Patrick O'Connor's body, Detective Sergeant Shaw communicated his recent discoveries in relation to Maria Manning's flight to Detective Inspector Haynes, his colleague at Scotland Yard. He told his superior that he had established that, after leaving some luggage at London Bridge railway station, she had alighted the cab at Euston station, which was the headquarters of the London and North Western Railway. Therefore, the detective assumed that she was planning to flee northwards. Inspector Haynes' first action was to try to locate her baggage.

London Bridge railway station was (and still is) on Tooley Street in Bermondsey, close to Minver Place. The capital's oldest running terminus, the first building dated from 1836. By 1849, it had been rebuilt and was now served by the South Eastern Railway on its Greenwich branch. According to the cab driver, William Kirk, Maria Manning had left two boxes in the left luggage office labelled 'Mrs Smith' on Monday 13 August.

Inspector Haynes entered the office and asked the two or three employees about the baggage. A Mr Day showed him the boxes, one of which was large and the other small. They both had labels with the expected details on. As described in the *Morning Advertiser*: 'The suspicions previously entertained by Mr Haynes now ripened into certainties.' The detective went straight to the secretary of the railway company, George Sowerby Herbert, to request that the luggage be opened. Mr Herbert conferred with the directors and finally agreed after the Metropolitan police commissioners intervened by telegraph in support of the detective's application. The boxes were removed to the secretary's office, where Haynes forced them open.

The larger box contained mainly household items, including fifty-two napkins, forty-five towels, twenty-seven pillowcases and eight sheets. There were also twenty-nine forks, seventeen knives and twenty-eight spoons of different sizes, such as for salt, gravy and eggs, as well as teaspoons. In addition, there was a teapot, a coffee pot, a sugar basin and tongs, a toast rack and a box of French artificial flowers. The few personal items in the box included three books, a silver pencil case, a work box, some hair pins, and letters and memos in French. There was also a tablecloth and a dressing table cover stained with blood.

The smaller box contained clothing, which included twenty-eight pairs of stockings, nineteen pairs of gloves, eleven petticoats, nine night gowns and three capes. Some of the clothes, such as two shirts, were marked 'Frederick Manning'. A tablecloth also bore his name and 'White Horse, Taunton'.

There was evidence of Maria's dressmaking skills, which she would have used as a lady's maid, with a work box containing ribbons and remnants of fabric. Most significantly, Inspector Haynes noticed a bottle of sulphuric acid, a gown, another dressing table cover and a piece of muslin, all with bloodstains. The detective later stated that the dress appeared 'to have been recently washed'.

After his examination of the contents of the luggage, 'that clever officer', as he was dubbed in the press, went to Euston station to continue his search for Mrs Manning. He soon discovered that a woman, whose luggage was marked with the name 'Smith', had boarded a train at 6.15 am on the Tuesday morning bound for Edinburgh. She had travelled in a first-class carriage.

At 12.50 pm, having now exhausted these new leads, Detective Inspector Haynes telegraphed the superintendent of the Edinburgh police with a full description of the female suspect. He had scarcely arrived back at the detective office, about an hour and a half later, when a messenger from the telegraph office brought him a communication from Scotland to say that Maria Manning had been arrested. Details of further items found on her person and in her belongings followed an hour later. Detective Haynes' timely investigative actions were praised in the newspapers:

> The activity displayed by this officer may be judged from the fact that scarcely an hour elapsed between the message having been sent, and the reply communicating the gratifying intelligence of the woman's arrest. (*Lloyd's Weekly*, 26 August 1849)

The arresting officer was the chief superintendent of the Edinburgh City police, Richard John Moxey. Aged 46, he was born in 1803 in the town of Haddington in East Lothian, two years before the establishment of the constabulary in which he would later serve. Richard began his judicial career in Edinburgh as a sheriff-clerk, which was a court official. In 1829, he was present at the confession of the infamous bodysnatcher, William Burke. Moxey was appointed chief superintendent of police in 1848.

Superintendent Moxey was not a detective. James McLevy, an investigating officer under Moxey's command, was quite scathing towards his superior. In a series of books based on his memoirs, which he published in the 1860s, McLevy recalled a case of stolen watches from a watchmaker in the city, in which Moxey had received some information which revealed that eighteen of the missing items had been recovered in Glasgow. McLevy commented sarcastically: 'Mr Moxey got the intelligence, and whether or not it was that he had been suddenly seized with the ambition of becoming a practical detective I cannot say.' The man who was found with the watches in his possession said, during his confession, that the thieves resided in a public house in Edinburgh belonging to a Mrs Walker. Superintendent Moxey rushed off to arrest them without referring the matter to McLevy. Unable to find the tavern, the superintendent soon gave up the search. However, McLevy knew where the public house was. He later went there himself and recovered the remainder of the watches. Interestingly, the detective makes no references to the Manning case in his published recollections, perhaps because he missed out on the action.

On Tuesday 21 August, when the Edinburgh police had received the telegraph about Maria Manning from Detective Inspector Haynes, they began by searching the railway station, but they could find no trace of the missing woman. Shortly after, Robert Dobson, a city stockbroker, came into the main police station with some new information; a woman answering the fugitive's description had visited his office and left her name and address, as Mrs Smith, 25 Haddington Place, Leith Walk. The broker gave a description of his customer. Superintendent Moxey compared it with that of Mrs Manning and decided that it was a match. The two men then proceeded to the address with another officer, Detective John Fallon, to investigate.

One of the longest streets in the city, which connects Edinburgh and Leith, in the mid-nineteenth century, Leith Walk was populated by fine mansion houses and market gardens. A contemporary sketch shows it to be genteel, with a wide paved boulevard bordered with gas lamps and trees. The smoking chimneys of factories are pictured in the far distance. Arriving at the lodging house, Moxey left Mr Dobson outside the room and entered with his plain-clothes companion. They encountered a well-dressed woman who was reading a copy of *The Times* from the previous day which, as *The Globe* pointed out, 'gave an account of the murder and a description of the parties supposed to have committed it.' According to *Lloyd's Weekly*, when the police entered the room, Maria Manning's 'face became deadly pale, and she bit her lip and showed other symptoms of uneasiness.'

Superintendent Moxey began by asking the woman to identify herself: 'I beg pardon for intruding; if you are really Mrs Smith, you are not the person I am in search of; may I request to ask, are you a married lady?' She confirmed that she was. When the police officer inquired about her husband, she replied, 'Oh, he is dead.' 'Mrs Smith' told them that she had been in Edinburgh for a few days, arriving the previous Tuesday or Wednesday. The superintendent asked if there was anyone in the city who knew her and who could verify the information. She replied that there was a neighbour called Mr Shaw, who had recommended the lodgings to her. Next, the police officer asked her where she had been previously and what her business was in Edinburgh. She replied, 'I last came from Newcastle, and the occasion of my visit is for the benefit of my health.' She then mentioned Portobello, a coastal resort about three miles to the east of the city, where she had been bathing.

The senior officer continued the conversation by inquiring about her finances, specifically whether she had any railway shares. The woman said that she did not. Moxey looked her straight in the eyes and said, 'My impression is, that you are the wife of Frederick George Manning.' Before she had chance to deny it, he sent for Mr Dobson who identified her as 'the lady who offered me scrip'. The officer asked if he could check her luggage, which consisted of a carpet bag, a trunk and a small box. At this point the landlady, Mrs Stewart, appeared and 'Mrs Smith' gave him the keys.

Moxey's fellow officer opened the small box, and his superior instructed him to look for 'any papers that will throw any light upon this'. One of the first items he found was a bill headed 'F. G. Manning' with the name of a Taunton hotel. With her identity confirmed, Superintendent Moxey charged Maria Manning with the murder of Patrick O'Connor, after which he asked her again if she had any railway shares with her. She directed him to the trunk, which was unlocked. Inside, he found some sovereigns and a piece of cloth containing several railway scrips. Mrs Manning commented that she had consulted Patrick O'Connor about purchasing the shares, and he had advised her to contact a stockbroker named Stevens, which she did. Some of the shares in her possession had been bought by O'Connor on her behalf.

Saying that he was anxious to track down her husband, the superintendent asked Maria about his whereabouts, to which she replied, 'Well, upon my honour, I don't know where he is; I came off from London suddenly, while he was out.' She described how she had left the city on the afternoon of Monday 13 August and had taken the cab to London Bridge station, where she had deposited some of her luggage in the name of 'Mrs Smith'. At that time, she had not decided whether to travel to France or Scotland. In the end, she had driven to Euston station and spent the night in the neighbourhood before catching the train to Edinburgh. She had changed trains at Birmingham and Newcastle as she navigated the rail network through the different railway companies, arriving in Edinburgh the next morning.

Mrs Manning reassured the officers that she had not murdered Patrick O'Connor: 'he was the kindest friend I had in the world; he has acted the part of a father to me.' She recounted how Patrick had dined with her on the evening of Wednesday 8 August. He had arrived 'the worse for liquor' and had left late. Maria told the police that she had invited him to dinner again the following evening, but he had not turned up. Indignant that he had failed to appear, she had gone to his lodgings in Greenwood Street that same evening to find out why. Despite a second visit on the Friday evening, she still could not discover the reason for his absence.

Maria also complained about her husband's mistreatment of her; Frederick had pursued her with a knife and threatened to 'cut off her head'. She added that they often quarrelled because she would not give him any of her money. Mrs Manning was taken to the police office with her luggage for further examination. Following the successful arrest, Superintendent Moxey was lauded in *The Scotsman* as 'our active and intelligent Superintendent of Police'.

When the police searched Mrs Manning at the station, they discovered several items of value on her person. These included a gold-plated chain and seal, three rings and two brooches. They also found a thimble, a purse containing 3 shillings, some postage stamps and a piece of paper with the name and address of her landlady, Mrs Stewart. Next, the officers opened her luggage.

Maria's large trunk contained mostly clothing; three dresses, fifteen handkerchiefs, nine pairs of gloves, four lace veils, lace collars, silk scarves, an apron and a fancy parasol. There were more than thirty pieces of silk and satin, some lace and ribbons, a bottle of eau de cologne and hair combs. More interestingly, the officers found shares from the French Boulogne and Amiens Railway, and the Sambre and Meuse Railway in Belgium as well as letters and papers, and a Spanish bond certificate.

Detectives also opened a large red carpet bag which contained a ticket from the London and North Western Railway excess luggage from London to Newcastle in the name of 'Smith'. Inside there was a gold ring and banknotes of various denominations amounting to £115 (about £12,000 in today's value). Finally, a search of Maria's rosewood work box yielded more personal items, including jewellery such as an antique gold watch, nine brooches, four rings, three breast pins and a coral necklace. There was more clothing: seven shirts, three lace veils, three pairs of kid gloves, and more lace and ribbons as well as fabrics. In addition, there was a crystal bottle containing an unknown liquid, her marriage certificate, a pawnbroker's ticket from January 1849, some of Frederick Manning's accounts, and letters between her husband and Lord Blantyre, the husband of Maria's former employer.

In addition to the items contained in her luggage, the police also removed any other belongings they found in her room at the lodging house. These included three bonnets, six petticoats, nine handkerchiefs, seven shifts, nine pairs of stockings and three pairs of ladies' boots. There were other personal possessions: a volume of sacred poetry, some psalms in French, a hat brush, a scent bottle, two pots of ointment, a comb, a box of lucifer matches, two pairs of scissors, a needle case, a French dictionary and a silk parasol. There were also lists of shares dated 1, 10 and 16 August 1849.

The railway shares in Maria Manning's possession were known to have belonged to Patrick O'Connor. However, there was even more incriminating evidence: when the Edinburgh police officers compared the numbers of the banknotes found in her carpet bag, five of them matched those circulated by Scotland Yard. It was clear that they had been given to Frederick Manning when he had cashed in the victim's cheque on Saturday 11 August.

The police then pieced together her actions since her arrival in the city four days later. On Friday 17 August, Mrs Manning bought some items from a draper on the High Street and enquired about local stockbrokers. After completing the purchase of a pair of stockings, the draper advised her to contact Messrs Hughson and Dobson whose office was at the Royal Exchange. She called on the stockbrokers the following day and discussed the possible sale of shares in railways at home and overseas. Maria told the stockbrokers that she had shares in the Boulogne and Amiens, and the Sambre and Meuse Railways, as well as between £300 and £500 in cash. The brokers offered to sell her stock through their London agents and, when she asked if she would be able to receive dividends overseas, they warned her against travelling abroad with a large amount of money and suggested that she deposit it in a bank account, to which she replied tapping her breast, 'I keep it here, where it is quite safe.' After telling them that her father, whom she referred to as 'Robertson', had lived in Glasgow and that he had lost a great deal of money in railway shares, she handed them a railway share certificate on which it was marked that one pound per share had already been paid. She asked them to find out whether any further payment was due. They gave her a receipt for the certificate, and she left.

On Monday morning, Mrs Manning returned to the office and spoke to Mr Dobson. Saying that she was leaving for Newcastle that day, she asked him to return the share certificate that she had given him two days earlier, which he did. She then tore up the receipt and asked if Dobson still held a record of her name and address which she had left with the certificate. He could not find it, so she left. The next day, when the stockbrokers received a letter from the police with the details of foreign railway shares that had been stolen in London and a description of the possible suspect, they realised that it had been Maria Manning who had visited their office. Robert Dobson found the note that 'Mrs Smith' had left with her details, and they immediately contacted the police.

As reported in *The Globe*, on Wednesday 22 August, 'Thanks to the energy and activity of our detective police force, in the first instance, and secondly, to the great invention of the age – the electric telegraph – the woman was arrested yesterday in the city of Edinburgh.'

Chapter 9

'Crowds of the curious'

Built in 1817 with crenellated turrets and a classic stone façade, Calton Jail was once the largest prison in Scotland. In 1849, Maria Manning was held there pending her appearance at the city's sheriff court. However, she was spared from the rather notorious conditions of the jail by staying at the governor's house, and it was from there that she was taken by cab to the court at 10 am on Wednesday 22 August, the day after her arrest, to be examined by Sheriff Patrick Arkley.

A report in *Lloyd's Weekly* described how she walked into the dock 'with a firm, unfaltering step'. She was dressed neatly, and the newspaper further commented that 'from her easy and graceful manner she is evidently a person who has mixed a good deal in society.' Superintendent Moxey read out the charges of murder and theft, after which Sheriff Arkley warned her of the seriousness of her charges and stated that she need not say anything if she did not wish to. Maria replied in a low but distinct voice, 'I have nothing to say.' She was then removed from the dock and taken to the police station with her luggage, from where she would be returned to prison later to await transportation to London. It was expected that one or more Metropolitan police officers would be arriving that day to take her into their custody and accompany her back to the English capital. As the awaited detectives did not appear, Mrs Manning remained in the police cell until 5 pm, after which she was transferred quietly by cab back to the Edinburgh prison.

As this was the first time that Maria Manning had attended a hearing, albeit very briefly and only with the sheriff and police officers in attendance, the press was keen to share a first description of the suspected murderer with their readers. The *Caledonian Mercury* observed: 'The prisoner, while at the bar, was perfectly calm and collected, and her demeanour was quite that of a lady.' However, *Lloyd's Weekly* printed a rather more disparaging description:

during the whole time she was at the bar her countenance did not
betoken the slightest symptoms of agitation or alarm … There
is a kind of dogged expression about her face, which, when
conjoined with her bold and somewhat callous manner at the bar
… led not a few of the on-lookers to say that she was just such as
woman as could assist in the devising and carrying out of such
a deed.

The Globe opined that it was 'a singular fact' that the Mannings had taken
every precaution to cover up their crime and yet Mrs Manning had retained
the railway shares in her possession which 'were certain to lead to her
identification as the murderess.' The commentator suggested that she might
have kept them as 'a peculiar sort of fascination' with the event or that she
had not realised she could not easily cash them like banknotes.

Back in London, people had been gathering throughout the day at Euston
station in the hope of seeing Maria Manning, as she was expected to return
to the capital that evening, following her appearance at the Edinburgh sheriff
court. *The Globe* reported that: 'A great crowd of spectators awaited the
arrival of the various trains at Euston station … under the impression that
Mrs Manning would arrive in town from the north' on the evening of Tuesday
21 August after her arrest. The first train that was considered possibly to be
the one in which she was travelling was the 9 pm service from Edinburgh.
When it arrived at its destination at 1 pm on Wednesday, 'the arrival platform
and the entrance thereto were crowded with people, all anxious to obtain a
glimpse at the accused woman.' Every carriage was eagerly scrutinised for
the accused and *The Globe* commented that 'it was really wonderful that some
very innocent lady passenger was not placed in the unpleasant predicament
of being mistaken for a murderess.'

After the passengers had undergone 'a rigid examination' of the carriages,
the spectators plied the guards with questions, who all pleaded ignorance
of when the prisoner was due to arrive. The crowd next considered the
possibility that she might arrive at 10.45 pm on the Wednesday evening, if
she had taken the express train that morning. However, once again, Maria
Manning did not alight the train. *The Globe* surmised that her delay was due
to the 'intense excitement'.

'A great deal of excitement' also prevailed in the vicinity of Scotland Yard,
according to the *Morning Advertiser*. Inside the detective office, the police
had been working hard to uncover more evidence with which to build the case

against the Mannings. On 22 August, Inspector John Perkins of Southwark Division confirmed that Maria Manning had been in correspondence with overseas contacts prior to the murder of Patrick O'Connor, perhaps to secure an escape route. He reported to Scotland Yard detectives that a grocer named Bundy, who kept a post office at 200 Bermondsey Street, had informed him that Mrs Manning had posted a letter on Monday 13 August, the day she left Minver Place. It was addressed to the 'British Hotel' in Boulogne. A week later, on 21 August, she had received a letter at the post office from Paris. This would substantiate the detectives' original assumption that she was intending to flee to the continent, and the correspondence might even offer some clues as to the whereabouts of her husband, who was still at large.

Also, additional details of the post-mortem examination on the remains of Patrick O'Connor shed some more light on the manner of his death. *The Globe* reported further on the results of the post-mortem undertaken on 18 August. The newspaper account described how a large bullet was extracted from the victim's skull which had apparently been discharged from an 'ordinary' pistol, rather than 'one of the large rifles used for shooting tigers'. The slug passed through the temporal bone in a slanting direction, which would not have caused death. It therefore seemed likely that, after receiving these wounds, Patrick 'must have struggled violently, and a period was put to his existence by repeated blows of a hammer or crow bar on the back part of the skull.' As previously stated, the blows were so brutal that his skull was smashed into ten or twelve pieces. The report added that the surgeon who had undertaken the post-mortem, George Odling, had retained possession of the skull fragments for display in court. Apparently, he had left some further pieces of bone in situ as he 'got quite weary' of removing them. Following his examination, Odling had concluded that the head injuries must have been caused by a broad, flat hammer. He also added that the murder must have taken place in the front kitchen, rather than the body having been moved from an upstairs room, as the noise of the gunshot would have been heard by the neighbours. This finally ended the speculation that he had been killed in one of the bedrooms and dragged down the stairs to the basement.

Furthermore, Mr Odling had also kept the victim's stomach with the intention of having the contents analysed, as he was convinced that O'Connor had been poisoned. A chemical analysis had not yet been undertaken, but *The Globe* revealed that the two bottles found at the scene of the crime had been confirmed as containing laudanum. One bottle was labelled, 'Poison, William Hill, chemist, 64 Bermondsey Street'. The other, which was made of cut glass and usually used for perfume, had contained about an ounce of the soporific drug. The newspaper concluded that these had been used by the Mannings 'in carrying out their deadly purpose'. One of the bottles was coated in quicklime, presumably due to it having been handled by someone with the substance on their hands. The journalist commented that it was surprising that there were no traces of blood found in any of the rooms at Minver Place as the scalp was 'dreadfully cut in many places, and, of course, a considerable effusion of blood must have taken place'. This new information was soon followed by even more incriminating evidence.

Inspector Yates, of M Division, had been coordinating further investigations on the ground in Bermondsey. On 22 August, the police discovered that Maria Manning had bought a shovel from a hardware shop belonging to a Mr Langley on Tooley Street, on Wednesday 8 August, the day before Patrick O'Connor was seen for the last time. The ironmonger's assistant, William Cahill, confirmed that Mrs Manning had come to the shop that afternoon to purchase a shovel. After he had showed several types of shovel to her, she said that she wanted a short-handled one. Cahill suggested several short-handled dust shovels, as well as some with longer wooden handles. Maria selected a short-handled one, which cost 15 pence, and asked for it to be sent to 3 Minver Place. The assistant took it to the specified address at 7 pm the same evening. William Cahill identified Maria Manning as the woman who had bought the shovel, and his employer, Mr Langley, declared that he was 'quite certain that the shovel in question was strong enough to remove any earth.'

Following the receipt of this information, Inspector Yates sent PC William Sopp to the house of Charles Bainbridge at 14 Bermondsey Square, in an attempt to recover the implement. When Bainbridge's wife handed the shovel to the police officer, the furniture dealer confirmed that it had been among the Mannings' belongings that he had recovered from Minver Place.

The evening after the police had recovered the shovel, which was likely to have been used in Patrick's murder, Charles Bainbridge sold the remaining furniture belonging to the Mannings by auction. When the lots were presented at the auction room in Prince's Street, it was not known at first from whom it had come. The items comprised four japanned chairs and an iron fender, a japanned chest with five drawers, two pairs of muslin curtains and two mats, a bronze fender and fire irons, a japanned French bedstead and mattress, a chimney mirror in a gilt frame, a set of eight mahogany chairs covered with satin hair cloth, and a mahogany-framed couch, which all sold for a total of £8 16 shillings. At this point in the sale, a person entered the room and informed the buyers about the identity of the previous owners. This increased the competition and the final lot, which was a four-foot mahogany table, fetched £2 2s. *Lloyd's Weekly* declared that the couch, which was sold at the auction, 'is supposed to have been that on which O'Connor used to smoke'. Unfortunately for the Bainbridges, despite the late interest in the items, they made a small loss on the sale.

While his furniture was being auctioned, Frederick Manning was still on the run and the police were desperately trying to find him. On the evening of Tuesday 21 August, when Detective Inspector Haynes had received the news of Maria Manning's arrest, Scotland Yard had received another telegram from the Scottish police at 11 pm asking, 'Is Manning in custody? Send back an immediate answer.' *The Globe* inferred from this that a person answering his description might have been spotted in Edinburgh. There was no further information about this request but, over the next couple of days, there were many possible sightings of the fugitive. The same newspaper later issued an update that the police believed Manning was 'lurking in some part of the west of England', likely in a coastal town or village. Two or three officers had been sent out in that direction as a precaution. There were also reports of sightings in London, but these were discounted by the police as it was quite certain that he had left the capital by the South Western Railway on 15 August.

As it was supposed that Frederick had taken the train to Southampton, two officers were despatched to the town to track him. In the meantime, it was discovered that a box had been left at Folkestone station, bearing the name of 'Manning'. Once again, this turned out to be a false lead. On Thursday 23 August, *The Morning Chronicle* reported that 'great excitement' had been caused in the area of Tottenham Court Road by the discovery of a man hanging from a tree in Bedford Square. The general public had jumped to the conclusion that the apparent suicide victim was Frederick Manning, even though he was five inches shorter and 'had the appearance of an Irish labourer'. The body was taken to St Giles workhouse to await possible identification. On the same day, a man also believed to have been Manning, but with his whiskers shaved, was arrested in Peter Street, Soho. He was taken to Vine Street police station where Detective Langley was sent for to identify him. The sergeant stated that 'although there was a great likeness', it was not Manning, and he was released.

One line of inquiry pursued by the police was to contact Frederick's family. At this time, four of his siblings were living in London. One of his oldest brothers, Joseph, was living in Grosvenor Square with their sister Elizabeth and her husband Peter Ralph, who was, in fact, a police officer. His fifth sibling Edmund (wrongly noted as 'Edward' in the press) was closer to Bermondsey, residing at 30 Frances Street, Newington Butts. His brother James was in Wiveliscombe, Somerset, and one sister, who was married to a man named Gandall, had remained in Taunton. Another sister, Harriet, was in Weymouth, where she and her husband, James Sly, ran the Cutter Inn. The detectives gave instructions to set up surveillance on all Frederick's brothers and sisters in case he should be hiding out in one of their homes.

The Globe revealed that the Scotland Yard detectives had also identified the boxes left by Maria Manning at London Bridge station as part of the luggage they had searched during the investigation into the mail robberies in 1848, in which her husband had initially been implicated. The newspaper described the apparent coincidence as 'one of those curious incidents which are perpetually occurring in the history of great crimes.'

Despite the ongoing endeavours of the police, the press lamented their continuing failure to catch Frederick Manning, as expressed in *Lloyd's Weekly*:

> Her [Maria Manning's] reputed husband continues at large, and although there is little doubt that he cannot long escape the keen pursuit of justice, yet it is remarkable that he has now for so many days baffled every effort to secure his person.

To that end, on 22 August, the Metropolitan police issued a new handbill, offering a £50 reward for information about Frederick George Manning, wanted for murder. It carried the same description of the fugitive as the previous communication and requested that information was to be submitted to any police station in the metropolis.

By Friday 24 August, crowds had been waiting at Euston station for three days for the arrival of Maria Manning from Edinburgh. The day before, *The Globe* had reported that a legal complexity had delayed her transfer back to London. The newspaper explained that, in their understanding, the Scottish authorities had no power to transport a person arrested for a crime in their country to England without a warrant from an English magistrate. At the time of the initial examination, Detective Inspector Field had the only warrant that had been issued. However, he was still overseas continuing his investigation into the case. The journalist pointed out that this issue might have been

67

solved by the use of the telegraph: 'It is somewhat strange that the facilities afforded by the electric telegraph were not called into action' by either police authority. Throughout the day, police officers had been sent to Euston station to receive the prisoner, but there had still been no news of her arrival.

Finally, after several hours, Detective Sergeants Walker and Shaw of Scotland Yard received a message from Superintendent Barker of the London and North Western Railway police regarding the situation, after which they passed it on to Chief Superintendent May of A Division. He in turn sought an interview with the chief magistrate at Bow Street, Mr Hall, who granted a second warrant for the arrest of Maria Manning. It was printed in the press that the new warrant had been given to Detective Inspector Haynes, who left by train for Edinburgh at 6.15 am on Thursday 23 August. He was due to arrive back in the capital with Mrs Manning later that evening. However, this was contradicted by *The Express*, who declared the published statement to have been 'erroneous'.

In the end, Maria Manning arrived in London on the Friday morning by the Caledonian mail train, which reached Euston station at 4.45 am. She had travelled from Scotland with Superintendent Moxey and two plain-clothes police officers who worked for the sheriff, John Milligan and John Fallon. They all rode together in the same first-class compartment. Inspector Darkin and Sergeant Sheppey, of Whitehall Division, were waiting on the platform at Euston to receive her.

As the train drew in, the crowd rushed towards the carriage. However, Superintendent Barker of the railway police 'had so perfected his arrangements ... that no confusion took place' (*The Morning Chronicle*, 25 August 1849) and Mrs Manning alighted freely from the train. After the door of the carriage was opened, she was ushered quickly into a two-wheeled cabriolet which set off at speed to Stones End police station in Southwark. *John Bull* reported that 'There was no manifestation of feeling on the part of the persons present, but great anxiety was shown to obtain a glimpse of the accused.' Mrs Manning was wearing a brown silk gown, a light shawl and a white straw bonnet. Unfortunately for the avid onlookers, she had covered her head with a thick white veil in anticipation of public curiosity, and she held it close to her face as she crossed the platform. Her luggage arrived with her, consisting of three black leather boxes and a carpet bag. The accompanying police transported the baggage to the police office in a separate cab.

On arrival at Stones End police station at 6.30 am, Maria Manning was taken into the prisoners' room, where Inspector Yates was waiting for her.

This was a small room with a stone floor, about 11 feet square, which had a desk and an easy chair. *Lloyd's Weekly* described how Maria 'appeared fatigued by her long journey and seemed indisposed'. She asked for some coffee as soon as she had arrived at the police station and, after she had drunk a cup and sat down, Inspector Evans read out the charge. The charge sheet stated:

> Twenty-seven minutes past five am, August 24. Maria Manning, aged twenty-eight, charged on suspicion of being concerned with another or other persons not in custody in the wilful murder of Patrick O'Connor, at 3 Minver Place, New Weston Street, in the parish of Bermondsey. Signed J. Yates, Inspector. Property found – three boxes, one carpet bag, nothing on the person. Reads and writes well.

The prisoner made no response, but simply bowed her head in acknowledgement that she understood the position in which she was placed. Inspector Yates proceeded with his questions to which she responded with 'the greatest calmness and self-possession', as noted in *The Morning Chronicle*. While the inspector was writing down her answers, she continued drinking coffee, occasionally turning her head to Superintendent Moxey, who was sitting beside her. According to the same newspaper:

> she made remarks in an under tone, accompanying them with a sickly smile, which exhibited, as far as outward appearance could indicate, a mind ill at ease ... There was, however, an utter absence of any such degree of depression as might have been expected under the circumstances, and her demeanour was altogether that of a woman of very masculine character.

When the inspector asked if she was aware of the crime of which she had been accused, she responded coolly, 'No, I know nothing.' Constable Wright interjected with a reference to Patrick O'Connor, to which 'she betrayed no remarkable feeling, but occasionally glanced around the apartment with a furtive look, as though to observe the different parties in attendance' (*The Morning Chronicle*, 25 August 1849).

Inspector Yates gave instructions for the prisoner to be taken to one of the cells and that the door should be kept open. A sergeant and a constable were placed outside 'to prevent her from attempting self-destruction'. Before she entered the cell, Maria was subjected to 'a very minute' search by the female searchers (usually police officers' wives), during which they found several letters and documents in her pockets. During the search, the prisoner expressed her reluctance to undergo the procedure, saying that all of her property had been confiscated by the police in Edinburgh. After the search, she was locked into the cell.

The conditions were very basic in the crowded cells of Stones End police station. The only ventilation was a small grating near the ceiling and an opening in the door of 6 by 10 inches, through which a small can of water could be passed. Detective Chief Inspector Timothy Cavanagh, who was stationed there as a constable in 1855, described the state of the cells as:

> Nothing more disgusting, nothing more revolting could possibly be imagined … there was only one bench in each, and upon this only room for about half a dozen to sit, the remainder had to stand or lie on the asphalt floor.

There was a toilet in each cell, but this had to be used by all the inmates in full view of each other. However, it is not known whether Maria Manning had to share a cell with other women.

During the rest of the morning, Inspector Yates visited Maria repeatedly in her cell and engaged her in conversation. She told the police officer about her early life and the occupations she had had, but never made any allusion to the nature of the crime with which she was charged. Between 8 and 9 am, she had a 'hearty' breakfast, consisting of broiled ham, coffee, and bread and butter. And at 10 am, she drank a small quantity of brandy to steady her nerves before facing the magistrate at Southwark police court.

Chapter 10

'Strong animal passions'

Southwark police court was on Blackman Street, which is now part of Borough High Street. Relocated from nearby Union Street in 1845, the court was close to Stones End police station, where Maria Manning had been taken on her arrival from Edinburgh. Before the day's proceedings began on Friday 24 August, just before 11 am, Superintendent Evans informed the chief clerk, Mr Edwin, that they had Mrs Manning in custody. He requested that the magistrate deal with this case first because he and the other witnesses had to attend the adjourned inquest into Patrick O'Connor's death, which was due to start at the same time. As reported in *The Morning Chronicle*, despite it not being widely known that Maria was in custody, rumours of her likely appearance soon began to circulate:

> neither the interior of the court nor the avenues leading thereto were inconveniently crowded at first, but as the hour for commencing business arrived a considerable number of persons filled the office and took up their position in the street at the front of the court, while others waited at the rear of the court-house in the hope that they might get a glance at the prisoner when she was removed.

After the doors of the court had been opened, Mr Edwin announced to the public that, when the prisoner was brought in, 'no expression of feeling might be given utterance to, otherwise the court would be immediately cleared.' This request was 'scrupulously attended to by the parties who were fortunate enough to gain an entry.'

Shortly before 11 am, the Metropolitan police magistrate for Southwark, Isaac Onslow Secker, took his seat on the bench and, after consulting with the chief clerk, he instructed that the prisoner was to take her place at the bar. *Lloyd's Weekly* described how Maria Manning walked in 'with the utmost calmness and firmness'. Appearing older than her stated age of 28, she was above average height with dark hair. The prisoner was 'respectably' dressed in a black silk visite (a fashionable outer garment like a wrap or shawl) with satin stripes, a matching gown made of the same fabric, a white straw bonnet trimmed with pink and green striped ribbons, and a white veil, which concealed her face as she made her way into the courtroom. When she had taken her place in front of the bench, she pulled back the veil revealing her extremely pale face and dark eyes. As was customary at the time, the publication printed a full physical description of her appearance, but with rather sinister overtones:

> She is a fine made, tall woman, with a full, fair, pale face, a large mouth, and full red lips. Indeed, her face is one which a physiognomist would pronounce as exhibiting strong animal passions.

The reporter observed that she stood erect in the dock and did not seem to be 'abashed' by the gravity of her situation, but was 'calm, apathetic, and resigned'. *The Times* also reported that she did not seem agitated, but suggested that this was due to her position in life as a lady's maid who had served the higher ranks of society, rather than her alleged crime:

> There is nothing about her which can be considered indicative of the monstrous crime with which she stands charged; and though there is little difficulty in seeing that she has been a woman of intrigue, no one from her appearance would fancy her a murderess.

The chief clerk opened the proceedings by asking the accused if she had any legal representation, to which she replied in a clear voice: 'No, I have sent for one this morning, but I understand he is ill.' Detective Inspector Field explained that she had sent for a Mr Games, who was unable to attend. The clerk reassured her that she would not be prejudiced by his absence.

Inspector Yates told the court that he had charged Mrs Manning with the murder of Patrick O'Connor. The magistrate immediately asked him for evidence. The police officer explained that he had viewed the body of the victim while it was still buried under the floor of the back kitchen at

3 Minver Place. He described how it had sustained fourteen wounds, mostly to the back of the head, and that also a bullet had been found in the skull. The magistrate then turned to the prisoner and informed her that she had a right to cross-examine Inspector Yates. However, he advised against it, as it was not necessary due to the purpose of the hearing being 'to take evidence merely of a preliminary character'. He explained that in the future, her legal representative would be able to question the witnesses. Maria confirmed that she had no questions.

The next witness was PC John Wright, Southwark Division, who had been involved in the initial investigation when Patrick O'Connor went missing. He explained that he had visited Minver Place with William Flynn, a friend of the deceased, on Monday 13 August. The police officer recounted how he had questioned Maria Manning about the last occasion on which she had seen the victim, on the previous Wednesday, when he had apparently been 'very tipsy'. He also said that she had admitted visiting O'Connor's lodgings in the days following his disappearance.

After PC Wright's testimony, Mr Secker suggested ending the proceedings, at which point the chief clerk asked Inspector Yates if he believed, from information received, that the prisoner was involved in the murder. After the police officer had affirmed that he did, the magistrate checked again whether Maria wanted to ask any questions. She replied that she did not. He instructed that she be remanded in custody for a week, and she left the dock 'composedly and apparently unconcerned', according to the press. She was driven in a cab to the nearby Horsemonger Lane Gaol.

After the prisoner had left, Superintendent Moxey, from the Edinburgh police, asked if his presence would be further required. Mr Secker gave him permission to leave, saying that he would notify him if his attendance were necessary in future hearings. The proceedings had lasted just a few minutes and the court was dismissed.

At 11 am, as the initial hearing was taking place, the adjourned inquest opened at the Leather Market Tavern on New Weston Street. As before, the room was very crowded. The coroner, William Carter, presided over the meeting, which comprised the testimonies of thirteen witnesses. The first half of the session was mostly focused on the disappearance of Patrick O'Connor and the discovery of his body at 3 Minver Place.

Customs clerk William Keating was the first to take the stand. He confirmed that he had been acquainted with the deceased and that he was familiar with his handwriting. Keating described how he and David Graham had seen

O'Connor on the evening of Thursday 9 August walking towards London Bridge and that he had 'appeared in good health and spirits'. They chatted for about two minutes before going their separate ways. During the conversation, Patrick had showed David a letter. William did not see the contents of the letter but noticed that it was marked with the name 'Maria'. Their companion had said, 'I suppose you are going to dine with Maria?' and although Keating did not hear the response, he assumed that this was the case. He reiterated that Patrick had been alone on the bridge when they met him and that it was the last time he had seen him alive. The next evening, he heard at work that O'Connor had not showed up for his shift. PC Burton confirmed that there was no evidence that Patrick had been off duty the following day, and therefore his absence was unexplained.

David Graham, who also worked for the customs and had known Patrick O'Connor for ten or twelve years, confirmed his colleague's statement. He told the inquest that the deceased had seemed 'quite well' and said that he was wearing a black neckerchief and a black hat on the evening they had met. He was carrying an umbrella. Graham told the coroner that the letter was an invitation to dinner from Maria Manning. He added that he had frequently seen Maria and Patrick together, both at the customs officer's lodgings and in the street. They were often walking arm in arm and 'appeared to be very well acquainted'. Although they worked in the same office, Graham had never discussed O'Connor's relationship with Maria Manning with him: 'I only know that they were very intimate.' Like William Keating, he did not see Patrick again after that date.

Another work colleague, John Younghusband, stated that he too had known O'Connor well, as they had worked together as gaugers. He revealed that he had also seen Patrick on London Bridge on the same evening. Younghusband had been travelling by omnibus towards Mile End Road when he spotted his colleague walking along at about 5.45 pm. He had not seen Keating and Graham but said that O'Connor 'appeared to be waiting for someone'. Finally, customs collector Thomas Wheatley said that he thought that he had seen him on 12 August but that he was not sure. As this was after the day of O'Connor's disappearance, it was not taken any further.

The next witnesses were Police Constables Henry Barnes and James Burton, who had found the deceased's body at 3 Minver Place on 17 August. PC Barnes, K Division, recounted that he went to the property with PC Burton after receiving some information. He described how they searched the house, noting in particular that all the furniture had been removed from the rooms, and that he had spotted the damp patch in the mortar between two flagstones in the back kitchen, which was underground. Pulling out their knives, they poked the mortar and found it to be wet. They then raised the flag using a shovel, a crowbar and a hammer. PC Barnes had commented to his colleague that 'the stone was never placed by a mason.' After lifting the two stones, they came across the piece of linen, which was about the size of the police officer's two hands. On pulling out the cloth, he held it to his nose: 'it very much smelt of death.' They carried on digging and soon came across 'something white', which they initially thought was another piece of cloth. The police officer shook it and said, 'Here is his toe; this is the toe of a man.' He dug deeper and found the whole foot. At this point, his colleague ran for help and two inspectors came to their assistance. The officers continued digging until they had excavated the whole body. PC Barnes confirmed that it was lying on its face with its legs tied up behind its back with strong cord. It had been buried in slack lime.

Before the body was removed from the hole, the surgeon Samuel Lockwood entered the room and extracted the false teeth. They carried the naked body to the front kitchen. Barnes said that he knew that it was a man due to its size and that 'it appeared to have been in the hole about a fortnight, judging from the smell.' PC Barnes then left the kitchen and went into the yard, so he did not see Mr Lockwood remove the bullet, but the surgeon showed it to him when he returned to the room. The police officer explained that the body had been lying about 20 inches below the surface of the floor and it was covered with 2 inches of lime, followed by 13 inches of earth. Following the discovery, the police called William Flynn, who identified the body as Patrick O'Connor. Another surgeon, George Odling, also arrived. When they had finished at Minver Place, PC Burton locked the house and left the body in situ.

Constable Barnes testified that he had searched Patrick O'Connor's lodgings in Mile End on Monday 13 August and again on the day they found his body. During their first visit, he had found only some memos and IOUs, and he confirmed that the deceased's money had been missing. O'Connor's friends had told the police officer that he had kept his money in the box that had been opened by William Flynn. PC Barnes also came across some personal letters at the lodgings, some of which were invitations from Maria Manning, but none of them had been written recently. In response to a juror's question, PC Barnes stated that he had been engaged to search for Patrick, but he did not say by whom. The next witness explained what had happened.

PC James Burton of M Division testified that on Tuesday 14 August, at about 8.30 pm, two friends of Patrick O'Connor, William Keating and David Graham, had come to Stones End police station to ask the police to inquire into his whereabouts. He went to Minver Place with Inspector Meade and found the house locked. Burton jumped over the wall of the adjoining house, intending to enter the property through the garden, but before he could gain entry, Meade acquired the key and let him in. He said that the house had been left in 'a very confused state'. A large portmanteau was lying open in the back kitchen and there was a quantity of clothing around the box, including a railway guard's coat. There were also personal items strewn about in the upstairs rooms. PC Burton rummaged through the clothing but did not find anything which seemed to belong to the deceased. The officers left the premises, locking the door behind them.

The police constable told the court that, the following day, furniture dealer Charles Bainbridge tried to enter the house but could not open the door. He came to the police station to complain that he had bought some goods from Frederick Manning for about £13 and had been prevented from retrieving them. He told the police that Manning had just left his house in Bermondsey Square. PC Burton returned to Minver Place with Bainbridge. This time, he found a copper shovel in the back kitchen, which he handed to Charles. The officer affirmed that he had not noticed the damp patch in the flags during this visit.

The officer next described the discovery of the body. He added that the stones appeared to have been freshly laid and that when he and PC Barnes had started to dig, 'we saw something which was soft and smelled sour.' Barnes disclosed to the inquest that, in lifting the flags, they had acted without waiting for instructions from their superiors. He said that the layer of lime was so hard that they could scarcely pierce it with the shovel. Constable Burton was not present when the body was taken out of the hole as he had left the house to seek assistance. On his return with Inspector Yates, he saw 'a portion of flesh belonging to a human body', but he could not tell whether it was from the front or the back of the cadaver. However, he reassured the coroner that any damage to the body had not been caused by the shovel or the crowbar that they had used to excavate it.

Inspector Yates instructed PC Burton to locate O'Connor's friends so that they could identify the body, and he later returned with William Flynn and the deceased's brother, Thomas. The police officer ended his testimony by stating that, when he had seen that the personal belongings of the Mannings had been removed from the house during their first visit, he had not been suspicious that the body of the missing man might have been there. Seemingly in contradiction of his earlier statement, he said that he had seen a necktie and a black stocking in an upstairs closet, which had belonged to Patrick, but again this had not raised any alarm. He did not see any blood and had only spotted one mark on the ceiling, which might have been caused by the top of a bedstead and which he considered not to have been important. Burton defended his actions by saying that he had been misled by a woman who had claimed she had seen O'Connor alive and, therefore, he had stopped looking for him.

The next witness was Samuel Lockwood, the surgeon who was the first medical doctor to attend the scene. He explained that he had been nearby in St Thomas Street when he heard the news that a body had been discovered at 3 Minver Place. He rushed over to the house to offer his assistance. On his arrival, two police officers were standing at the door and when he announced that he was a surgeon, they admitted him into the house. When he went down into the back kitchen, he saw a police officer and a labourer, who had been engaged for the purpose, digging the hole. He helped remove the dirt as the body was revealed and then taken out. The surgeon concurred with PC Barnes' account of the position and condition of the body and said that, on first inspection, he could feel a 'very extensive fracture on the superior part of the head', which was so large that he could put two fingers into it.

Mr Lockwood had then remembered that the missing man wore false teeth, as had been stated on the handbills. Raising the head with one hand, he felt inside with the other and found a full set of teeth, which he extracted and handed to the summoning officer, who was also in attendance by this time. As the body was removed from the grave, he saw that it was 'quite blue and excoriated, and decomposing'. He could not say how long it had been in the grave and found no instruments nearby which might have caused the injuries. Later, he and George Odling located another fracture on the right side of the head. Mr Odling examined the body and discovered a small hard lump over the right eye. Lockwood cut it open and took out a large bullet. At this point in his testimony, he produced the bullet, which looked like it had been cut in half, and handed it to the coroner and jury. He ended his statement by saying that there was a hole in the back of the victim's head and the bullet had passed directly through to the forehead.

Charles Slow, the summoning officer, added some more details regarding the extraction of the body. He explained how he had sent for some ropes to place under it. He had also pulled down one of the shutters to put the body on to carry it into the front kitchen for examination. Slow noted that Mr Lockwood had washed the teeth before he handed them to him. The summoning officer showed the teeth, which were an entire set, to the coroner, and they were identified by Mr Lockwood as the same ones that he had taken from the body.

After a 30-minute break for refreshments, the second medical doctor involved in the case gave his statement. George Odling was the divisional police surgeon for Southwark. He had arrived at 3 Minver Place at 3 pm. His description of the body tallied with that of Samuel Lockwood. During his formal examination, he found the foreign body under the skin above the right eye and instructed his colleague to remove it with a lancet. Mr Odling discovered no other external wounds on the body, other than the fractures of the skull which, in his opinion, was the cause of death. He then examined the head externally and removed a large amount of hair. The scalp had as many as eighteen severe wounds, some of which were deeper than others. They were mostly sustained to the back and the top of the head on the right side, and he estimated that they were about an inch and a half in length. The surgeon concluded that the wounds had been made with a blunt instrument rather than a sharp one, as the latter would have sliced through the bones. To demonstrate his theory, he produced a model of a similar instrument, which had a sharp head like a hammer but was not divided in two.

Surmising that the bullet must have caused an entry wound, Odling re-examined the head. He removed the scalp to expose the remains of the skull, which had been smashed into many pieces. He brought out sixteen pieces of bone to show to the jury. He explained that, as the skull had been so severely damaged, it was not possible to say where the bullet had entered, although he had found a mark on the back of the head which could have been made by powder, presumably from a firearm. The course of the bullet could not be traced due to the damage, and Odling commented that 'The brain was quite soft and perfectly decomposed.' He told the jury that he next opened the abdomen but found 'nothing unnatural'. However, as he was not able to undertake any further analysis of the organ, he sent it to Alfred Swaine Taylor, lecturer in medical jurisprudence at Guy's Hospital, in the hope that it could be tested for poisoning following the discovery of a laudanum bottle at Minver Place, which PC John Wright, who had found it, now displayed to the jury. Mr Odling conjectured, however, that even if the victim had been given laudanum, as well as being shot, the fractures of the skull were sufficient to have caused death. Mr Lockwood was recalled to corroborate Mr Odling's statement and he added that, in his opinion, the blows had been made with a hammer similar to one used by a metalworker. He told the coroner how he had helped to remove the scalp and that he too was unable to determine the track of the bullet. Lockwood concluded that the fractures in the skull had been fatal and that the injuries had been inflicted prior to the victim's demise. He added that there was no possibility of them being self-inflicted.

Having ascertained the identity of the deceased and the cause of death, Mr Carter suggested considering the chain of evidence. The first witness was James Coleman, who had built and owned Minver Place. He had received information that the Mannings had vacated the property on Tuesday 14 August. After making some inquiries of the neighbours, he visited the house and found it empty. While he was there, he met the furniture dealer's assistant who asked him if the couple owed him any rent, which they did not.

Mr Coleman confirmed that Frederick Manning was his tenant and that Manning and his wife had lived there since 25 March, which was Lady Day. He had paid a quarter of the rent in advance and the landlord was not expecting another payment until September. Coleman had watched Manning sign the papers, and he had also received a reference for him. He declared that he had never entered the house while the Mannings were living there and that he knew nothing 'of his domestic circle, nor of any person who was in the habit of visiting the house'. After James Coleman left the stand, there were only three more witnesses to be examined before the proceedings were adjourned for the day. *Lloyd's Weekly* noted that the evidence of the next witness was 'listened to with the greatest interest.'

Chapter 11

King Cholera

The Mannings' former lodger, William Massey, who had been unavailable until now, had finally arrived in the capital to give his version of the events. The medical student confirmed that Frederick Manning had been his landlord and that he had stayed at 3 Minver Place for nine or ten weeks until mid-July. He explained that he had sometimes dined with the Mannings while he was lodging there, and that they did not keep a servant. As far as he was aware, Patrick O'Connor was the only visitor to the house during his stay, and he had dinner with the Mannings three times: 'Mr O'Connor appeared to be on friendly terms with Mrs Manning, but nothing more.' William had also spent an evening with the threesome at Patrick's lodgings in Mile End, but he had no suspicions that there was anything going on between the customs officer and Maria: 'there did not appear to be any improper intimacy', although he later admitted that he had seen Mrs Manning going into Patrick's bedroom once. However, he knew that O'Connor was a wealthy man and he believed that, in the eventuality of his death, Maria Manning would inherit £20,000 (about £2 million today). As soon as he heard about the murder, he had returned to London.

William Massey had little to say about the characters of the Mannings, but he reported some unusual conversations that he had had with Frederick. On one occasion, while Manning had been talking to him about O'Connor's will, he had told the lodger that when Patrick had shown the document to Maria, who was apparently the beneficiary, he had been intoxicated. This appeared to contradict other statements from Patrick's friends that he had been a teetotaller. Manning explained that O'Connor drank port and brandy because he had been afraid of contracting cholera.

While this case was taking place, London was in the grip of an epidemic. Cholera is an infectious disease of the small intestine. Symptoms, which begin between two to five days after exposure, include diarrhoea, vomiting and stomach cramps. Typically, a victim of the disease has sunken eyes and bluish skin, and is cold to the touch. In the late 1840s, it was still believed that cholera was transmitted through poisonous air, which the Victorians referred to as 'miasma'.

In 1849, Bermondsey was densely populated with some 35,000 inhabitants crammed into tenements which housed four or five families in one dwelling. Just 15 minutes' walk from Minver Place was the infamous Jacob's Island, which had been immortalised by Charles Dickens in his novel *Oliver Twist*, serialised less than a decade earlier. When Bill Sikes meets his grisly end, Dickens describes the notorious slum:

> crazy wooden galleries common to the backs of half a dozen houses, with holes from which to look upon the slime beneath; windows, broken and patched, with poles thrust out, on which to dry the linen that is never there; rooms so small, so filthy, so confined, that the air would seem to be too tainted even for the dirt and squalor which they shelter ... dirt-besmeared walls and decaying foundations, every repulsive lineament of poverty, every loathsome indication of filth, rot, and garbage: all these ornament the banks of Jacob's Island.

Little had changed in this squalid area by the time of Patrick O'Connor's murder. Dickens further wrote in *Household Words* that, when the tide rose in the Thames, the streets in Bermondsey 'became rivers', and cellars and kitchens were flooded. It is not surprising, therefore, that it was a breeding ground for diseases such as cholera.

The previous year, more than 1,000 lives had been lost to the infection, leaving the capital's graveyards full to bursting. Cholera began to take hold again in the late spring of 1849, resulting in the deaths of more than 14,000 Londoners. Most of the victims were those living in the cramped and airless accommodation on the south bank of the Thames, in the poorest quarters of the city. Bermondsey had the second highest death rate, with a total of 591 inhabitants lost, which was a ratio of 1 in 59. At the height of the epidemic, novelist Charles Kingsley visited Jacob's Island. He observed the ravages of cholera with horror: 'people having no water to drink ... but the water of the common sewer stagnated, full of dead fish, cats and dogs under their windows'. Kingsley described how the church bells tolled all day long, as the mass burials took place, and that mourners would return to their homes after a funeral only to find that another family member had succumbed to the illness.

Journalist Henry Mayhew also visited Bermondsey and he published his experience in *The Morning Chronicle* in September 1849. Mayhew dubbed Jacob's Island the 'very capital of cholera':

> On entering the precincts of the pest island, the air has literally the smell of a graveyard, and a feeling of nausea and heaviness comes over anyone unaccustomed to imbibe the musty atmosphere.

The reporter described the 'rotting bridges over the reeking ditch', where the mephitic air was charged with 'deadly gas'. He also recorded the appearance of the local inhabitants, whose faces were as white as parchment, their cheeks flushed and their eyes sunken. It would be another five years before epidemiologist John Snow would trace another outbreak of the disease to a contaminated water pump, which supported his theory that cholera was a water-borne infection, rather than being transmitted through the air.

In the three days before Patrick O'Connor's body was discovered, 3,015 people had contracted cholera in London, 1,253 of whom had died. There were 53 deaths in Bermondsey. On 22 August, twenty-two cases and six deaths were added to the district's tally, followed by thirty-six new cases two days later. A third of these were fatal. On the day of the inquest, the General Board of Health recorded thirty-seven more people had succumbed to the disease with two fatalities. Between July and September, 12,800 Londoners died, including 6,500 in Lambeth, Southwark and Bermondsey, where at least a hundred victims fell prey to the disease every month adding to, as described by Mayhew, 'the fearful catalogue of mortality'. This was a terrifying period, and residents lived in a constant state of fear.

People resorted to all sorts of treatments to stave off the disease, including opium, chloroform, carbonic acid, ammonia and ether. They ingested mustard, cayenne pepper and other 'hot' substances, as well as drinking wine and brandy like Patrick O'Connor. Frederick Manning suggested to William that they frighten Patrick with scare stories of the disease and that, once he was in a state of fear, they could offer him some brandy to which they would have added a stupefying drug. Not surprisingly, the medical student declined.

Massey also told the coroner about a conversation he had had with Frederick Manning, during which the landlord had asked him about poison. One night, the two men were sitting in Massey's room smoking a pipe. Frederick inquired whether laudanum or chloroform 'would produce stupefaction or partial intoxication, so as to cause a person to put his hand to paper.' William responded with a casual remark that such drugs were often used for 'bad purposes'. Furthermore, Frederick had asked the student, who had been reading a medical textbook at the time, if he knew 'which part of the skull was the most dangerous to hit'. Massey had replied that it was the ear. On another occasion, Frederick questioned William about whether he had ever fired an airgun. When he said that he had seen one fired during a philosophy experiment, Manning inquired whether it had made any noise.

As the spectators in the public gallery listened avidly to Massey's testimony, even more damning evidence came to light. The medical student revealed that Manning had mentioned the murders of Isaac Jermy and his son at Stanfield Hall, near Norwich, which had taken place the previous year, and for which James Blomfield Rush had been convicted and executed in April 1849. Born in 1789, Rush was a tenant farmer on Jermy's estate. Also an auctioneer and a land agent, by 1836 he held the tenancy for two farms, but when his landlord noticed some irregularities with the leases, he had them redrawn, which resulted in Rush paying higher rents. By the early 1840s, the tenant farmer had fallen into debt. This was compounded by the death of his wife in 1842, which left him with nine young children to care for. Initially, Rush borrowed money from his late father's wife but when she died, she left her money to her grandchildren. After paying for a governess to look after his children, Rush decided to expand his tenancies and bought the lease for Potash Farm, also from Isaac Jermy, using a loan from him, which was due to be repaid on 30 November 1848. Rush had already failed to pay the rent on another of the farms and had been evicted. Jermy had also brought a suit against his tenant for poor cultivation of the land, which he had won. In May 1848, Rush declared bankruptcy, after which he began plotting his revenge against Jermy by helping other claimants to the estate to retrieve the title and property. They in turn promised to reduce his rent. His efforts soon led to a desperate act.

On the evening of 27 November 1848, when Isaac Jermy slipped out onto the porch for a cigar while his son and wife were playing cards indoors, a man with a piece of black cloth wrapped round his head suddenly appeared and shot him. After shooting Isaac Jermy senior, the attacker entered the house and fired at his son, Isaac Jermy Jermy, who was rushing out of the dining room after hearing the commotion. He was killed instantly. Isaac junior's wife was shot in the arm and their maid in the thigh. Despite his attempt to disguise himself wearing a cloak and a mask, the identity of the perpetrator was obvious.

Following the shootings, the quick-thinking butler, who had been in the stables, swam across the moat and raised the alarm. A telegraph was sent to the Norwich police, who staked out Potash Farm, and, when Rush returned at 5 am the following morning, they arrested him.

James Blomfield Rush was tried on 26 March 1849. He was convicted of the double murder and hanged at Norwich Castle on 21 April. As many as 13,000 people attended his public execution. Charles Dickens had visited the crime scene the previous January, which he described as having 'a murderous look that seemed to invite such a crime.' The writer had watched as the police searched for the murder weapon and had been unsurprised when they found it in a manure heap in the farmyard near the house.

The Rush case was linked with the Bermondsey murder in the press, and a letter to the editor of *The Illustrated London News* suggested that the Manning case was even more depraved than the murders at Stanfield Hall:

> Such crimes as those committed by Rush, and by the Mannings –
> the latter in its cold-blooded hideousness, even surpassing in
> accumulated horror the fearful tragedy of Stanfield Hall – make
> Englishmen blush that such things should occur in the bosom of
> a civilisation that boasts to be so advanced as ours.

During the continuing inquest into Patrick O'Connor's death, William Massey recounted how Frederick Manning had referred to the wax image of Rush at Madame Tussaud's. He then asked William if he believed that a murderer could enter heaven. Massey replied in the negative.

Although Frederick Manning had asked these seemingly incriminating questions, William Massey maintained that they had not aroused his suspicions, even when his landlord quizzed him about the stupefying effects of laudanum and chloroform. He told the court that Manning said he hated O'Connor because he had once sued him for 30 shillings. According to Frederick, the feeling was mutual. Massey concluded his testimony by saying that, during the final three weeks of his tenancy, both Maria and Frederick had been keen for him to leave Minver Place to the extent that they were not anxious about him settling his bill. He added that he had never seen any weapons or a hammer at the property, only some garden tools which included a large hoe. After moving out of Minver Place, Massey spent eight days with the Bainbridges before he left London for Derbyshire.

The final two witnesses testified about the Mannings' purchases of the lime and the shovel. Richard Welsh related how Frederick had visited his employer's building yard on 23 July and ordered a bushel of lime to be sent to 3 Minver Place. It was unslacked (dry) yellowstone lime. When the boy had arrived at the address with the consignment, he had noticed that there was no furniture in the kitchen except an old square basket with a cover, into which he had poured the lime.

Ironmonger's assistant William Cahill stated that Maria Manning had come to the shop to buy a coal shovel. He described the implement that she selected as 'wrought iron, plain, without holes'. The handle was also made of iron and was about a foot long. He said that she was wearing a black dress with three or four flounces, and a black bonnet. She had 'a slight foreign accent'. Cahill identified the shovel in court, adding that it was marked with their private stamp, which was a scratch with a bradawl (a tool used for woodworking).

At the end of the statements, the coroner consulted with Detective Inspector Haynes and then announced that there were several more witnesses to examine but, as it was now 6.30 pm and they had been sitting since 11 am, he proposed adjourning the inquest until the following Monday, which would give the police enough time to prepare the remaining evidence.

The day after the latest sitting of the inquest, the coroner issued an order for Superintendent Moxey, of the Edinburgh police, and witnesses William Massey and Ann Armes to attend Southwark police station to examine the property found on Maria Manning. The police opened four chests in their presence, which contained silk dresses and haberdashery, her marriage certificate, an illustrated edition of the Psalms of David in French, and the railway shares that she had allegedly stolen from Patrick O'Connor. It was hoped that his acquaintances could identify any items belonging to him, which could be used as evidence against Mrs Manning.

While he was at the police station, Scotland Yard detectives further questioned the Mannings' lodger William Massey, who stated that Frederick had spoken to him about the cheapness of living in Guernsey or Jersey. Manning had asked him whether he would like to accompany him to the islands. He then gave the medical student the card of an innkeeper in Guernsey, whom he knew well, and advised him to go and see him. As Manning had shared his intentions of returning to the island, under the pretence that he was a representative for a wholesale paper warehouse, Massey firmly believed that his absent landlord had fled to Guernsey. Acting on this new information, a description of the wanted man was sent to the governors of Jersey and Guernsey for circulation, and A Division officers Detective Sergeant Edward Langley and Police Constable Henry Lockyer travelled to the Channel Islands to investigate the lead.

Massey also confided that Frederick Manning had sent a letter to his parents in Derbyshire informing them that their son was 'comfortably settled' with him and his wife, who were 'pious people'. Manning asked if William's sister could come to London for a few days. *Lloyd's Weekly* reported that 'what the object was in inviting this young female to the house is at present a mystery; but there is not a shadow of a doubt in Mr Massey's own mind but that the Mannings intended to make her an instrument in taking away the life of Mr O'Connor.'

Despite this new information, Frederick Manning was still on the run and the newspaper reports, such as shown in the update in *Lloyd's Weekly*, were incredulous that he was still evading justice:

> It certainly is singular that the artful, resolute woman who fled to Scotland, where no one ever thought of flying before, except perhaps for a clandestine marriage, has been taken; while the man, who when last seen was brutally intoxicated, and without any self-control, is still at large.

However, there were numerous sightings of the fugitive. A report was circulated by Southwark Division to several police stations throughout the capital that Frederick had been seen in Clerkenwell. Also, the landlady of the Rodney's Head public house in Pentonville had disclosed to the police that a man who looked like Manning had entered her establishment for some refreshment. He had asked her for a newspaper. Mrs Whitehorn noticed that, on reading it, he began to tremble and looked agitated. On receipt of this information, plain-clothes officers were sent out across the divisions to make inquiries and, as was stated in the press: 'The result leaves no doubt, that such a party was seen by several persons, and so sanguine are many of the police, that they anticipate a capture during the night.'

Around the same time, the police commissioners received information that Manning was at Wimbledon railway station but, when they investigated, they found that the individual 'did not in the least degree answer his description' (*Lloyd's Weekly*, 26 August 1849). By Saturday afternoon, despite several false trails, including leads that suggested that Frederick Manning had absconded overseas, the prevailing opinion was that he was still in London, especially as when he had been last seen in the company of Charles Bainbridge, he had been drinking, which led the police to believe that he was still holed up in a tavern somewhere.

Later that evening, the Metropolitan police received information that Maria Manning had also taken a cab to Waterloo station, as had her husband, but she had then changed her mind and instructed the driver to take her to London Bridge. Thus, the police surmised that the Mannings were intending to take the South Western Railway to Jersey or Guernsey, as they had initially thought.

This theory seemed to have been finally confirmed when Scotland Yard obtained intelligence that Frederick Manning had made his way via Southampton to Jersey. Four months earlier, Manning had lodged in the neighbouring island of Guernsey for about a fortnight, at the house of a builder named Mr Robin, under the guise of being a representative for the General Steam Navigation Company. Due to the timing of his visit, it is possible that he was keeping out of the way during the investigation into the mail robberies committed by Poole and Nightingale. After two weeks, he departed from the island in great haste following the arrival of a letter. Frederick left for Southampton and that was the last Mr Robin had seen of him. On Thursday 16 August, Mr Robin's sister-in-law was returning to Guernsey on the steamer from Southampton, and she saw Manning on the journey but, as the murder had not been discovered at the time, she thought nothing of it. She was sure it was him, as she had met him several times at her sister's home on the island. However, on this occasion, she did not speak to him because she was suffering from seasickness. The woman landed in Guernsey, but Frederick continued the crossing to Jersey. When news of the murder hit the headlines the following week, Mr Robin immediately informed the crown solicitor, who sent a message to the authorities in London.

It was further supposed that ultimately Manning was trying to get to France. *The Express* commented:

> By these circumstances the police are put on the right track, and although the pursued has many days the start of his pursuers, yet, unless Manning be a good French scholar (which is doubtful), he will have much difficulty in eluding the vigilance of our detectives in whatever part of France he may have escaped to.

Chapter 12

Motive for Murder

While the police were still searching for Frederick Manning, the final session of the inquest into Patrick O'Connor's death opened at 11 am on Monday 27 August at the Leather Market Tavern. A large crowd was present to hear the remaining sixteen witnesses give their testimonies before coroner William Carter.

The first to take the stand was PC William Sopp, of M Division. He told the jury how, on Wednesday 22 August, he was instructed by his superior officer, Inspector Yates, to visit the Bainbridges at 14 Bermondsey Square. He asked the furniture dealer's wife whether there had been a shovel among the Mannings' possessions. Mary Ann Bainbridge subsequently handed him the iron shovel, which was now produced in court in its original state. PC Sopp identified it as the same one. He described how, when he had first seen it, he had observed 'marks of mortar' on the shovel and 'something which had the appearance of blood and ashes and human hair attached.' Before he removed the shovel from the Bainbridges, the police officer asked Mary Ann if she had seen the shovel before and, if it had, to her knowledge, ever been used by any member of the household. She replied in the negative to both questions. At this point, the coroner intervened to ask whether her husband Charles Bainbridge was present in court. The summoning officer told Mr Carter he had promised to be there by 10.30 am. PC Burton explained that Mr Bainbridge was currently on the other side of the city.

The following four witnesses gave a detailed account of Maria Manning's flight from 3 Minver Place on Monday 13 August. Firstly, cab driver William Kirk described how Mrs Manning had approached him in Joiner Street at 3.30 pm, after which he had taken her back to Minver Place. Kirk had helped her to remove three boxes from the property, which were so full that he had to ask a passer-by for assistance. Two of the boxes had been in one of the upstairs bedrooms and the third in the kitchen. One was locked, one had a rope tied

88

Minver Place, New Weston Street, Bermondsey. (Source: *The Progress of Crime or the Authentic Memoirs of Marie Manning*, Robert Huish, 1849)

NO. 3, MINVER-PLACE, THE SCENE OF THE MURDER.

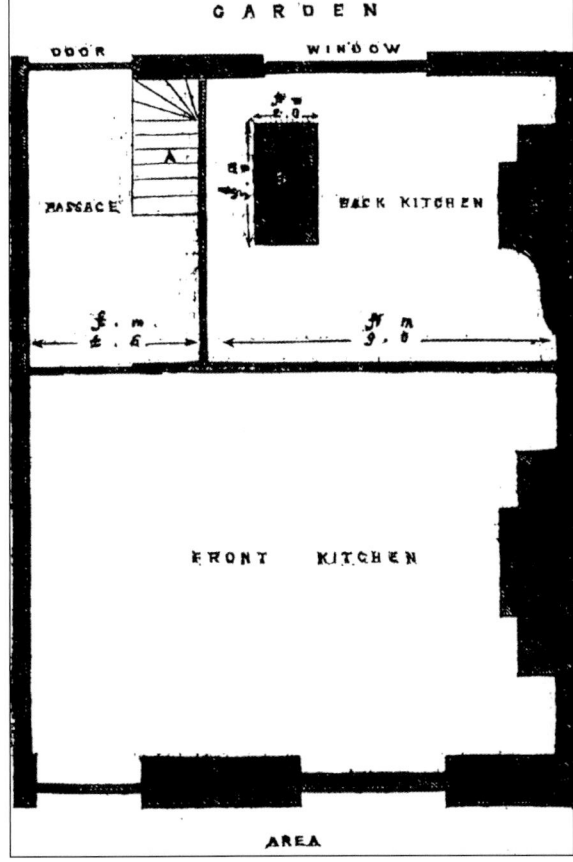

Floor plan of 3 Minver Place. (Source: *The Bermondsey Murder: A Full Report of the Trial of Frederick George Manning and Maria Manning for the Murder of Patrick O'Connor*, W.M. Clark, 1849)

DISCOVERY OF O'CONNOR'S REMAINS (p. 368).

Top: Discovery of Patrick O'Connor's body at 3 Minver Place. (Alamy)

Above left: Patrick O'Connor. (Source: *The Progress of Crime or the Authentic Memoirs of Marie Manning*, Robert Huish, 1849)

Above right: Frederick George Manning. (Alamy)

Left: Maria Manning, née de Roux. (Alamy)

Above: Lausanne,
Switzerland, birthplace
of Maria de Roux.
(W. Courthope Forman)

Right: London Bridge
station, 1849, where
Maria Manning left
her luggage after
fleeing Minver Place.
(W. Courthope Forman)

Leigh Walk, Edinburgh,
where Maria Manning
was arrested at
25 Haddington Place.
(W. Courthope Forman)

Governor's house, Calton Prison, Edinburgh, where Maria Manning was detained after her arrest. (W. Courthope Forman)

Left: Frederick Manning travelled to Jersey after leaving Minver Place. (W. Courthope Forman)

Below: Prospect House, Jersey, where Frederick Manning was arrested. (W. Courthope Forman)

Horsemonger Lane Gaol, where the Mannings were detained. (From a drawing by A.D. McCormick). (W. Courthope Forman)

Right: The Old Bailey in 1849, where the Mannings were tried. (W. Courthope Forman)

Below: The judges who tried the Mannings at the Old Bailey, October 1849. (L to R: Mr Justice Cresswell, Chief Baron Pollock and Mr Justice Maule). (W. Courthope Forman)

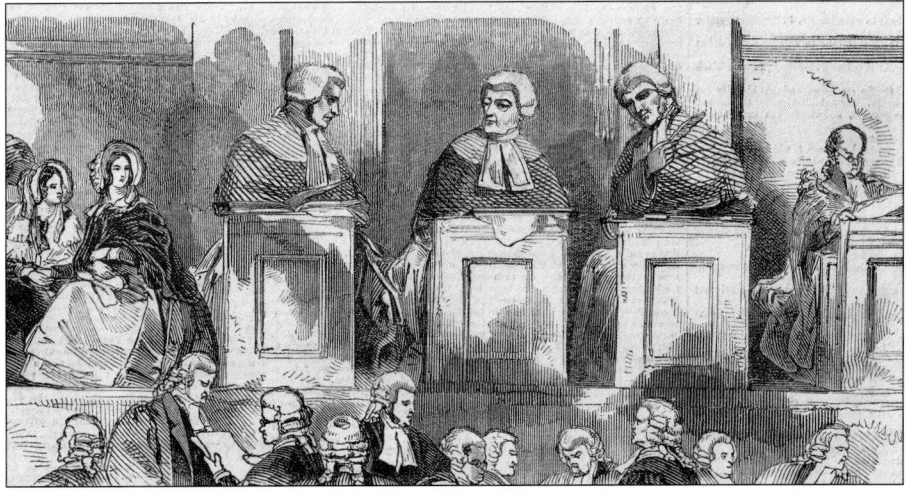

Above left: William Bodkin, counsel for the prosecution, October 1849. (W. Courthope Forman)

Above right: Charles Wilkins, counsel for Frederick Manning, October 1849. (W. Courthope Forman)

Left: William Ballantine, counsel for Maria Manning, October 1849. (W. Courthope Forman)

Exterior of Horsemonger Lane Gaol, on top of which the Mannings were executed in November 1849. (W. Courthope Forman)

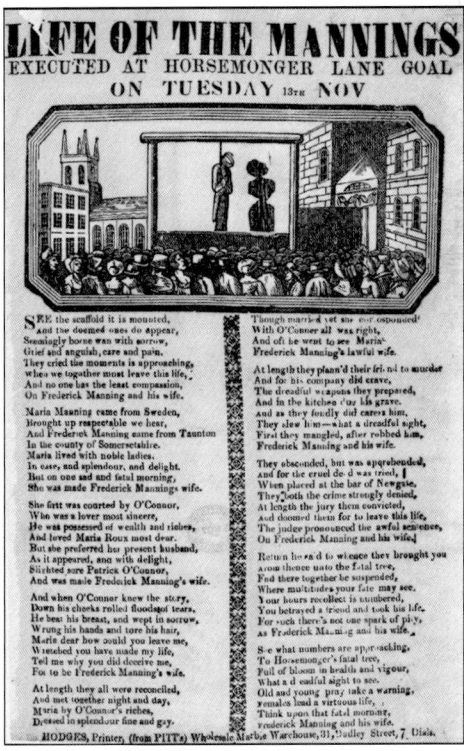

Above left: Bath Terrace, from where Charles Dickens viewed the Mannings' execution. (From a drawing by A.D. McCormick). (W. Courthope Forman)

Above right: Broadside featuring the Manning trial and execution, November 1849. (Source: British Library. (Public domain))

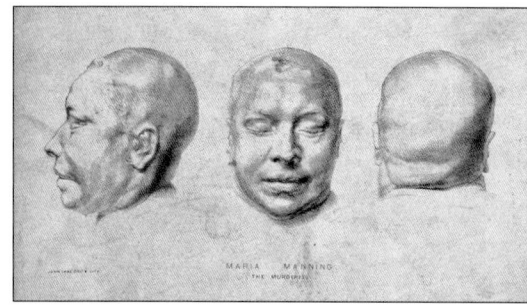

Maria Manning's death mask.
(Lithograph by John Lane).
(Source: The Wellcome Collection.
(Public domain))

INSPECTOR FIELD.

Right: Detective Charles Frederick Field, the inspiration
for Inspector Bucket in *Bleak House* by Charles
Dickens. (Public domain)

Below left: China figurine of Maria Manning.
(W. Courthope Forman)

Below right: China figurine of Frederick Manning.
(W. Courthope Forman)

around it and the third remained unlocked, as they could not close it properly. As well as the boxes, Kirk stated that there was a carpet bag and several more items, including coats, cloaks, shawls and a couple of baskets. He loaded everything into the cab and drove back to London Bridge station, stopping en route to buy the luggage labels, which the porter later attached to the boxes. After depositing the luggage, Mrs Manning instructed the cab driver to take her to Euston station. William Kirk estimated that he had spent about an hour and a half with Maria, and he told the court that she was wearing a bonnet and a veil. He thought that she was from the countryside or that she was 'a woman that came from Essex or Sussex, a person who could not speak the English language.' Laughter erupted in court at this last comment. Kirk ended his testimony by confirming that she had paid her fare in full.

Porter William Day took up the account. He deposed that when Mrs Manning had arrived at London Bridge station, he had opened the cab door for her to alight. Following her instructions, he had unloaded two of the boxes, apparently with the aid of a police officer, and taken them into the cloakroom. She had then produced some nails and asked him and the officer to fix the cards onto the luggage, which they did. The porter attested that the address on the labels was 'Mrs Smith, passenger, Paris'. After a futile attempt to close one of the boxes, Day stowed them in the office. The whole process took about ten minutes. William Day said that Mrs Manning 'appeared to speak cheerfully. She did not speak like a London lady'. William Dyne, a clerk at London Bridge station, completed the narrative by stating that he had received the two boxes into the cloakroom. He recorded the details in a ledger and gave Mrs Manning a ticket with a number corresponding to one placed on the items. The number was 456.

The ensuing discovery of the boxes left at London Bridge station was recounted by Detective Inspector John Haynes of Scotland Yard. The following day, on receiving information (possibly from the previous witness whom he knew), he sent for William Kirk and then went to the railway terminus to recover the luggage. Haynes searched the two boxes, which contained mostly clothing, household items, letters and papers. The detective made special mention of Frederick Manning's will, which was dated 6 January 1848 and was signed by Henry Poole, one of the railway robbers, and Robert Steele. (Other accounts state that the will had been drawn up in June 1849. However, there is no reference to this document in the surviving Metropolitan police files.)

Haynes also pointed out that, in the smaller box, he had found a skirt and the body of a dress, which had been separated. Where the cut had been made between the skirt and the bodice, there were 'several marks of blood' on the dress lining, and it seemed as though the garment had been recently washed. Also, two dressing table covers and a piece of muslin were marked with 'splashes of blood'.

The next witness was Superintendent Richard Moxey, of the Edinburgh police, who shared the details of Maria Manning's arrest in his city on Tuesday 21 August. He explained how he had visited 'Mrs Smith's' lodgings with the stockbroker, where he had asked her about her husband, whom she had claimed was deceased. After the stockbroker had identified her as Mrs Manning, Superintendent Moxey had searched her luggage and discovered the incriminating evidence, notably the linen marked with Frederick Manning's initials, the railway shares and the banknotes that had been stolen from Patrick O'Connor. After she was searched at the police station, the superintendent telegraphed Scotland Yard with the details of the items found.

Superintendent Moxey told the court about his conversations with Maria after her arrest. During the evening, he had entered her cell to check that she was comfortable – she had requested some extra bedding – and he asked her if she knew where her husband was, to which she replied that she did not. She then told him what had happened to make her leave London:

> I left town suddenly; I came off on Monday when he [her husband] was out. I have left him as I have done before. I was afraid of my life. He has maltreated me for a long time past. His threats generally were, that he would cut off my head, all of which can be proved by servants who lived with us at Taunton; and he has pursued me with a knife.

Mrs Manning had told the police officer that, after leaving Minver Place, she had spent a night in the neighbourhood of Euston Square and had set off for Edinburgh the following day, where she had passed another night in the company of two women she had met on the train. Following his statement, a juror asked Superintendent Moxey if any of the clothing that had been found in Maria's lodgings were 'discoloured in any way'. He answered that they were not.

Next, stockbroker Francis Worrell Stevens of the Royal Exchange, London, stated that he had known Patrick O'Connor for three years, on whose behalf he had bought railway shares. When shown the scrips (share certificates) found in Mrs Manning's belongings, he identified his own signature on the documents; he had purchased them for Patrick on 11 May and 6 August 1849. The shares were further identified by Superintendent Moxey. Mr Stevens said that, on 1 August, a woman had entered his office and asked about the purchase of some shares, after being recommended by O'Connor. As she told the stockbroker that she was planning to travel to France, he showed her a list of appropriate businesses in which she might like to invest. She indicated her interest in the Sambre and Meuse Railway in Belgium. When Mr Stevens asked for her details, she gave her name as 'Maria Manning', after which she left the office. The witness did not see her again.

Francis Stevens informed the coroner that, during their conversation, 'Some words fell from her which excited some little suspicion', as she said that she wished to purchase some scrip without her husband's knowledge. He thought that she was perhaps intending to elope with Patrick O'Connor, but when he reflected on 'the steady character of Mr O'Connor', he decided that it was not likely. Superintendent Moxey added that Maria Manning had told him that she had her own money, which Frederick had been keen to get hold of, and that this had been the cause of the couple's arguments.

After a 30-minute break, the inquest resumed at 3.45 pm with statements about Patrick O'Connor's behaviour and habits. Firstly, his landlady deposed that he had lodged with her in Greenwood Street for five years and had occupied two 'ready-furnished' rooms on the first floor. She last saw him alive on the morning of Thursday 9 August, when he left at 7.30 am: 'He then appeared in good health and very comfortable.' He was wearing a black coat, a plain black satin neckerchief tied with a bow, check trousers, Albert shoes and a black hat. According to Ann Armes, Patrick was a man of 'particular' habits; he went out at the same time every morning for work but did not always return at 5 pm. He mostly dined at home, and sometimes relatives and acquaintances visited him at his rooms.

Patrick had known the Mannings for about a year and they used to drop in on him together, although Maria came more often than her husband. Miss Armes said that Maria had visited O'Connor frequently during the fortnight or so before he went missing. Sometimes she came alone while the customs officer was absent on business and, after waiting some hours, left before he returned. On other occasions, both the Mannings visited in the company of their lodger, William Massey, and the four took tea together. This happened about once a month. Ann observed that Maria and Patrick were on friendly terms, but that the former 'appeared particularly attentive to him.'

91

However, she further declared: 'I had no feeling that there was any improper conduct existing.' The landlady told the court that the Mannings had tried to borrow money from Patrick O'Connor on several occasions, but she and her sister did not know if he had succeeded.

On Thursday 9 August at 6 pm, Maria Manning visited Patrick's rooms and left again an hour and a quarter later. That night, Miss Armes had stayed up waiting for him until 2 am, but he did not return. This was not entirely unusual behaviour, because the lodger occasionally stayed out late with Pierce Walsh, as he had done on the previous evening when he had come home from Minver Place about midnight slightly worse for wear.

After his absence on the Thursday, the landlady said that several people had arrived at Greenwood Street looking for him; William Keating had come the following day and said to her that he was surprised at his friend's absence. Maria Manning also arrived on that day and spent some time in his room. When she passed through the shop afterwards, she had seemed 'all of a-shake and pale'.

The next day, Saturday 10 August, a notice arrived from the docks reporting O'Connor's absence from work. Miss Armes checked his room and could find no signs of his having been there for a while. She also noted that his trunk was still in the same spot, despite Mrs Manning having visited twice during his continued absence. The following Monday, John Bassett, a stockbroker, visited and told Ann that he had seen Patrick ten days earlier at the Royal Exchange. When she explained that he was missing, the man offered to contact Patrick's brother. He later informed the police and identified O'Connor's body at 3 Minver Place.

Following Ann Armes' lengthy testimony, acting Inspector of Customs, William John Ready, took the stand. He too had seen Patrick for the last time on Thursday 9 August at the docks. He also confirmed that O'Connor had been on duty the following day, but he had not turned up. He described O'Connor as 'a tall broad-shouldered man, about five feet ten or eleven inches' and weighing between 13 and 14 stone. He had light grey eyes and 'did not wear much [*sic*] whiskers.'

There followed statements from two stockbrokers who had had dealings with the deceased. The first was John Bassett, who was a clerk at the firm Killick and Co., Whitechapel. On about 31 July Patrick came to the office for the first time to inquire about shares. He returned on 11 August and, as the manager with whom he had spoken previously was absent due to illness, John Bassett had dealt with him. O'Connor produced twenty shares in Eastern

Counties Consolidated Stock, for which he received £110 from the clerk. The banknotes were later discovered in Maria Manning's luggage. Bassett said that Patrick 'appeared in excellent spirits and was very talkative.' He told the clerk that he was planning to go fishing in Exeter and that he would bring him a box of salmon. John Bassett also confirmed to the court that he had visited O'Connor's lodgings on Monday 13 August because he had forgotten to get his signature on a memorandum relating to the transaction, but Patrick was not at home. The clerk ended his testimony by recalling that he had seen the deceased's body after it was discovered at Minver Place: 'I could not swear that the body I have seen was the body of Mr O'Connor. It was so mangled and decomposed.' Another employee of the same firm, Richard Hammond, corroborated his colleague's testimony. He declared that the dead body was that of Patrick O'Connor, adding that he had seen 'persons in a worse condition in the cholera time.'

By this time, Charles Bainbridge had finally arrived at the tavern. The furniture dealer was late due to business 'at the west end of the town', for which he apologised. He testified that he had only known the Mannings for about seven weeks and was introduced to them by a Mrs Hornby from Bermondsey, who had told him that they wished to sell some furniture. Bainbridge had called at the Mannings' house a couple of times to make the arrangements. After a series of negotiations, during which Mrs Manning pushed for a higher price, they settled on £13 for the lot. Frederick Manning also asked if the dealer would lend £10 to their lodger William Massey against his medical certificate, and Charles agreed to consider it. On Monday 13 August, Bainbridge and Manning finalised the agreement for the furniture and the dealer handed over a deposit of 15 shillings. He agreed to take the items the following morning. Frederick was not present during the removal and, when he returned to the property later, he asked Charles if he had any rooms to let, as he wished to rent some accommodation for a fortnight. Bainbridge asked for 10 shillings, and it was agreed. Frederick then sent for his wife to inspect the temporary lodgings, but she never arrived.

After the furniture removal, Frederick went back to Bermondsey Square with the dealer, who told the court that Manning 'drank a good deal' during the evening. Bainbridge returned to Minver Place the next day to collect the remainder of the Mannings' belongings, which included the railway guard's coat. However, when he arrived at the house, it was locked from the inside and he could not gain entry. After speaking to the owner, James Coleman, he contacted the police and PC Burton let him into the property to recover the final items. These included the iron coal shovel, which Bainbridge identified in court.

The last witness's wife, Mary Ann, confirmed his statement, adding that among the belongings was a dress that seemed to have been washed 'in a hurry', as it had been put away before it was completely dry. PC Burton interjected that the dress had bloodstains on it. Mrs Bainbridge continued by stating that Frederick Manning had left their home on the Wednesday morning. During the two evenings that he had spent with them, he had been several times to The Horns Tavern in the square and came back 'very tipsy'. While drunk, he had asked her to get a lobster for his supper. The dealer's wife asked him if he would sleep in his own house, but Manning replied: 'I would not sleep in that house for £20.' After her testimony, William Cahill, the ironmonger's assistant, identified the shovel as the one he had sold to Maria Manning, and the surgeon, Samuel Lockwood, confirmed that there appeared to be human hair on it. He also said that the stains on the dress seemed to be blood.

The final two witnesses recalled their visits to Minver Place. William Flynn gave the details of the conversation he had with Maria Manning there on Monday 13 August. On that occasion, after commenting on how strange it was that Patrick O'Connor had gone missing, Mrs Manning had told him that some friends of hers, including William Keating, had seen him on the bridge the previous Thursday. She added that it was customary for Patrick to come and go, as he was 'very fickle-minded'. Sometimes he stopped at Minver Place for a minute or two and then he would jump up suddenly, take his hat and leave. On the mention of Patrick, Flynn detected 'a slight change on her countenance' and she seemed flustered. She explained it away and he did not give it any further thought: 'Nothing occurred to excite suspicion that the man [body] was there.' Flynn also recounted his visit to O'Connor's lodgings in Mile End Road. He told the court that the cash box, which was found in his room, was a gift from him to Patrick. He revealed that it was the state of the money box that had induced him to approach the magistrate with his concerns for his missing friend. At the end of his statement, Flynn attested that Patrick had told him that he was worth between £4,000 and £5,000 (about £500,000 today).

William Keating, who had testified at the previous sitting, deposed that he had been to the Mannings' home on Sunday 12 August to look for O'Connor. When he entered the house with his colleague David Graham, Mrs Manning was sitting with her back to the window and 'she seemed rather slovenly in her dress'. When asked if Patrick had dined there on Thursday evening, she appeared 'to show no anxiety' and said that he had not. Before they left, Keating inquired as to the whereabouts of her husband and their lodger. Mrs Manning replied that Frederick had gone to church and William Massey was away in the countryside.

After the last witness stepped down, William Carter addressed the jury. He reminded them that they should dismiss any information that they may have heard about the case outside the court. He then presented the main questions for the jury to consider; whether the deceased was Patrick O'Connor, the cause of his death, whether his injuries could have been self-inflicted and, if not, who had inflicted them. After summarising the evidence against Frederick and Maria Manning, he raised the issue of motivation and suggested that financial gain might have induced the couple to end O'Connor's life. In relation to Mrs Manning's likely part in the crime, Mr Carter reminded the jury that she had bought the shovel which had been used to bury the body under the kitchen floor.

The jury retired at 9.30 pm, returning 45 minutes later to deliver their verdict: the deceased was Patrick O'Connor, and he had been wilfully murdered by Frederick George and Maria Manning.

At the same time as the inquest was taking place, some further evidence against Mrs Manning came to light. Following the discovery of the bloodstained clothing in the trunks that she had left at London Bridge, PC James Burton returned to Bermondsey Square to examine some old clothing in the possession of the furniture dealer Charles Bainbridge. There he discovered a plaid dressing gown with large patches of blood which had been partly washed out. The officer showed it to William Massey, who identified it as belonging to Maria Manning. PC Burton also found the black waistcoat, which had been worn by Patrick O'Connor. It was torn from the left arm across the chest and down to the bottom of the garment, suggesting that there had been a violent struggle before his death.

While the police were gathering evidence, the Scotland Yard officers were still looking for Frederick Manning. On Monday, Detective Inspector Field was despatched to Plymouth following information that Manning had boarded the *Constant*, an emigrant ship bound for Australia. A few days earlier, a man matching his description had called at the shipping agent's office and inquired about the passage, which cost £15. The traveller offered £13 and said he would return later. Although the agent did not see him again that day, he believed that he had boarded the vessel, as someone had paid that exact sum for a ticket. The ship was due to leave from Plymouth that evening, so Inspector Field travelled to the coast with a letter for Admiral Sir William Hall Gage, who was commander-in-chief at Devonport, to request permission to search the docks.

There were other sightings of Frederick Manning elsewhere. On Tuesday 28 August, a boy ran into Southwark police station with a note from two men in the Strand, who were allegedly acquaintances of Manning. They had met him the previous evening at a public house in Poland Street, where he was believed to be hiding. The police recognised immediately that this was a ruse, as the tavern was a 'flash house' notorious for pickpockets who were trying to make fools of the officers.

The same evening, there was intense excitement in Waterloo Road after a rumour circulated in the neighbourhood of the Cut that Manning had been arrested there. A few weeks earlier, a man who resembled Frederick had acquired some carpenters' tools from a shopkeeper under false pretences. When he was arrested, the officers believed that they had caught the missing murderer. A mob gathered, and the police had to make their way through the crowds to the station, where they ascertained that it was not him. There was a similar case in Dublin, in which the prisoner was called 'Manning' but it was not Frederick.

On the evening of Wednesday 29 August, Scotland Yard received a telegraph informing them that, after twelve days on the run, Frederick Manning had finally been arrested in Jersey.

Chapter 13

A Game of Cat and Mouse

Frederick Manning had arrived in Jersey on Thursday 16 August, the day after he had left Bermondsey Square. After departing London, he had spent a night at the Oxford Arms Inn, near Southampton railway station, before taking the passage at midnight to the island on the South Western Steam Packet Company's paddle steamer, the *Courier*. Built in 1847, the vessel was especially used for services to the Channel Islands. Manning spent most of the crossing in his cabin, drinking copious amounts of brandy, and rarely appeared on deck. On reaching Jersey, he disembarked with a fellow passenger named Mr Turk, with whom he had struck up an acquaintance. The two men walked into St Helier together, and made for the Navy Arms in Mulcaster Street, which was at the centre of the town near the port. According to *The Jersey Times*, the neighbourhood was 'by no means one of its most inviting streets', and the houses were 'high, dark and gloomy'. On their arrival at the tavern, Mr Turk asked for his usual accommodation and the landlady, Mrs Berry, told them that she only had a double room available. The two travellers took it and Manning agreed to pay his companion 8 shillings per week. Also, on arrival at the hotel, Frederick immediately asked to see a copy of *The Times*.

The next day, Mr Turk showed Manning around the island, after which they took tea with Mrs Berry and her husband. According to a Jersey reporter, the landlord of the Navy Arms did not like Frederick and considered him to be rather peculiar. The other guests also disliked him, finding him overbearing and argumentative. He even fell out with Turk and, on the Friday evening, they had a dispute about money, with Manning trying to outdo his companion with the amount of cash he was apparently carrying with him. On the Sunday, Frederick asked the landlord where he could attend church. He also told him that he needed to go to Paris to settle his affairs, as he had lost all his money during the French revolutions of 1848. Mr Berry asked how much it would cost to sail to Granville in Normandy and, when he learnt that it would be about

20 shillings, he implored the landlord to travel with him to act as interpreter. Berry declined and advised him to go to France via London instead. Manning agreed and asked for an alarm call in time for the packet leaving Jersey for Southampton the following morning. However, when Berry roused him the next day, Frederick declined to leave and stayed in bed, which, by then, he had to himself as Turk had already departed.

On the Sunday afternoon, Manning had taken a trip on an omnibus to the parish of St Lawrence, about 5 miles west of St Helier. During the ride, he waved to an old friend from five years earlier who happened to be walking along the roadside. The driver told him that the man was staying at the British Lion Inn. Frederick asked to be dropped there and entered the tavern to look for his old acquaintance, whose name was Ford – they had met through Manning's sister when she was working as a barmaid in London. Manning asked if Ford would accompany him to France, but he declined. They made an appointment for dinner during the next week, but Ford did not turn up. However, it was while he was at the British Lion that Manning spotted Prospect House, where he would move to next. The cottage belonged to an elderly couple called Berteau. After he left the British Lion, Frederick called at the house and agreed to rent a large bedroom for 4 shillings a week. But, for the time being, he remained at the Navy Arms.

Later that evening, after his trip, Manning visited the Bath Hotel, one of the most prestigious hotels in St Helier, where he entered into conversation with a number of local tradespeople. He complained to them about the difficulty of finding work on the island and said that he had only had one decent meal of conger eel during his stay so far. His new companions took exception to his condescending manner, and a Mr Purkis quipped: 'I tell you what, sir, you'll find Jersey a very healthy place, for where there is one die there are twenty bolt.' When Manning asked him what he meant by 'bolt', the man told him it referred to 'absconder', at which Frederick threw himself back in his chair and laughed heartily.

During the course of the evening, one of the men mentioned that he was from Derby. Manning asked if he knew the Massey family of Swarkestone. He told his new acquaintance that the family's son, William, had lodged in his house in London while undertaking his medical studies. He even showed him that he was wearing William's hat. As news of Patrick O'Connor's murder had not yet reached the island by this time (his body had been discovered only two days earlier), no one knew who Manning was. He continued the evening drinking brandy and boasting of his alleged business as a representative for a textiles warehouse; he showed them a card but carefully covered the name so that it could not be seen properly. Frederick called again at the Bath Hotel the following day and spent another afternoon in the bar. This time, he told the landlady, Mrs Seward, that he worked for a gin company. When she replied that her husband ordered gin from the same business, he laughed and narrowly avoided mentioning his real name. He told Mrs Seward that he liked the island so much that next time he would bring his wife. As later highlighted in *Lloyd's Weekly*: 'Had he desired to secure his own apprehension he could scarcely have taken a more likely course to secure it.' Later that day, after he had left the Bath Hotel, Manning met a man in St Helier, whom he knew from Taunton and who was spending his honeymoon on the island, and it was perhaps this encounter that encouraged him to move on.

After a week's stay, on Thursday 23 August, Manning settled his bill at the Navy Arms, telling the landlord that he would be away until the Saturday. As he left some clothing at the tavern, Mr Berry fully expected him to return. He then moved into Prospect House, which was near St Aubin's Road, close to the coastline and near to the village of Beaumont. This was a much more picturesque part of the island, and the thoroughfare ran from St Helier to the beautiful bay of St Aubin, which was the island's second most important town. Not far from Manning's new lodgings was the fortress of Elizabeth Castle which was accessible only at low tide on foot or horseback.

However, the fugitive would have been more safely concealed in this secluded place, were it not for his need for alcohol; Manning sent out for brandy so frequently that suspicions began to be aroused.

On Monday 27 August, two brothers, John and George Heulin contacted Detective Sergeant Langley in St Helier. The Scotland Yard detective had arrived on the island two days earlier with his colleague, Police Constable Lockyer.

Information about the murder of Patrick O'Connor and the subsequent search for Frederick Manning had reached the island, three days earlier, on 24 August, after the Metropolitan police commissioners had written to Sir James Reynett, the lieutenant governor of Jersey, following the sighting of the felon on the steamer from Southampton. Sir James had immediately conferred with the island's chief justice, Sir Thomas Breton, who had consulted with his colleagues in the law, and then placed the matter in the hands of Chief of the Honorary Police, Mr Chevalier, who was already apprised of the situation due to having received a letter from Detective Sergeant Thornton of Scotland Yard. In his ensuing investigation into the matter, Mr Chevalier had ascertained that two individuals had acquired a small steamboat to travel to Saint Malo, one of whom bore a striking resemblance to Frederick Manning. The chief police officer set a watch on the travellers and brought them in for questioning. As he was dissatisfied with their statement that they were going to France to attend the funeral of a relative who had died of cholera, he passed them onto the mayor, who later released them. That evening, Chevalier received information that Manning had been seen in St Helier by a man named Trenchard who knew him from Taunton.

On their arrival in Jersey, Detective Sergeant Langley and PC Lockyer proceeded straight to the police station where they met Mr Chevalier. They soon discovered, from information received, that Frederick had lodged at the Navy Arms, which was opposite the police station, until Thursday 23 August. Shortly afterwards, they found Frederick Manning's discarded belongings in the tavern, which were packed into a carpet bag. The contents were mostly clothing; shirts, handkerchiefs, stockings, neckerchiefs and two pairs of boots. The police also found six memorandum books, a pocket book, a cheque book and five character references for the fugitive. When Detective Langley spotted a dark green shooting coat, he exclaimed, 'That's Manning's coat; we are on the right scent.' In the pocket he discovered some loose tissue paper and brown paper, and some gunpowder. However, there were no clues as to Manning's whereabouts.

In the next few days, the police officers interviewed Frederick's former acquaintance, Mr Ford, whom he had met while on the omnibus excursion. They spoke to him at the British Lion Inn, unaware that they were only 300 yards from where Manning was hiding out. Mr Chevalier concluded that the suspect must have fled the island from its northern coast, so he applied to the lieutenant governor for a steamboat to take him to Granville to see if he could locate the felon. The chief of police made the crossing on Sunday 26 August but, finding no trace of Manning there, he returned to Jersey.

The following day, the London officers were still busy making inquiries. They visited public houses along Manning's supposed route and followed up inquiries. Unbeknown to them, Frederick was still at Prospect House, drinking brandy and chatting to the landlord and the other boarders. On the Sunday, a friend of Madame Berteau had visited, and she had commented that Manning's behaviour seemed very strange. She added that she hoped he was not the perpetrator of the dreadful murder in Bermondsey. Madame Berteau had not heard about the incident and therefore dismissed her friend's concerns.

However, a local man, George Heulin, who was providing brandy to the household during Manning's stay there, became suspicious. He questioned the serving girl who came for the alcohol, after which he discussed the matter with his brother John, who had met Frederick at the Bath Hotel in St Helier. They decided to contact Detective Langley.

Officers Langley and Lockyer had retired to their rooms for the evening when they received the message from the Heulins. After speaking to them, Langley immediately informed Mr Chevalier. Although the chief of police raised concerns about the lateness of the hour, Langley persuaded him that it was better to act immediately, rather than to delay the arrest. The three police officers, together with the Heulin brothers and Mr Purkis, the cab driver who had met Manning, went to Prospect House, where the fugitive was believed to be staying. They alighted from the cab some 200 yards away from the house and continued their journey on foot, so as not to create any noise. Mr Chevalier and George Heulin proceeded to the back of the property and told Monsieur and Madame Berteau that they were planning to arrest their lodger. Leaving the brothers outside to keep watch, in case the prisoner escaped, Chevalier knocked at the front door. As arranged, Monsieur Berteau opened it and handed the officer a candle. Langley, Lockyer, Chevalier and Purkis, the driver, went inside.

When they entered the room, Langley stepped forward and shouted, 'That's the man – seize him!' Taken by surprise, Manning said, 'Hallo! What are you all about, are you going to murder me?' Then he remarked, 'Sergeant, is that you? I am glad you are come; I was going to London to explain it all.' According to the press reports, Frederick appeared to be very nervous and there was a bottle of liquor and an open razor by his bed. He asked, 'Is the wretch taken?' to which Langley replied that he did not know, but he believed so from the newspapers. Frederick said, 'I suppose they found a great deal of money upon her, £1,300 or £1,400.' Again, the detective did not know whether that was the case. He cautioned Manning and took him into custody, to which Manning offered no resistance. He simply said, 'Oh, very well, I am willing to explain it all; I am perfectly innocent.' When Detective Sergeant Langley instructed Lockyer and Chevalier to put handcuffs on him, Frederick complained, 'Surely you will not put the handcuffs on me, you know me so well?' Langley replied, 'As an officer you must excuse me; I must put them on, it is my duty.' After allowing Manning enough time to get dressed, Lockyer pinioned him while Chevalier snapped the cuffs onto his wrists.

The officers took him downstairs to the waiting cab and drove him to the prison. While they were travelling, Manning said:

> She [Maria Manning] shot him; she invited him to dinner, the cloth was laid when he came in; she asked him to go downstairs to wash his hands, and when at the bottom of the stairs she put one hand on his shoulder and shot him at the back of the head with the other.

After this startling revelation, Mr Chevalier asked him what had become of the body and, despite Langley nudging him to indicate that he should not answer any further questions, the prisoner replied, 'She had a grave dug for him.'

Frederick Manning was placed in a cell overnight. After telling the medical officer that he was feeling ill, the prisoner was provided with some brandy and water, which revived his spirits. The following morning, he asked Detective Langley how long he was going to be kept there, as he was keen to get to London to explain everything. However, it was not possible for the police officers to convey Manning back to England immediately, as the authorities in Jersey were not permitted to release a prisoner on the basis of a magistrate's warrant and required an order from the Metropolitan police commissioners before he could be transported to London. The transfer was therefore expected to take place the following Monday.

Soon after Manning's arrest, news had been sent to Southampton where it had been received by Detective Sergeant Whicher, who was waiting in the coastal town. He telegraphed the secretary of state on Wednesday 29 August to inform him of the arrest and his colleague, Detective Sergeant Haynes, had set out for the coast straightaway with a magistrate's warrant. Realising later that they needed a special order from the police commissioners, Haynes immediately wrote to the Home Office and suggested that they send the special order in the mail to the coast in time for him to take it across to Jersey on the Friday evening, which was the next crossing to the island. In the end, the administrative issue was resolved due to an outbreak of cholera in the prison, which culminated in one death and three prisoners being admitted to hospital, after which the authorities decided to release Manning without waiting for the official permission.

While Frederick Manning was waiting behind bars for his transfer, crowds of islanders applied for admission to the prison to see him. Those who were permitted to enter observed that he was sitting on a bench or walking about the prison yard. *Lloyd's Weekly* reported that:

> [He] seemed to gaze with something like an expression of indignation at those who came to stare at him like as they would at a wild beast, but he took no notice of the other prisoners, or of the persons connected with the gaol, whose anxiety to get a sight of him, seemed, however, as intense as that of the visitors from without the prison walls.

The lieutenant governor Thomas Le Breton also visited Manning while he was incarcerated. The prisoner plied him with questions about his transfer to London and was particularly interested in trying to find out if his wife had confessed.

At 7 am on Friday morning, Mr Chevalier and the Scotland Yard detectives arrived at the prison to convey Manning to the vessel that would take him back to face justice in London. Frederick requested that he be allowed to walk to the port through the streets of St Helier. Chevalier agreed, as it was early in the day, and no one was around. According to the press, during the walk Manning further asked if he could smoke a cigar, to which the officers also consented.

Frederick Manning set sail on the steam packet for Southampton from St Helier at 8 am on Friday 31 August, accompanied by Detective Sergeant Langley and Police Constable Lockyer. On the crossing, Manning asked Langley whether he would be freed, were his wife to confess. The detective replied that he was unable to answer his question. Manning said, 'I am sure she will confess when she sees me, particularly if a clergyman is with her.'

On their arrival at the Southampton Docks at 7.10 pm, throngs of people were gathered in the hope of seeing the now famous prisoner. The party was met by Detective Sergeant Haynes, who had been waiting for them. As the last train for London had already left Southampton due to the late hour, Manning was conveyed by a special train. By this time, Detective Langley was feeling unwell as he had been awake for so long, and he fell asleep in the carriage while Manning and Haynes conversed. Frederick asked the detective if he had seen his wife. Haynes answered that he had not, after which Frederick asked, 'Do you think I shall see her tomorrow?' The detective said, 'I don't know, but I don't think you'll be allowed to see her.'

Before the prisoner could ask any more questions, Haynes cautioned him: 'This is a very serious affair, Manning; I am an officer, don't say anything to me that will prejudice yourself.' Frederick replied, 'I am perfectly aware of all that; I was very foolish to go away, for I ought to have stayed and explained all.' Manning then said, 'If I could see her in the presence of a magistrate and a clergyman, she would confess all, for it was her that shot O'Connor.' He explained to the officer that she had invited Patrick O'Connor to dinner and shot him as she was walking behind him down the stairs. He said that she was a very violent woman and would think no more of killing a man than she would of killing a cat. Frederick had frequently been afraid for his own life and, on one occasion, she had followed him with a knife. He said she was determined to exact revenge on O'Connor, for it was he who induced them to take the house in Minver Place, and it had cost them £30 to furnish it. When Manning had finished his explanation, Haynes simply observed, 'It appears by the papers that there were several other wounds in the head', to which the prisoner made no reply. The train arrived at Vauxhall station at 10 pm, where a cab was waiting to take them to Stones End police station in Southwark.

The headlines announced that the fugitive had been captured at last, and the press agreed unanimously that confidence in the police had finally been restored:

> The means by which the officers of justice have succeeded in tracking his guilty steps, show how small are the chances of escape now left to those who commit enormous crimes ... the police by more systematic and skilful means follow in the trail of the fugitive. The dexterity and unwearied industry with which, in this instance, they have pursued the perpetrators of a most atrocious murder, are deserving of the highest commendation. (*Lloyd's Weekly*, 2 September 1849)

The Times summed up the result of the tireless efforts of the detective police:

> Both the perpetrators, or supposed perpetrators, of the Bermondsey murder are now in the hands of the law, and so far, the public indignation will be satisfied in reference to a crime as diabolical in its conception and execution as any in that black catalogue which of late years we have had to record.

Chapter 14

Behind Bars

The Surrey County Gaol in Southwark, known as Horsemonger Lane Gaol, took its name from the street on which it was built between 1791 and 1799. The construction, which replaced several older local prisons, included a courthouse which faced onto Newington Causeway. Behind the squat gatehouse, on which the gallows were erected, was a quadrangle comprising four three-storey wings; three for remanded or convicted criminals and the fourth for debtors. It had capacity for 300 inmates. There was an infirmary to the left of the gatehouse, behind which were the women's quarters, including a laundry and baths. In the centre of the prison was a kitchen and segregated exercise yards. A chapel and schoolrooms were located at the far side of the quadrangle, opposite the entrance. In 1800 the prison reformer, James Neild, reported that Horsemonger Lane was an 'excellently well-regulated gaol.' In his inspection, he had found it to be clean and well organised, with two surgeons in attendance. The prison closed in 1878 and the building had been completely demolished by 1945. There is now a public garden and playground on the site.

Maria Manning had been admitted to the prison on Friday 24 August. On entry, the prison doctor used scissors to cut her hair short 'foreseeing some improper use might be made of it.' He later reported to the police that 'she had very little hair, most of it being false.' Despite her treatment, it was reported in the press that: 'The prisoner possesses the most extraordinary nerve they [the prison authorities] ever witnessed' (*Lloyd's Weekly*, 2 September 1849). After eating her meals 'heartily', Maria went to bed each night at 11 pm and slept through without waking until 8 am. However, when she received the news of her husband's arrest, apparently she blanched and trembled for a few seconds and said, 'The villain! It was him that did it, not me', after which she resumed her usual calm demeanour. On being informed that Frederick Manning had accused her of firing the pistol that had killed Patrick O'Connor, she declared that it was untrue and denied all knowledge of the murder.

On Friday 31 August, Mrs Manning returned to Southwark police court for the next session of her hearing before the magistrate. Long before 10 am, the usual starting time for such proceedings, the thoroughfare in front of the court was already crowded and a double row of police officers was deployed to keep the road from being completely obstructed. By this time, the public houses in the vicinity were all full and the windows of the houses overlooking the entrances to the court were populated with well-dressed people, most of whom, according to the press, were women who had gathered to watch the prisoner's arrival. Inside the courtroom were more 'fashionably attired ladies' and on the bench were several county magistrates and their friends, all keen to follow the events that were about to take place.

Just after 10 am, the sitting magistrate Isaac Secker took his seat at the bench. He spent the first hour dealing with other charges that had come to his attention overnight. This was followed by an hour's break, after which he instructed the court officials to clear a space so that Maria Manning could make her way to the bar. Outside, confusion broke out as the prisoner was driven into the courtyard, where hundreds of people were congregated, all jostling for the best view. By 1 pm, order had been restored and the bench was full; those present included the chief secretary to the Austrian ambassador, the rector of St George's, Bermondsey, and other local clergymen.

At a few minutes past 1 pm, the solicitor for the Treasury, John Hayward, entered the court with Maria Manning's solicitor, Joseph Solomon. Five minutes later, the long-awaited prisoner finally entered, attended by a female prison warder, and walked slowly to the dock. She was wearing a black satin outer garment trimmed with black lace, a white straw bonnet adorned with a pink and white plaid ribbon and a black lace veil, which covered her face. Mr Hayward rose from his seat and declared his intention to prosecute on behalf of the Crown. A Mr Blandford said that he was in attendance on the part of Patrick O'Connor's friends.

The four main witnesses repeated their statements from the inquest. Cab driver William Kirk identified Maria Manning as the woman he had taken to London Bridge and Euston railway stations: 'I can swear that that female is the same', even though her face had been partly covered by a veil. William Day, the railway porter, described the boxes that had been left at London Bridge, after which he too identified Mrs Manning: 'To the best of my knowledge the prisoner is that lady.' The cloakroom clerk who had ticketed and stored the luggage, William Dyne, stated that he had 'some slight recollection' of the passenger, but he 'would not undertake to swear positively to the fact.' Finally, Superintendent Richard Moxey repeated his evidence relating to Maria's arrest in Edinburgh. All four witnesses signed their depositions and were bound over to appear for the prosecution at the Old Bailey. The current hearing was then adjourned to Thursday 6 September at midday, and Maria Manning was to be returned to Horsemonger Lane Gaol. At this point, some of the spectators tried to leave but the court was so packed that it was impossible to convey Mrs Manning back through the crowds to the van that was waiting for her outside. In the end, the police officers forced their way through, and she was taken back to the gaol.

As Maria Manning waited for her next appearance in court, the newspapers continued to comment on her appearance, as was customary in relation to female offenders who were sensationalised and often demonised in the press. In the edition of *Lloyd's Weekly* that was published the following day, the commentator contradicted earlier descriptions of the female prisoner, who had originally been depicted as a fine woman with 'a good figure' and 'a lady-like appearance'. After having been scrutinised in court, she was now deemed to have:

> an almost masculine figure, and to be possessed of considerable strength. Her brow is large and heavy, and her face, which is long and broad, and scarcely feminine, has, altogether, a coarse and vulgar appearance.

The journalist further observed that 'her self-possession was somewhat remarkable', especially considering the intense attention that she had attracted. Mrs Manning had stood up for the entire proceedings, which had lasted two and a half hours, only leaning lightly upon the dock, having refused to take a chair:

> Scarcely an emotion was visible in her countenance from the beginning to the end of the tedious examination; but a slight tremulous shake of her body, as she stood, was observed by one or two persons. Beyond that, however, nothing could be seen which indicated that she was other than quite composed. She had her veil drawn over her face and did not once lift it up. On being asked if she wanted any water, she shook her head and said, 'No.'
> (*Lloyd's Weekly*, 2 September 1849)

Later that evening, Frederick Manning had arrived in London and been taken to Stones End police station. On his arrival at 10.30 pm, Inspector Yates read out the charge, to which the prisoner replied, 'Very well, sir.' He was searched, and a comb, a Bible, and 1 shilling and 4 pence were found on his person. After that, he was placed in a cell overnight, closely guarded by two police officers. The next morning, he was to appear at Southwark police court, the day after his wife had been before the same magistrate.

On Saturday 1 September, due to Frederick Manning's arrival in London having been published in the press, an immense crowd had gathered once again in front of the court, and extra officers were deployed to prevent their entering the courtroom. Shortly after 10 am, the magistrate arrived, and the prisoner was placed in the dock. As this was his first public appearance, Manning was described fully in the newspapers:

> He is a stoutish man, with a long thick head, and sandy hair, with small whiskers; his chin is rather long, and he has a very stupid appearance. He seemed to feel his awful position but made no allusion to the crime. (*Lloyd's Weekly*, 2 September 1849)

It was noted in *Bell's New Weekly Messenger* that he appeared agitated, which was in contrast to his wife's demeanour when she was examined the previous day. *The London Evening Standard* summed up Frederick's appearance as 'repulsive-looking'.

The accused stood erectly in the dock, with a sullen demeanour. According to observers, he looked very tired and was dressed in a shabby, blue overcoat buttoned to his chin and a red check neckerchief. He was wearing a black hat, which he removed. During the examination Manning's eyes were fixed intently on the magistrate. He held his hat in his right hand, with his other placed lightly on the rails of the dock.

The session opened with Inspector Yates reading the charge against the prisoner. The police officer confirmed that Patrick O'Connor had been murdered, as he had viewed the body, which bore several wounds to the head and had also been shot. The magistrate asked for evidence that Mr and Mrs Manning lived at Minver Place. In response, medical student and former lodger William Massey stated that the Mannings lived at 3 Minver Place and that he had seen O'Connor frequently at the house: 'he seemed on familiar terms with Manning and his wife.' Massey had last seen the couple at the property at the beginning of August. Inspector Yates added that he had found items belonging to the victim at the house on the day of the murder.

The magistrate explained that, as Maria Manning was remanded until the following Thursday, he would not proceed with her husband's hearing. He asked if the prisoner wished to ask any questions, but Frederick declined. He too was remanded until Thursday 6 September and conveyed to Horsemonger Lane Gaol. On arrival at the prison, Manning asked the governor, John Keene, if he could see his wife in the presence of Inspector Yates and his officers, but permission was denied. Manning responded that he was 'sorry for it, as his wife could exonerate him from all participation in the crime.' He was led into one of the cells reserved for those charged with serious offences, and he later asked for some ink and paper so that he could write to Maria. Once again, his request was denied.

That weekend, now that both the prisoners were behind bars, the newspapers continued to print numerous additional pieces of information about the case, which they had apparently gleaned from interviews with their sources. Along with many other publications, *Lloyd's Weekly* shared titbits with its readership. Following the first appearance of Maria Manning at the police court on 24 August, the newspaper disclosed details which had not been mentioned so far in the formal proceedings.

Allegedly, during the conversations that had taken place between Mrs Manning and Superintendent Moxey, while she was still at Stones End police station, he had mentioned to her that it was believed that Patrick O'Connor had been murdered on the evening of 9 August. The prisoner had replied: 'Well, if a murder was committed in the house on the Thursday night, it must have been during my absence, for I went out at four o'clock, and did not return till late in the evening.' Moxey told her that the police had discovered that she had visited the victim's lodgings during that time, for which she would have needed to have taken his keys. Maria responded: 'Well, I know nothing about the keys, but hearing he was missing I certainly went to his house and took the property, which was my own.' She did not reveal the nature of the items taken.

Later that day, while Mrs Manning was in the charge room at the police station, a police constable noticed that she was reading a handbill offering a reward for her husband's arrest. The officer took the opportunity to ask her if she knew where Frederick was. She said: 'No, but it's no use your looking after him, for he's a long way from here. In fact, he is out of the country.'

However, despite Maria Manning's declaration that she was unaware of the events that had taken place at 3 Minver Place, the newspaper had found evidence of the murder being premeditated, based on letters which had been received by William Massey's sister, Mary. On 5 August, four days prior to Patrick O'Connor's estimated death, Frederick Manning had written to Mary Massey at her home in Swarkestone, Derbyshire. He wrote that he was trying to locate her brother William, as the medical student owed him 10 shillings after he had settled his debt with Patrick. In William's absence Manning wanted Mary to reimburse him urgently. Mary Massey did not send the payment as her brother had now arrived back home and he had advised her not to, claiming that Manning had increased the original amount of the debt from £13 to £15, to extort additional money from him. Three days later, Frederick wrote directly to William, threatening him that if he did not send the balance immediately, he would take action against him and besmirch his character. William Massey did not send the cash either, as he was broke due to not having been able to borrow from anyone else.

The most entertaining snippet that appeared in the press was a story connected with Detective Inspector Charles Field of Scotland Yard. The French newspaper, the *Gazette des Tribunaux*, reported that, when Maria Manning was arrested in Edinburgh, the inspector was still searching for her husband in Paris. After it became obvious that it was unlikely that Frederick Manning was in the French city, he decided to return to London. While he was waiting at the Gare Saint-Lazare terminus, a passenger who was also in the queue discovered that his pocket had been picked. The traveller called out the theft and Field, 'after having cast an investigating glance at the persons present', approached a young man. He was elegantly dressed and nonchalantly playing with his cane. Recognising him as a felon called 'Wood', the inspector cried out, 'This is the thief.' The suspect protested loudly that it was a case of mistaken identity, but the detective insisted. When the alleged thief was taken to a private room and searched, the stolen watch was found on his person. Before alighting the train, Detective Inspector Field took the time to give a description of five or six London pickpockets who were in Paris that week, hoping to 'do business' at the International Peace Congress, which was taking place between 22 and 24 August, presided over by Victor Hugo.

Back in London, the detective's colleagues at Scotland Yard were working hard to find additional evidence to strengthen their case against the murderous couple. On Saturday 1 September, while Frederick Manning was at his first hearing, the police made an important discovery. Following Manning's abortive attempt to purchase a crowbar on 13 July, it transpired that almost a fortnight later, he made a visit to another supplier on the same street. On 26 July, he called at the ironmongery warehouse belonging to Messrs Evans at 33 King William Street, London Bridge, and asked to see a small crowbar. The shop assistant informed him that they did not keep such items in stock but that he could have one made for him. Manning agreed and ordered a crowbar weighing about 7 or 8 pounds. He left his name and address so that it could be delivered to him. Two days later, the tool was ready following Frederick's instructions, and one of the company's porters delivered it to 3 Minver Place.

A few minutes after the employee had started out to Bermondsey, Manning called at the shop again to check that his order was ready. On learning that it had already been despatched, he hurried out of the shop and managed to overtake the porter in Tooley Street. When he had ascertained that the man was carrying his custom-made crowbar, he expressed his concern that it was not wrapped. Saying, 'One don't [*sic*] want everybody to see such things', he ushered the porter into a stationer's where he bought a sheet of brown paper in which he wrapped the implement. Manning then returned the crowbar to the porter and asked him to take it to his address.

When the porter arrived at 3 Minver Place, the door was opened by a tall, well-dressed woman. She asked how much there was left to pay and gave the porter the balance of 3 shillings and 6 pence. Fortunately, the ironmonger's assistant had kept the slip of paper on which Frederick Manning had written his details, which was later confirmed to be his handwriting. Also, the porter was taken to Horsemonger Lane Gaol, where he identified both the prisoners. The police had not managed to locate the crowbar, which resembled a large ripping chisel, with a long, flat steel-tipped point.

In relation to the two medicine bottles, which were found with Patrick O'Connor's body, the police discovered that they belonged to John Packer, a surgeon, who had also helped lift the body out of the hole in the floor. One bottle contained laudanum and the other chloroform, and they had fallen out of his pocket as he bent down. Thus, this ended speculation that they might have been used to poison the victim.

On Tuesday 4 September, the Metropolitan police commissioners gave orders for a more detailed search of Minver Place, especially of the water closet at the rear of the house, which had not yet been properly examined. The police had felt around it with a boathook, while searching for Patrick O'Connor's missing clothes, but it was still possible that the crowbar and firearm had been thrown into it. As the water closet opened into the sewer, which was 16 feet below, the commissioners wished it to be opened in order to complete the search. At midday Detective Inspector Haynes and PC Burton went to the house, along with several labourers who were deployed to help. However, when they arrived at the property, they found that a family had already moved in, and the officers were denied entry. They appealed to the landlord who also refused them admission due to concerns about further damage, as a search of the water closet would involve digging up the garden and dismantling the lower section of the house. Undeterred, Haynes acquired an interview with the magistrate who was reluctant to interfere in a matter which, in his opinion, should be decided by the police commissioners.

That same afternoon, Inspector Yates also visited the magistrate to request permission for a tradesman to be admitted to Horsemonger Lane Gaol to see the prisoners. The inspector told Mr Secker that, on 6 August, a man answering Frederick Manning's description had called at the stationer's shop of Messrs Eastman and Yeo, in Cheapside. He had asked to leave a small airgun wrapped in cloth for safekeeping. The shop assistant had agreed and placed the firearm behind the counter. At midday, on the day of the supposed murder, the same man had called again at the shop and reclaimed it. On reading about the incident in the newspapers, proprietor Thomas Yeo had contacted the police. The magistrate gave his permission and Mr Yeo, accompanied by Inspector Yates, visited the prison. At the gaol, the warders gathered a group of male inmates from various wards together and Yeo was invited to take a good look at their faces to see if he could identify the man who had left the airgun. Frustratingly for Inspector Haynes, he did not recognise any of them.

However, later in the day, the owner of a pawnbrokers' shop in Bermondsey produced a pair of pistols, which had been pledged in his shop by a man who also resembled Frederick Manning. The man had given his name as 'Jennings' and he had pawned the pistols for 4 shillings. On examining them, the pawnbroker had found that one had been recently fired. He gave the weapons to the police and, the following day, they tracked down the owner, a Mrs Bliss, who was a dealer in Lambeth. Through interviewing her, it was discovered that a man, who also might have looked like Manning, had sold them to her two months earlier. As, by this time, the magistrate had left the court, Inspector Haynes was unable to obtain permission to take the pawnbroker and the dealer to the prison in another attempt to identify the suspect, but he was confident that eventually these leads would result in his finding the missing pistol.

Finally, it also came to light that Mrs Manning had employed a young woman to clean the back kitchen of 3 Minver Place after the body had been laid under the floor. As the Mannings did not keep a servant, the neighbours had noticed the woman on the Saturday after Patrick O'Connor had disappeared. She had been washing the passage, while Maria was sweeping the front steps. When she had finished her day's work, she had remarked to a servant who worked next door that she had had 'a filthy job' and that the kitchen had been 'in a beastly state'. The police were very anxious to speak to this unknown person. As noted in *Lloyd's Weekly*, the pressure was on to find this crucial witness:

> As yet the police authorities have failed in eliciting evidence to establish the fact of Mrs Manning's presence in the house on the night the murder is reported to have been committed.

Chapter 15

A Double Event

While the police were busy chasing the final pieces of evidence, Frederick and Maria Manning were behind bars at Horsemonger Lane Gaol. During the week leading up to their first joint hearing, Frederick seemed unsettled. He drafted letters to his wife, with whom he was not allowed any contact, and he constantly pestered the prison warders and any visitors for extra privileges, such as tobacco. His requests were always refused.

Maria Manning had recovered from her agitation over her husband's arrest and was conducting business related to her defence. She had a meeting with an inspector from Southwark Division, with whom she agreed to release £20 to pay the solicitor who was going to act on her behalf. Her demeanour was positive and business-like and, when the police officer was about to leave, she shook his hand vigorously and said, 'I thank you and the worthy magistrate for this assistance; I am much obliged to you.' Despite her cordiality, Mrs Manning was irritated that she and Frederick were to appear together at the hearing, and she quizzed the warders about what the newspapers were saying about the case. Rarely talking about the matter herself, she devoted most of her time to preparing what she would wear to the next court session. Having gained permission from the magistrate to have some of her clothing restored to her, she set about sewing and made a double veil for her bonnet to conceal her face. Maria seemed relatively content in prison and was appreciative of the prison authorities and their provision: 'I have plenty of room, plenty of air, and plenty of food, and am not without society.' She asked to see Superintendent Moxey so that she could thank him and, when she discovered that he had already left for Edinburgh, she was disappointed, but stated that she planned to visit him in Scotland 'as soon as I have got over this difficulty.' It was evident that Maria Manning was confident of her exoneration, and she even expressed some concern about her husband, saying: 'Ah poor boy, he ought not to have been taken.'

Frederick, on the other hand, was not faring so well as the week wore on. His appearance and behaviour changed for the worse and he became depressed. Once again, he asked for an interview with his wife, but the prison governor refused. While Maria attended both the morning and afternoon services in the chapel on Sunday, her husband did not. However, despite his low spirits, he maintained his innocence and declared that Maria was the sole perpetrator of the crime.

On Wednesday 5 September, the day before their hearing, Mrs Manning received a letter, which had been forwarded to the prison from Minver Place. It had a French postmark. Before it could be passed onto the prisoner, the magistrate was obliged to open it. He discovered that it was from Maria's sister, who was completely unaware of Patrick O'Connor's murder and the situation in which her sibling was now placed. As the correspondence referred solely to domestic matters, it was handed to Maria who 'perused it with great eagerness, and seemed to derive much pleasure from its contents' (*Lloyd's Weekly*, 9 September 1849). Mrs Manning, at least, was optimistic about the future.

The next day, outside Southwark police court, the anticipation of the crowds had increased, due to the forthcoming appearance of both supposed murderers together for the first time. The applications to attend the hearing were so numerous that by 10 am, every part of the room was completely full except for the bench, which was saved for the magistrate and those with special reservations. Isaac Secker arrived a few minutes later. After the magistrate had assessed further applications to attend the hearing, all of which he declined, the rest of those with seats on the bench arrived. The long and illustrious list of attendees included Austrian diplomats, colonels, Irish politicians, and several other dignitaries and ministers of the church. As before, the newspapers pointed out that there were many 'ladies' present. The lawyers, who had been at the previous two separate hearings, were again in attendance, with the addition of barrister and former MP, William Bodkin, who joined John Hayward for the prosecution.

Before entering the court, the Mannings were granted five minutes together but, according to Inspector Yates, neither party had anything to say to the other. Maria, who remained as composed as usual, said: 'I don't wish to say anything to him.' In response Frederick shook his head and made a similar remark. At midday, the spectators surged forward as the couple entered the courtroom and made their way to the dock, where they were placed with a small table between them. Their lawyers sat behind them, and the governor of Horsemonger Lane Gaol stood by.

Maria Manning was dressed in a similar manner as before, with the same thick black veil which she raised when required. Her husband was wearing a blue topcoat, buttoned to the throat, and a red and white neckerchief, which had been carelessly tied. Without a short collar, the observers could see his rather unusually-formed chin. After they were placed in the dock, Frederick sat on a chair to the right. He leaned back with his hat in his left hand, appearing calm and collected. Maria was placed on the left. She declined the use of a chair and 'appeared as impassive as on former occasions' (*The Times*, 7 September 1849). The police finally succeeded in managing the crowds both inside and outside the courtroom, and the hearing was ready to begin.

The first of the twenty-nine witnesses on the first day of the proceedings was PC Henry Barnes, who repeated his evidence from previous sessions about discovering Patrick O'Connor's body at 3 Minver Place. Frederick Manning's solicitor, Thomas Binns, asked the police officer if he had taken any notes of his evidence, to which Barnes replied that he had not. Mr Binns put the same question to Barnes' colleague, PC James Burton, who was the next to testify. The constable said that he had taken some notes but that he did not know where they were. After another question about his powers of memory, the rather rattled constable promised to try to find them.

After the police officers, the medical experts gave their statements. Surgeon Samuel Lockwood presented the findings of the post-mortem examination. He informed the court that he still had possession of the bullet, which he had extracted from the victim's skull, but he did not produce it as evidence. At this point, the court clerk interrupted to ask Mrs Manning if she would prefer to sit down. After initially declining the offer, she sat down briefly but stood up again when the next witness, Charles Slow, stepped up. The parish summoning officer showed the false teeth, which had been extracted from Patrick's body, to the court but offered no further evidence or comments. Following this, the other surgeon, George Odling, who had performed the post-mortem, was called but he did not appear, which caused a brief delay in the proceedings.

While waiting for Mr Odling, Pierce Walsh told the court about his acquaintance with the deceased and their frequent visits to Minver Place to see the Mannings, including the evening before Patrick disappeared. He also confirmed his identification of the body as that of his friend. By the time he had finished, Mr Odling had arrived. The surgeon described how, with the police officers, he had found the body under the floor. He summarised O'Connor's injuries and added that the blows to his head would have rendered him unconscious immediately.

The following witnesses were Patrick O'Connor's friends and colleagues, who testified to the last sightings of him on Thursday 9 August. Customs clerk William Keating added to his earlier statement that Frederick Manning had referred to Patrick as 'very ungentlemanly' when he allegedly did not turn up for their dinner engagement that evening, which led to Maria going to O'Connor's lodgings in Mile End to look for him. Manning's defence, Thomas Binns, inquired about the letters purported to have been sent between Mrs Manning and the deceased, but Maria's solicitor countered that he had no knowledge of any. Keating's colleague William Flynn relayed his visit to Minver Place to look for their missing acquaintance when Mrs Manning had paled at the mention of his name. Under cross-examination from Mr Binns, Flynn confirmed that Patrick had worn false teeth and said that he had seen him 'pull them out both at his lodgings and at the docks at different times.'

Next followed the testimonies of Patrick O'Connor's landladies, sisters Ann and Emily Armes. As stated at the inquest, Ann gave the details of his daily habits and his amicable relationship with the Mannings, as well as Maria's visits to the lodgings after their tenant's disappearance. Emily Armes added that Mrs Manning had borrowed money from O'Connor and that she had overheard conversations between the pair, during which he gave her advice about which railway companies to invest in. When Maria's lawyer asked her about the frequency of Maria's visits, she replied: 'He [O'Connor] requested me not to let her in, as she came oftener than he liked.' Mr Solomon also asked her if Patrick and Maria were 'on terms of the closest intimacy', to which she answered that she did not know, and that she only saw them together in the sitting room and never in his bedroom. However, Mrs Manning visited O'Connor for tea frequently without her husband.

After the Armes sisters left the bar, the Mannings' lodger William Massey stepped up. He gave the details of his stay at 3 Minver Place and told the court that the couple were anxious for him to move out because they wanted to leave town. The medical student shared the conversations that he had had with Frederick Manning about the impact of stupefying drugs and O'Connor's fear of contracting cholera. He stated that Manning had wanted to try to coerce Patrick into signing a promissory note for £500. Also, Frederick had not believed that the customs officer would have left everything to Maria in his will, which had led to a quarrel between the married couple in Massey's presence.

William explained that, after he had left Minver Place, he had stayed with the Bainbridges for eight days, during which time he had seen Frederick two or three times at his former digs, but that they had only discussed the settlement of his bill. However, when questioned by Mr Binns, he admitted that he had also written two or three letters to O'Connor, at the Mannings' request, to invite him to dinner. He said that there had been a dispute between him and his former landlord over money, which had still not been settled.

After the medical student's statement, the prosecutor William Bodkin proposed that the inquiry be adjourned to the following day, as he thought that all parties must be quite exhausted after such a long day. His request was granted, and the prisoners were remanded until 11 am the next day. They were transported back to Horsemonger Lane Gaol, with a throng of people following behind the van.

According to the press reports, neither of the prisoners had spoken to each other throughout the day, nor had they shown the slightest emotion. Maria Manning had conferred occasionally with her solicitor, but her husband had not said a word to anyone. The journalists from *The Illustrated London News* commented:

> He [Frederick] appears to have fallen away very much since Saturday last, and we thought we noticed an expression of despair in his countenance. His wife, however, continues to display the greatest confidence in her manner, and we observed her to smile more than once during the investigation.

On the morning of Friday 7 September, there were fewer people outside the court, but the inside was just as full. Again, the press commented on the presence of female spectators which, according to *Lloyd's Weekly*, lent an inappropriately festive air to such a serious occasion:

> amongst the assemblage were a great number of well-dressed women, many of whom were accompanied by their daughters, and, from their demeanour, a person unacquainted with the nature of the proceedings they had attended to witness, would have thought they had met for some purpose of festivity, so unbecoming was their behaviour.

At 11.10 am, once the magistrate and lawyers were in place, the prisoners entered. Frederick Manning came in first. Wearing the same clothes as the previous day, but with a pink neckerchief, he looked very pale, although he did not seem nervous. Maria was also dressed the same as before but had raised her veil so that her face was visible to the court. She cleared her throat several times before the session began.

First, builder's assistant Richard Welsh identified Frederick Manning as the man who had bought some lime from his employer on 23 July. He confirmed that Maria Manning was the woman who had paid him for the purchase three days later, when he had returned to 3 Minver Place for the money. However, under questioning, he seemed less sure about her identity: 'I will not swear that the female prisoner is the woman who gave me three halfpence. I am not positive about it. I did not see her at all.' When William Bodkin pressed him on this point, Welsh admitted that he did not know Maria Manning at all, and he could only confirm that the woman he had seen at 3 Minver Place was about the same size as the prisoner. This deposition was followed by that of William Cahill, the ironmonger's assistant from whom Maria Manning purchased the coal shovel, in which he repeated his previous evidence. PC William Sopp then produced the shovel as he had done at the inquest.

Next, William Danby, the ironmonger's porter who delivered the crowbar to Frederick Manning, presented new evidence, which had not come to light during the inquest. He told the magistrate how Manning had overtaken him on the way to Minver Place and insisted that they go to the stationer's shop to buy some brown paper to wrap it in. As soon as Danby was asked to identify the prisoner, he did so without the least hesitation. The surgeon Samuel Lockwood attested that the crowbar could have caused the injuries to the victim's head. He mentioned the one strand of human hair that he had found on the implement and said that it was too long to have belonged to Patrick O'Connor.

Furniture dealer Charles Bainbridge repeated his testimony from the inquest. Next, his wife said that the shovel had been with the Mannings' belongings when she and her husband had bought them, and she had since used it to rake cinders. Frederick had also given her some of his wife's clothes, including dresses and stockings, which had been washed in a hurry and had become mildewed due to them not having been dried properly. One of the garments was scorched. Finally, cabman William Kirk, porter William Day and William Dyne, cloakroom clerk, all gave identical statements to those submitted before the coroner. No questions were asked.

The tension increased as the detective officers testified next. Detective Inspector John Haynes, who had discovered Maria Manning's boxes at London Bridge station, reminded the magistrate of the details, with a specific focus on the bloodstains found on the prisoner's clothing. He described the smear of blood on the skirt of the dress, 'as if the fingers had been wiped on it'. As he held up the dress, Mrs Manning looked at it with a slight smile. The police officer also produced a piece of muslin and two dressing table covers, both of which were marked with blood. He described Frederick Manning's arrest on arrival in Southampton and the prisoner's subsequent declaration that his wife was the one who shot O'Connor. After an objection from Mr Solomon about the appropriateness of the evidence, which was eventually overruled, he continued. He said that Manning had been afraid of his violent wife: 'She would think no more of human life than a cat,' and that she and Patrick had arranged the lodgings at Minver Place. When the customs officer had reneged on his agreement to move in with the couple, Maria had threatened revenge. Inspector Haynes concluded his statement by adding that, when he had pointed out to Frederick that the deceased had suffered many other wounds in addition to his having been shot, the prisoner made no reply and afterwards seemed to be in low spirits.

When questioned about his use of protocol in the questioning of Frederick Manning, Haynes responded that he had received no communication from his superiors on how to interview him, nor had he taken any notes of the conversation at the time. He admitted that he had only written the evidence down the night before the hearing, and he had not conferred with his colleagues.

Detective Sergeant Edward Langley recounted Frederick's capture in Jersey on 27 August at Prospect House. He repeated the conversation he had had with the felon after he caught him unawares while he was in bed, during which Manning had declared his innocence and placed the blame for O'Connor's murder firmly on his wife. Langley relayed the discussion he had had with Manning during the sea crossing from Jersey to England, in which he had insisted that Maria would confess, especially if a clergyman were present. Finally, the detective attested that he had brought Frederick's luggage into the Scotland Yard office, where he had examined the contents in the presence of O'Connor's landlady. The detective had found some gunpowder, wrapped in tissue paper, in a coat pocket. Once again, Thomas Binns asked about the procedure, to which Langley replied that during the train journey from Southampton to London, he had sat opposite the prisoner, who was handcuffed to PC Lockyer. Langley spoke to Mr Hayward, Maria's defence solicitor, about the case, but he did not confer with Inspector Haynes. Like his colleague, he did not make any notes. PC Lockyer corroborated his colleagues' evidence, adding that he had heard Frederick Manning say that Maria would escape the gallows as her former employer the Duchess of Sutherland would intercede for her.

The following five witnesses gave evidence about the railway shares acquired and sold by the Mannings. Clerk John Bassett identified Frederick Manning as the man who had sold him some railway stock after presenting himself as Patrick O'Connor. Bassett explained that he had picked out Manning in Horsemonger Lane Gaol from among twenty-six or twenty-seven other inmates: 'I had no hesitation in identifying him and am quite certain that the prisoner at the bar is the very same man.' The clerk showed the railway stock to the magistrate. The certificates were made out in O'Connor's name and had been signed by Manning in Bassett's presence. As at the inquest, his evidence was confirmed by his colleague, Richard Hammond.

Two other clerks gave additional evidence. First, Archibald Griffith, who worked at the Bank of England, produced the banknotes which had been exchanged by Manning on 11 August. He had written his signature on the back of the notes. However, he could not recall who had brought in the money and could not say whether it was a man or a woman. His testimony was confirmed by Joseph Reece Adams, who was also an employee of the bank.

The identical notes, which had been found in Maria Manning's belongings on her arrest in Edinburgh, were now shown to the magistrate. Solicitor Henry Webb Shillibeer, who was acquainted with Frederick Manning, confirmed that the writing on the back of the £100 note was that of the prisoner. Finally, stockbroker Francis Stevens stated that he had delivered the shares to Patrick O'Connor on 6 August. He identified them as those found by Superintendent Moxey in Maria's possession and described how she had visited him in early August to inquire about purchasing overseas railways shares.

The last witness was William Byford, who also testified for the first time. He told the magistrate how he had driven Frederick Manning in his cab from Bermondsey Square to Waterloo station on 15 August. Byford said that he had visited the prison that morning to identify him: 'I think he was the person I took.' Under questioning, he conceded that the prisoner closely resembled his passenger and that he remembered him because he had instructed him to take an indirect route to the terminus, which he had thought was 'very curious'.

After the cab driver had finished, William Bodkin proposed that the prisoners be remanded until the following week to give time for new evidence to be collected. Magistrate Secker agreed and adjourned the hearing until Saturday 15 September.

Frederick Manning had remained seated throughout the proceedings. He looked generally unconcerned, with occasional glances at the witnesses. Maria stood with her chin resting on her hand and her elbow on the bar. At some points, she appeared to twitch nervously, especially when the evidence concerned her directly. As observed in *Lloyd's Weekly*:

> During the whole of the examination to-day Manning and his wife maintained the coolest indifference to each other, not so much as exchanging a single look. They appeared like man and wife upon the worst possible terms.

Chapter 16

The Shadow of Death

As Maria and Frederick Manning prepared to face the magistrate again, the cholera outbreak continued to rampage unchecked through London. Of the 2,796 deaths registered in the capital during the week leading up to their next court session, almost 60 per cent of them were attributed to the disease, which was still causing 300 to 400 deaths each day. This seemingly unstoppable infection also had an impact on the hearings at Southwark police court. John Bassett, the stockbroker's clerk who had identified Frederick Manning as having bought railway shares under the pretence of being Patrick O'Connor, was taken ill during the night following the session on Friday 7 September. He died of cholera the following morning. John was one of the 432 people who succumbed to the disease in the metropolis that week and one of the 24 who died of it in Bermondsey. The next day, another witness, Bassett's colleague Richard Hammond, became infected. The epidemic's progress and its deathly toll would dominate the remaining hearings.

With a week's break between sessions, the police had more time to prepare the evidence against the couple, and members of the general public offered their assistance. Inspector Yates received a letter from a person in Bolton, Lancashire, who had engaged the services of a clairvoyant. The anonymous writer asserted that the missing revolver used in the murder was buried beneath the hole in which Patrick O'Connor's body had been found in the cellar of 3 Minver Place. The clairvoyant, who described the cellars accurately, could not see the exact location of the firearm, but the correspondent said that if she turned out to be correct, they would provide further information. PC Burton returned to the property to look for the pistol. The officer conducted the search in the company of the landlord's son. They did not find the weapon, but they noticed some spots of blood opposite the back kitchen door, which had been overlooked in previous searches. As the marks were thick and quite obvious, it was surprising that they had not been discovered before.

However, they seemed to confirm Frederick's statement that his wife had encouraged O'Connor to go down the stairs to wash his hands and, while he was doing so, she shot him; the marks might have been made when Patrick slumped against the wall, where he was bludgeoned to death. With regards to the firearm, the police concluded that the clairvoyant had been deluded.

The police interviewed the neighbours again and found out more about the Mannings' movements between Patrick's murder and when they fled. Maria had asserted that her husband had sent her away on Monday 13 August. However, PC Burton, who was following up the information she had given him, found that she had left Minver Place while her husband was absent. The Bainbridges' servant, Matilda Weldon, told the police that Frederick had come to her employer's house in Bermondsey Square at 8 am on that morning. He had stayed there until 10.30 am, after which he disappeared for five hours. On his return, he had inquired about the availability of rooms to let, and he had sent Matilda to Minver Place to fetch Maria. As the servant could not locate the address, Manning said that he would go and find his wife himself. He went out but came back 20 minutes later with a bottle of brandy. He seemed excited and, when the Bainbridges asked about Mrs Manning, he said that she had left him and gone to the countryside.

At 5.30 pm that same afternoon, Mary Ann Schofield, who lived opposite 3 Minver Place, told the police about Frederick arriving at the house. When he found that his wife was not there, he approached Mrs Schofield, who informed him that she had left two hours earlier. He then went through the house next door to his and accessed no. 3 through the garden. He was then seen smoking his pipe on the wall by Sophia Payne. Mrs Payne informed the police that Frederick had talked to her about railway shares that he was intending to dispose of. As they were chatting, they heard a loud knock at the door and Manning jumped off the wall exclaiming: 'Oh, I forgot that I have an appointment with a gentleman this evening.' Sophia did not see him again that day, but she heard a great deal of scuffling in the kitchen that night. Just after midnight, a noise coming from the house woke her up. When she looked out of the window, she saw a light in the back kitchen of the Mannings' house and the shadows of a man and a woman stooping over something. The police passed this new evidence to the prosecution.

During the interval between the court hearings, the police also interviewed Mr Wells, the bricklayer who had sold the lime to Frederick Manning. On further questioning, he said that he could not swear that the man who had bought the lime was the prisoner. However, PC Burton ascertained that

Mr Wells' daughter was in the office that day, and she took particular notice of the customer because of his rude and abrasive manner. She told officers that she was confident that she could identify him. Accordingly, Inspector Yates arranged for the girl to attend the prison, where she instantly picked out Frederick from a group of twenty inmates in the exercise yard.

Finally, since the last hearing, the police had been desperately looking for another young girl, who had been engaged to clean 3 Minver Place by Maria Manning. After considerable difficulty and many fruitless efforts, PC James Burton managed to locate her. This new witness was Hannah Firman (also recorded as 'Furman' and 'Fermor'), who lived with her family in Bermondsey.

At 9 am on Saturday 11 August, Mrs Manning had asked Hannah to clean the house. When Hannah was scrubbing the upstairs rooms, she had seen spots of blood on the passage wall leading to the kitchen. She tried to wash them off. After she had finished the upper part of the house, she had gone to the back kitchen and was about to start cleaning, when Maria pulled her away and shouted: 'I cleaned this place yesterday, and it don't [*sic*] want scrubbing anymore.' The girl told the police that she saw a square basket in the room, which was covered with lime, which Maria told her to wash. While she was doing so, she ran out of water so she left the basket, which was later found by PC Burton.

Hannah said that, while she was in the house, Mrs Manning went out two or three times and, at midday, her husband came downstairs and stamped his feet 'as if in a passion'. He called to Maria: 'Give it me directly,' to which she answered, 'Yes, I will directly.' Hannah was unsure what he was referring to. She went upstairs and did not hear the rest of the conversation. Manning remained in the house while his wife fried some beefsteaks in the kitchen for their dinner. The girl said that the back kitchen was very wet and that the stones on the floor of the passage seemed to have been rubbed recently with a brick or a stone. She also said that the dust-hole was full of mould and dirt, mixed with water.

All three new witnesses were taken to the Home Office to give their statements to the crown prosecutor. PCs Burton and Barnes were so successful in their investigation into Patrick O'Connor's death that the local inhabitants of Bermondsey considered drawing up a special testimonial to award them for their active part in bringing the perpetrators of this shocking crime to justice.

The inquiry into the Mannings resumed on Saturday 15 September at Southwark police court. Although the examination was originally set for

3 pm, it was moved to 1 pm, to accommodate a hearing rescheduled for later that afternoon on behalf of the members of the local Board of Health, who had taken out a summons against the churchwardens of the Crossbones burial ground, who had not complied with an order to close the post-medieval resting place (it is still in existence today). The chief clerk sent for the prisoners once the day's schedule had finally been settled.

As usual, the court and the surrounding streets were very crowded, but there was ample space for the press inside. The Mannings entered just before 2 pm. Frederick's face looked deathly white as he gazed nervously at those gathered in the courtroom. There was a marked change in his attire since the previous week, and he was much more neatly dressed, with a new black suit and a black silk neckerchief above his clean collar and shirt front. Maria looked much the same as on her last appearance; she seemed quite unconcerned and was in good health. After it was stated that Frederick was unwell, he was given permission to sit during the proceedings, whereas Maria only sat down while the depositions were being read over and signed.

William Bodkin, the crown's prosecutor, had already taken his place at the bar, where he was joined by Thomas Binns for Frederick's defence. Maria's solicitor was absent. While they were waiting, Mr Bodkin proposed reading the depositions which had already been taken. The governor of Horsemonger Lane Gaol, who was once again standing with the prisoners, passed on a complaint from Mrs Manning about her representative not being present. It transpired that Mr Solomon had not been informed of the change of time. A message was sent to him, and he arrived soon after.

The chief clerk read over the witness statements already given and made a few alterations in response to the lawyers in attendance. When Samuel Lockwood was about to sign his deposition, both defence attorneys suggested that the matter as to whether the substance on the shovel was blood or not should be cleared up. In response, Mr Lockwood stated: 'I said I could not make it out; it seemed like rust and might have arisen from blood.' (A test for human blood would not be available for another fifty years). He added that the hair, which he had found on the shovel, was a woman's: 'at least, I should think so; at all events, it was not the hair of O'Connor.' Neither statements were contested further.

The clerk then called Mary Ann Bainbridge, to which her husband replied that she was too ill to attend. When questioned as to the nature of her illness, he answered: 'She has been confined since she was here a week ago.' Laughter erupted in court at his response. It was also mentioned that James

Coleman, the Mannings' landlord, was also absent due to sickness. When Richard Hammond was called, it transpired that he too was not in court. Inspector Yates told the magistrate that the clerk had contracted cholera at the bedside of his dying colleague, John Bassett. Fortunately, he was recovering but he was still too ill to attend the hearing. Bank of England clerk Archibald Griffith had also succumbed to cholera during the week and was therefore absent too.

The reading and signing of the depositions took two hours and, just as the formal hearing was about to begin, against all expectations, Richard Hammond arrived in court. He had recovered quickly from the disease but was still very weak. He was able to sign his statement.

The proceedings opened with the summoning officer, Charles Slow, who produced the false teeth which were found on the body buried under the floor at Minver Place. Dentist William Comley identified them as having been made for Patrick O'Connor in June 1847: 'The set I now hold in my hand are the same. I can swear to them.' There followed the new witnesses, who had been located by PC James Burton since the last session.

The bricklayer's daughter, Mary Wells, recounted Frederick's visit to her father's business to buy some lime. She said that he had bought 6 pence worth of lime for the purpose of killing slugs in the garden. She could not remember the date of the purchase, but she knew it was on a Monday in July. Mary told the court that she had offered Frederick white or grey lime, and he had asked for that which burned the quickest. As they did not have any white lime, he ordered the grey and it was delivered to his address two days later. Under cross-examination by Thomas Binns, Miss Wells said that she had heard about the murder from her father's assistant, Richard Welsh, who had delivered the lime to Minver Place. When Miss Wells was asked to identify Frederick Manning in court, she looked around the room for some time, without appearing to recognise him. After the clerk asked the prisoner to stand, she declared that he was the man who had bought the lime.

Next to take the stand was Hannah Firman, the young girl who had been engaged to clean Minver Place. She told the magistrate that she was 12 years old and that she sold lucifer matches and stay laces on the streets in Bermondsey. While she was in the neighbourhood on 11 August, she had seen a woman cleaning the windows of the property. When she pointed at Maria Manning saying, 'That is her', the defendant cleared her throat. Hannah offered to take on the cleaning work for the prisoner for 5 pence. She described how she had suggested cleaning the kitchen but that

Mrs Manning had told her she had already done it. Hannah also said that she had been unable to wash the basket of lime because she had cut her hand, as well as there being insufficient water. The girl was asked if she could identify Frederick Manning in court. At first, she picked out a man from the crowd, who bore a striking resemblance to the prisoner, but when Manning stood up, she said, 'No, that is the man,' and pointed to him.

The Bainbridges' servant, Matilda Weldon, gave her testimony regarding Frederick Manning's arrival at Bermondsey Square, after which he had sent for his wife. Under questioning, she admitted that she did not know whether Manning had said that Maria had left for the countryside or not.

The following two witnesses described seeing Frederick at Minver Place on Monday 13 August. Mary Ann Schofield attested that Maria had left the house at 4 pm and her husband had arrived an hour and a half later. She relayed her conversation with Frederick after her departure, during which he had asked whether his wife had taken any luggage with her. Then Sophia Payne told the court that she had seen Frederick that same evening and she had allowed him to pass through her house so that he could gain access to no. 3 through the garden. She also gave the details of her meeting with him on Thursday 9 August when he talked about buying railway shares. Mrs Payne said that she thought that he was a commercial traveller, but she did not know how he earned his money. There were no further questions for either of the witnesses.

The court's attention turned to the final sightings of Patrick O'Connor before his death. Customs gauger John Younghusband repeated his evidence from the inquest about seeing the deceased on London Bridge on the evening of Thursday 9 August. He said: 'He was walking slowly and looking round him. He looked undecided as to which way to go.' Another customs employee, James Jarvis Coleman (not to be confused with the Mannings' landlord) deposed that he had known O'Connor for eight or ten years. On 9 August, he had seen him in Weston Street at about 5.10 pm, walking in the direction of Minver Place. Coleman, who was on the opposite side of the street, did not stop to speak to him.

At the end of the day's testimonies, William Bodkin asked for a further adjournment until Wednesday 19 September because of the prevailing epidemic. This would allow sufficient time for all the depositions to be read and signed just in case any more witnesses were lost to the disease. He also needed time to summon the witnesses who lived in Scotland. The magistrate agreed and the prisoners were remanded yet again.

Four days later, the prisoners were due to appear to Southwark police court, but by then the mood had become more sombre as cholera continued to sweep through the district. As reported in *Lloyd's Weekly*: 'The day had been set apart for humiliation and prayer, on account of the ravages of cholera, all the shops in the neighbourhood were closed, and the streets were comparatively deserted.'

However, at 3 pm, the masses were still present outside the police court, and they were just as anxious to see the accused couple as they had been at the previous sittings. The newspapers commented that there was no decrease in the number of women in attendance. There was little change either in the defendants' appearance and behaviour as they were placed in the dock, although it was noted that perhaps they were starting to become more aware of their precarious position. Throughout the process, Frederick Manning had showed signs of alarm, but today they were even more obvious; his face looked bloodless, as he strove hard to conceal his anguish. He hurried quickly to his seat, as if to avoid any attention. Maria was wearing her veil down over her face, under which observers noticed the sickly hue of her face. The press concluded that she had started to lose some of her habitual confidence.

As the prisoners stood in the dock, it became apparent that the crown prosecutor, William Bodkin, had not yet arrived. The magistrate was reluctant to start without him, so the court was forced to wait. He finally arrived an hour later. Despite their initial apprehension and the exasperating delay, both the Mannings recovered their composure as the proceedings began. Seemingly recovered from his illness, Frederick stood at the bar with his wife. They did not look at each other as they consulted their respective solicitors. Maria also spoke frequently to the female warden and the prison governor, who accompanied them.

Before the next series of testimonies, builder and landlord, James Coleman, and bank clerk, Archibald Griffith signed their depositions, as both had been ill with cholera at the previous session. Superintendent Richard Moxey, of the Edinburgh City police, repeated his evidence from Maria Manning's examination on 31 August. As soon as Mrs Manning had seen that the superintendent was in court, she had requested permission to speak with him, but this was denied. The senior police officer told the court how she had at first denied having possession of the railway shares. At this, Maria shook her head as if refuting his statement. Her husband watched intently as Moxey described how she had accused him of cruelty. Following his testimony, Maria's solicitor challenged the admissibility of his evidence in the hearing, which was for both prisoners, as it had been originally heard in relation to his client only. The magistrate responded that any evidence was permitted, but that any prior accusations made by Mrs Manning against her husband would not be considered.

Following this, stockbroker's clerk Richard Hammond was re-examined. After confirming that his colleague John Bassett had 'ceased to exist', he explained how he had gone to the Bank of England to intercept a £100 banknote which had been given to Bassett by the man pretending to be Patrick O'Connor. He identified Frederick Manning as that person. Next, the court clerk summoned Francis Worrell Stevens, the stockbroker who had given evidence at the inquest. Despite having promised to attend, he had travelled to Kent with his son instead and was not in court. The day's proceedings finished, and the final hearing before the magistrate was set for Thursday 27 September.

Chapter 17

'I have nothing to say'

As the initial examination of the Mannings before the magistrate drew to a close, the police continued their tireless efforts to search for more evidence. On Saturday 22 September, Inspector Yates and PC Burton discovered that Patrick O'Connor had been seen in Maria Manning's company on the evening of his murder. At 5.40 pm, a woman who ran a tobacco and newspaper shop had noticed them walking arm in arm past her business in the direction of London Bridge. Behind them followed Frederick Manning and another man. The police officers found further witnesses who had seen the group during that evening, and it transpired that the three men had entered a public house while Mrs Manning continued to O'Connor's lodgings in Mile End Road. While she was absent, apparently Frederick and his companion took Patrick back to Minver Place, where they were later joined by Maria. At this time, there was no further evidence of the identification of the third man, but it was clear that the press was expecting another arrest in this complex case.

While the matter of a possible new suspect was being referred to the Home Office, the police made another discovery. This time, there was no doubt as to its importance. The same officers found two pistols at a pawnbroker's shop in Bermondsey, which had been pledged along with a bullet mould. PC Burton examined the firearms and the surgeon, Samuel Lockwood, made some bullet casts with the mould. These were the exact same size and weight as the one found in Patrick O'Connor's skull. As reported in the press: 'There is no doubt one of these pistols was used to shoot O'Connor' (*Lloyd's Weekly*, 23 September 1849).

No other evidence came to light during the week leading up to the next session of the hearing, but the Bermondsey murder was never entirely out of the news. One report outlined a case linked to that of the Mannings in Clerkenwell. A man named Kent was brought before the district's magistrate for threatening to assault a young woman called Elizabeth Langley. A few days earlier, Miss Langley had been visiting two female friends one evening, when the conversation had turned to the ongoing examination of Maria and Frederick Manning. When Elizabeth expressed her abhorrence of the event, Mr Kent became agitated. He retorted that he was acquainted with Frederick and that he believed him to be innocent. Miss Langley repeated her opposing view, at which Kent seized her and began hitting her. He threatened to strike her again if she did not retract her opinion. When questioned by the magistrate, the defendant claimed that he had not struck her, but he had pushed her aside as a rebuke. He was bound over to keep the peace for six months.

On Thursday 27 September, when the prisoners were due back at the magistrate's court, the public interest in the case was as intense as ever. By 11 am, the usual throng of hopeful observers was assembled in front of Southwark police court, all anxious to try to gain admission. One young man even tried to get in through the window and was promptly ejected. By the time the regular court business had been dispensed with, all seats in the gallery were full. As they waited for the prisoners to arrive, the magistrate warned that any disturbance from the public gallery would result in his clearing the court completely.

At 2 pm, the Mannings entered to take their places in the dock. Frederick walked in rather nonchalantly, but his wan face belied his fear. He still looked unwell, with a sallow complexion, but less so than at the previous appearance. He sat down on the right side of the dock and his glazed eyes stared out dreamily into the court, as if he were in a trance. The newspapers were again quick to point out the difference in the demeanours of the two defendants. In contrast to her husband, Maria was described as looking 'shrewd'. Wearing a black satin dress with a brightly patterned plaid shawl and a white veil, she appeared cool, calm and collected. She too looked less pale this time, and the reporters went so far as to say that she seemed to be in 'rude' health. As before, Maria chatted with the prison governor and the female warder, even laughing at times. She did not look at her husband, who engaged in an earnest conversation with his solicitor while they were waiting for the proceedings to begin.

Firstly, Francis Stevens, the stockbroker who had been missing from the previous session, signed the deposition he had given at the inquest. Following this, medical certificates were issued for Mary Ann Bainbridge, who was still confined (her child, named Charles after his father, had been born on 15 September – he died on 18 October), and share dealer George Nash Linthorne, who was too ill to leave his bed. The crown's prosecutor,

William Bodkin, said that, in the absence of these witnesses, that it was not worth taking up any more of the magistrate's time. As the lawyer was keen to press ahead to the committal of the defendants to trial and, as there did not appear to be any new evidence to present, he proposed a further remand of a week. The magistrate agreed and the defendants were formally remanded again. The proceedings had barely lasted a quarter of an hour.

With the final hearing before the inevitable trial looming, both parties' defence solicitors stepped up their efforts to gather as much support as they could for their clients. Later that week, on Maria's instructions, Joseph Solomon attended Southwark police court to apply to the magistrate for an important letter which was being held by the police, after being taken from her in Edinburgh by Superintendent Moxey. Mrs Manning believed that the letter, which she had received from Patrick O'Connor while she was in service with Lady Blantyre, was vital to her defence. Mr Solomon told the magistrate that the document would explain the reasons why his client had had certain items in her possession when she was arrested. Magistrate Isaac Secker denied the solicitor's request, as he felt that the police might also need the letter for the prosecution but, following a suggestion by the court clerk, he allowed a copy to be made for Mr Solomon, for which he could apply to Inspector Yates.

Following the granting of permission for a copy of the letter, Inspector Yates visited Maria in prison to ascertain which missive she was referring to. She told him that she had received the letter from Patrick shortly after she had made his acquaintance and that it contained a request from him for her to buy some railway and overseas stock. The inspector informed her that he had made a minute examination of all her confiscated possessions and that he was unable to find such a letter. She asked him to search the boxes again in case it had fallen to the bottom.

Later that same day, the magistrate received a letter from a Mary Dible, claiming that Maria Manning had spent three days at her house in Southampton after she had left Minver Place on 13 August. Given that she had written the communication on the basis of a description of the female prisoner in the press and that Maria had been in Edinburgh during that time, Mr Secker dismissed it as evidence.

Frederick's solicitor, Thomas Binns, applied on behalf of both defendants to the Metropolitan police commissioners for the remainder of the cash which had been confiscated from Maria on her arrest in Edinburgh. Binns claimed that he would be unable to defend Frederick Manning without the money, and he assured them that he would give half to his colleague Joseph Solomon for Mrs Manning's defence. The request was later denied, and Mr Secker told the solicitor to apply to the government for his expenses.

While Frederick's representative was busy securing the funding of his defence, the prisoner remained in Horsemonger Lane Gaol, where he had been engaged in writing poetry. He even presented one poem, entitled 'The Prison Bell', to his solicitor. When a letter penned by Frederick was reproduced in *Lloyd's Weekly*, the journalist quipped that 'although he professes himself to be a poet, his orthography is far from being correct.'

Manning made no further attempts to speak to his wife, and nor did he mention the murder. Despite this, he maintained lively conversations with other inmates, although he grumbled at having to spend time with them in such close quarters, as it hampered his poetic endeavours. Frederick was now eating more heartily and seemed to be in better health, as well as spirits.

Manning's more positive attitude did not last long and the evening before the next hearing, a rumour was circulated in the press that he had tried to take his own life. He had allegedly attempted to hang himself with a handkerchief, which he attached to one of the bars in his cell. There was no foundation to this rumour, but the prisoner had become more despondent during the week, and the prison authorities had placed a warder on watch in case he made any such desperate attempt. As he faced another appearance in court, Frederick continued to place all the blame for Patrick's murder onto his wife, telling his solicitor that she ought to confess and thus liberate him.

At 2 pm on Friday 5 October, the Mannings came to Southwark police court for the final time. Even though they had made several appearances over the previous weeks, the courtroom was just as busy as on earlier occasions. Outside, however, there was less interest, with just a few persistent stragglers and a few extra police officers on duty in the street in front. The newspapers opined that the loss of interest might have been due to the futility of trying to catch a glimpse of the couple as they came back and forth.

The solicitors took their seats and the prisoners entered just before the appointed hour. Both were wearing the same clothes as at the last hearing. The reporters noted that Frederick seemed to be getting stouter during his incarceration and, even though he seemed to affect an air of nonchalance, he looked anxious and depressed. As expected, they also observed that Maria looked much healthier and unconcerned than her husband. When they were ordered to stand, she raised the white veil covering her face, arranging it carefully over the edge of her white straw bonnet, which she then tied under her chin.

Before the examination began, Thomas Binns informed the press that there was not the slightest foundation to the rumour that Frederick Manning had 'contemplated self-destruction'. He said that his client was 'never in better spirits'. While the journalists present accepted the falsity of the rumour, they strongly refuted the solicitor's claims that Frederick was in good spirits, which had been contradicted by their sources.

The hearing opened with a new witness. John Green, a clerk at the Eastern Counties Railway Company, produced a statement of transfer for twenty shares from Elizabeth Parkinson, of Stancliffe Hall, near Matlock in Derbyshire, to Patrick O'Connor, for the sum of £147 10 shillings, dated 16 May 1849. On receiving the shares, O'Connor had been given a certificate, for which he had signed the company's ledger. Green showed the book to the magistrate.

Next, another stockbroker, Alexander Lamond, told the court that he had bought twenty shares for O'Connor in the Eastern Counties Railway Company. He confirmed that the signature in the ledger book produced by the previous witness was that of the deceased. Lamond had also purchased ten shares in the Sambre and Meuse Railway on Patrick's behalf on 27 April. He identified them as the ones found in Maria Manning's possession. His testimony was confirmed by Donald Wenham, a broker's clerk, from whom Lamond had bought the shares. Wenham said that he had delivered the stock three days after the purchase.

Finally, two witnesses were re-examined. Mary Ann Bainbridge, the furniture dealer's wife, responded to further questions by prosecutor William Bodkin. She told him that she had not seen all the items brought from Minver Place after the sale, but she did see the dresses. Mary Ann recalled that she remembered Frederick going to help her husband remove the furniture on a Wednesday morning, after which he had sent the maid back to the property to fetch his wife. As she repeated her earlier evidence that, when she had asked Manning if he would return to the house to sleep, to which he replied that he would not do so even for £20, Frederick bit his lip, and a strong flush came over his face. The Bainbridges' servant Matilda Weldon then told the prosecutor that, before the furniture was removed from Minver Place, Frederick Manning had instructed her not to tell anyone of his plans and that if anyone asked after him, she should inform them that she had not seen him for a fortnight.

William Bodkin concluded that, given that there was sufficient evidence against the defendants, he would propose that they be committed for trial. He reminded the magistrate that the law required that the depositions be read out once again in the presence of the prisoners before they had the opportunity to respond to the charge against them. Thomas Binns said that his client did not wish to hear the statements again as he had understood them the first time. However, the magistrate insisted on sticking to the legal requirements and he instructed the court clerk to read them through one more time. This took a further two hours, during which time both prisoners remained seated.

As the testimonies were read out, the journalists watched the defendants' expressions carefully. They observed that they both paid attention, with Frederick looking particularly serious. Maria was reported to have smiled sarcastically when her husband's allegations against her were referred to, and she remained completely impassive during the recounting of the details of Patrick's murder. After the reading was finished, the magistrate asked each defendant in turn if they wished to say anything. Frederick replied, 'I have nothing to say, sir.' Maria answered, 'I leave all in the hands of my attorney, sir.' The hearing ended at 4.45 pm, after which they were transported back to Horsemonger Lane Gaol, where they were to wait for their removal to Newgate Prison.

After their final appearance, the pencil sketches of the prisoners made by artists in court were published in the press. They show Maria looking quite serene with her dark eyes fixed ahead and her gloved hands gently resting on a handkerchief. She is wearing a black shawl and a white bonnet trimmed with ribbons. Her veil is pinned up revealing her pretty face. Frederick is also staring, his round face framed by his fair hair that almost reaches his collar. He has a black neckerchief tied at his throat under his jowly chin and above his thick, dark overcoat. His hands look tense, with one fist clenched.

Ten days after the end of their hearing, on Monday 15 October, the Mannings were moved unexpectedly to Newgate Prison, prior to their trial which was due to begin a week later. After breakfast, the governor of Horsemonger Lane Gaol, John Keene, informed them that the authorities had decided to move all the prisoners for the next Old Bailey sessions on the same day. At 10 am, Frederick Manning left the prison in the county van with fourteen others. Maria left shortly afterwards in a cab, accompanied by the governor and his assistant. As news of Mrs Manning's removal to Newgate had got round, a few people had congregated near the entrance to the gaol to watch her leave. And, by the time she had arrived at Newgate, there was a large number of spectators assembled in the precincts to await her. Maria Manning arrived just before 11 am and hurried into the prison with her veil covering her face.

Both prisoners thanked John Keene for the kindness shown to them while they had been under his care in Horsemonger Lane Gaol.

Newgate was one of London's most notorious prisons. The original building, which dated from the twelfth century, was constructed on the site of a gate in the capital's Roman wall. After it was destroyed in the Great Fire of London, the prison was rebuilt by Sir Christopher Wren in the 1600s. During the following century, it was enlarged and became the place for public hangings, after they were moved from Tyburn, at the northeast corner of Hyde Park, to the prison. The courtrooms attached to the infamous prison formed the Old Bailey, the present building of which, now known as the Central Criminal Court, occupies the former gaol site, after its closure in 1902 and subsequent demolition.

During the decade before the Mannings were incarcerated there, Charles Dickens wrote about Newgate in his series of articles, *Sketches by Boz*. The writer shared his memories of seeing the prison during his childhood:

> We shall never forget the mingled feelings of awe and respect with which we used to gaze on the exterior of Newgate in our schoolboy days. How dreadful its rough heavy walls, and low massive doors, appeared to us – the latter looking as if they were made for the express purpose of letting people in, and never letting them out again.

After visiting Newgate, Dickens described the condition of 'the unhappy beings immured in its dismal cells'. The prison buildings formed a square, with one side abutting the Old Bailey. The space in between was divided into several paved yards for the inmates' exercise. The women's quarters were on the right-hand side of the prison. The whitewashed wards were spacious, airy and well-lit by windows which overlooked the central yards. The inmates slept on mats, which were rolled up during the day. In each ward, prisoners were appointed as wardswomen or wardsmen to maintain order, for which they gained the privilege of sleeping on a bedstead.

Following a tour of the cells and schoolrooms, Dickens had proceeded to the prison chapel, where he was struck by the condemned pew, in which those facing the gallows were placed on the Sunday preceding their execution to hear the prayers for their souls and so that others could take heed of their fate. He entered the condemned ward located in one corner of the prison building. The ward formed a long, narrow court with a cistern at one end and a double grating at the other, through which the prisoners were able to speak to their friends and relatives. Dickens encountered twenty to thirty condemned prisoners while he was there. He observed that the majority of them did not appear to be unduly anxious or depressed, which he attributed to the final decision about their fate having not yet been confirmed.

Further along the yard were the condemned cells, which were entered via a narrow, dark staircase. Once the warrant for a prisoner's execution was granted, they were removed from the communal dayroom into the cells, where they were confined until they left for the scaffold. Described by Dickens as 'a stone dungeon', they were 8 feet long by 6 feet wide, and had a bench, rug, a Bible and a prayer book. There was no other furniture. An iron candlestick was fixed onto the wall and there was a small, high window to let in a little light and air. As the writer stood in the cell, he imagined how it must have felt to be awaiting death: 'Conceive the situation of a man, spending his last night on earth in this cell … an overwhelming sense of his helpless, hopeless state rushes upon him, he is lost and stupefied.'

On arrival at the prison, Frederick Manning was allocated to no. 19 ward, which housed men remanded for, or convicted of, murder. A report in *Lloyd's Weekly* described his accommodation:

> It is a spacious stone built room, looking through a strongly barred window into a small yard; which, although within several other walls, has high walls looped with strong iron *chevaux-de-frieze*. The furniture consists of a large strong table, with just sufficient chairs to accommodate the prisoner and his keepers.

The inmates slept in compartments, one above the other, like berths on a ship. When Frederick entered the ward, he did not seem downcast and engaged the warders in conversation. When asked about his case, he responded that he was certain that he would be acquitted. Maria Manning was similarly optimistic and, at first, she too seemed to settle easily into her new surroundings. However, as the week drew on, there was a notable change in the spirits of both prisoners, as their thoughts turned to the trial that lay ahead.

At the end of the week, summonses were sent to the witnesses, requesting that they arrive in court on Tuesday 23 October at 10 am. It was confirmed that the crown prosecution would be led by the attorney general, Sir John Jervis. It was not yet known who would be defending Frederick Manning, but his wife was to be represented by William Ballantine and John Humffreys

Parry. There was some concern over the funding of Maria Manning's defence, as a significant sum had already been spent on her behalf, but it was assumed that the authorities would grant further access to the money which had been confiscated from her on her arrest.

The Old Bailey sessions were due to open on Monday 22 October with the expectation that the Mannings' trial would begin on the Thursday and last until the Saturday. As the general public waited with bated breath for the culmination of this sensational crime case, *Lloyd's Weekly* expressed the collective sentiments shared throughout the country:

> Never, perhaps, has a crime of a similar nature to that of the late murder of Mr Patrick O'Connor, in Miniver-place, Bermondsey, created so much sensation in the public mind. A husband and wife have been placed at the bar of justice, charged jointly with the crime of murder under circumstances of aggravation calculated to arrest attention in no ordinary degree.

Chapter 18

'This barbarous transaction'

London's Central Criminal Court, known as the Old Bailey, dates from the seventeenth century and, although the courthouse was rebuilt many times since its opening in 1674, the basic design had not changed by the time of the Mannings' trial. The courts were arranged so as to accentuate the contest between the defendant and the rest of the court, with the accused being placed at the bar, facing the witness box. The judges were seated on the other side of the room, below whom were the lawyers, clerks and scribes at a table. The jurors sat in stalls to the right of the defendant. A second courtroom had been added to the building in 1824, which had ample seating for attorneys, law students, court officers and spectators. Deemed inadequate, these buildings were demolished, and King Edward VII opened the current courthouse in 1907. Charles Dickens described the proceedings at the Old Bailey, in the mid-nineteenth century, in his *Sketches by Boz*: 'There is a great deal of form, but no compassion; considerable interest, but no sympathy.'

On Monday 22 October, the recorder read the calendar for the forthcoming sessions to the grand jury, including the charge against the Mannings, in order for them to decide which cases had sufficient grounds for a trial. The schedule comprised 208 prisoners. However, according to the recorder, this number was likely to increase, with further committals during the sessions. The list included five charges of murder, all of which would probably be tried. In addition, there were fifty cases of common larceny. After a summary of the lesser charges, the recorder proceeded to give the details of the more serious offences. In one of the homicides, a man was accused of having killed his wife and child, and in another, a father was alleged to have murdered his child by drowning. Another involved a victim who had been kicked to death. There was also a case of manslaughter, in which an unqualified medical student had given a homeopathic treatment to his brother, who was suffering from cholera, which had denied him sufficient food and resulted in his death.

In relation to the Mannings, the recorder reminded the grand jury that in the case of a joint charge of husband and wife, if the husband was present at an alleged crime, other than murder or manslaughter, the wife could be acquitted on the presumption that she was coerced by her spouse. However, in this instance, as it was such a heinous crime, this legal consideration did not apply. If, however, the wife was present at the time of the offence and her husband was not, she could be considered to be the sole perpetrator and he might be tried as being an accessory before the fact. Whereas, if it was found that a wife had procured her husband to commit a felony, she could also be indicted as an accessory before the fact.

Therefore, the main question for the grand jury to consider, in this case, was the extent to which each party was involved in the putative murder. The recorder added that he had noted in the depositions that the couple had made declarations against each other, but that these should not be taken into account, as it was clear that they both appeared to have been actively involved in the act and were present at the time. This contention was supported by the sequence of events leading to the murder, as well as the motive and means. Finally, the recorder exhorted the grand jury to examine the circumstantial evidence to ascertain whether the victim was deliberately lured to the place where he died, or whether the meeting was accidental; how soon after his disappearance did his death occur; whether the clothing and possessions of the accused exhibited any bloodstains; when, and under what circumstances, they left the scene of the crime; and the nature of the account each of them gave. The grand jury withdrew to make their initial judgement.

The following day, the jurors returned to the courtroom and requested the assistance of the treasury solicitor, John Hayward, who had participated in the earlier hearings before the magistrate. The recorder agreed and Mr Hayward was sworn in as a witness for the prosecution. The grand jury withdrew for another hour, after which they returned with a true bill (a document stating that there was sufficient evidence for prosecution) for murder against both Frederick and Maria Manning.

During the afternoon, in an unusual move, Mrs Manning's belongings were seized by an order of the sheriff's office, following a legal suit by her husband's solicitor, Thomas Binns, who was still trying to obtain reimbursement for representing Frederick at the previous hearings. In assembling the counsel for the defence, he had already committed £100, with other expenses costing an additional £30, which was not covered by the money he had already received. Therefore, he had applied to the police commissioners and the secretary of state for the remainder of Maria's possessions, which he intended to sell in order to fund Frederick's defence. On Monday, he had received a judge's order to that effect and the sheriffs had been instructed to seize the property, which consisted of Maria's clothing and jewellery.

On Wednesday 24 October, the judges who were to preside over the Mannings' trial took their place on the bench, accompanied by the lord mayor. On the application of the attorney general Sir John Jervis, Chief Baron Pollock and Mr Justice Cresswell agreed to schedule the trial for the following day at 10 am.

Due to the intense appeal of this case and the notoriety of the alleged perpetrators, it was not surprising that a large throng had congregated outside the Old Bailey ready for the first day of the Mannings' trial on Thursday 25 October, although it was not quite as extensive as on previous occasions, due to the excellent arrangements made by the under-sheriff. Entry was limited and tickets for admission could only be purchased from the sheriffs, which helped to reduce any confusion and chaos. The inside of the courtroom, on the other hand, saw one of the greatest assemblages ever, with people arriving an hour before the opening to secure a good spot from which to view the proceedings.

Notable attendees included dignitaries from Sweden, Austria, Prussia and Sardinia, as well as members of the English aristocracy and clergymen such as the Reverend Gibson of the local church of St Mary Magdalen in Bermondsey. As recorded in the *Evening Standard*: 'It has been many years since the Old Bailey was so much filled with gentlemen learned in the law, a great number of whom were compelled to stand the whole of the time, it being impossible to find a sufficient number of seats.' Touts targeted those without tickets, offering entry for exorbitant prices. After being fleeced of their cash, the final few observers managed to squeeze into the already overcrowded space. As usual, the press commented on the large number of women, who were on raised seats near the judges, from where they waited in expectation of the unfolding events.

At 10 am, after several other prisoners were arraigned, the legal representatives involved in the Mannings case entered the courtroom, followed by the lord mayor and the three judges: Lord Chief Baron Pollock, Mr Justice Maule and Mr Justice Cresswell. Tory politician and lawyer Sir Jonathan Frederick Pollock, formerly attorney general, had been appointed Lord Chief Baron of the Exchequer in 1844. Sir William Henry Maule was appointed King's Council in 1833. Prior to his legal career, he had been a mathematics tutor at his alma mater, Cambridge University, where one of his students had been Sir Cresswell Cresswell (born Cresswell Easterby), with whom he now shared the bench in this case. Like Pollock, he had served as a Tory MP until he was appointed as a judge in 1842.

Before the judges sat the lawyers; Attorney General Sir John Jervis, William Bodkin, William Clarkson and Mr Clerk for the prosecution; William Ballantine and John Humffreys Parry once again in defence of Maria Manning, and Sergeant-at-Law Charles Wilkins, Mr Charnock and Mr Saunders, who were to defend Frederick Manning.

Once everyone was assembled, the prisoners arrived. Frederick entered the courtroom first. Dressed in black, he seemed in better health and spirits than previously. He looked sullen and indifferent as he approached the dock with his eyes downcast. As he moved closer, he lifted his gaze to the judges and scrutinised them. *Lloyd's Weekly* observed:

> There was nothing in his physiognomy peculiarly to denote him capable of perpetrating the crime of which he is accused. It is evident, however, that the animal are largely predominant over the intellectual faculties of the man. The whole expression of the face is of a repulsive character, though it lacks the appearance of determination and ferocity.

Frederick did not cast as much as a glance at his wife as she entered the courtroom and was seated some 10 feet away from him at the bar.

That morning, Maria Manning had woken up early in her cell and spent the next two hours preparing her dress carefully so as to make the best impression she could. However, by the time she had arrived at the courtroom, she seemed anguished and melancholy, in contrast to her husband's demeanour. As she made her entry, those seated in the public gallery raised their opera glasses to gain a closer look. Maria's outfit was plain but respectable; a black silk gown, which was fitted to the throat, a brightly-coloured plaid shawl and a headdress with long strings and a fine white lace veil. She was wearing primrose kid gloves and lace ruffles on her wrists. She approached the bar with her gaze lowered, as her husband had done. She too peered at the judges, casting a brief glance around the room before taking her place. *The Times* noted that both prisoners appeared much older than their recorded ages.

With the judges sitting solemnly in their wigs and scarlet robes and the lawyers in black, the formal proceedings began with the swearing in of the jury. The twelve jurors included a greengrocer, a carpenter, a straw hat manufacturer and an egg importer. Next, the clerk of arraigns read out the indictments to the prisoners for their response. Frederick replied in a firm voice, 'Not guilty.' Maria made the same answer but seemed less sure.

Before the trial could begin properly, Mrs Manning's defence lawyer, William Ballantine, made a formal objection to her being tried with her husband. Due to her being a foreign national, he argued, she had a right to be tried separately by a jury *de medietate linguae* (equally divided as to language) which meant that half the jurors must also be from other countries. This was in accordance with a statute which had been enacted in 1355 during the reign of Edward III. However, the attorney general countered that, due to a recent change in the law, she was now legally considered to be the wife of a British national, and therefore was not eligible for a separate trial. As the statute had only become enshrined in law the previous year, the lawyers discussed the matter for a while, after which the three judges conferred. After half an hour's deliberation, they concluded that Maria Manning had become a British citizen on her marriage and should be treated as such. After further agreement that the objection should be recorded, so that it could form the basis for an appeal should she be convicted, the trial proceeded.

The attorney general opened the case against the two prisoners. He stated that he was conducting the prosecution personally due to the notoriety of the case. After calling on the jury to dismiss any previous knowledge of the events from their minds, he summarised the facts, beginning with the background of the couple and their marriage. John Jervis then described the discovery of Patrick O'Connor's body under the cellar floor of 3 Minver Place, concluding that his death 'was the result of a deliberate, long-considered scheme.' At the end of his summary, he posed the principal question: 'Are both or either of the prisoners guilty of the crime for which they are about to be tried?'

Sir Jervis added that the charge in the indictment was that Frederick Manning had murdered Patrick O'Connor, either by hitting him with a crowbar or by shooting him with a pistol or airgun, and that Maria had aided and abetted him. However, this would not prevent Mrs Manning from being found guilty of murder. It would be the same case if she had committed the act in her husband's presence. After a discussion of the legal nuances, he presented the chain of evidence in the case, which comprised the relationship between the Mannings and the deceased; the conversation Frederick Manning had had with their lodger, William Massey; the purchase of the lime, the crowbar and the shovel; the letter inviting Patrick to dinner on 9 August;

and the clearing of the furniture from Minver Place after his disappearance. The attorney general further described how both Maria and Frederick had left London and had been arrested in Edinburgh and Jersey respectively. After highlighting Manning's contention that his wife had committed the act, he concluded that it would be up to the jury to determine the guilt of each party in regard to 'this barbarous transaction'. The chief prosecutor reminded them that some of O'Connor's possessions were found on one prisoner, and the other had sold shares in the deceased's name, after which he called his witnesses.

PC Henry Barnes, of Stepney Division, was the first witness. He began by recounting the discovery of Patrick O'Connor's body on 17 August at Minver Place and his subsequent visit to the deceased's lodgings in Mile End Road, where he found the empty cash box. On cross-examination by Frederick's defence barrister, Mr Sergeant Wilkins, explained that one of the flagstones, under which Patrick had been buried, was 2 feet square and the other was about 3 feet long and 2 feet wide: 'They were thick, heavy stones. I lifted them with a crow-bar,' which his colleague PC Burton had borrowed from a neighbour. The soil underneath the flags was wet and composed of lime core and clay, as was customary in foundations for houses. The police officer described the premises at 3 Minver Place, adding that he did not know whether any noises in the house could be heard by the adjoining neighbours. Mr Bodkin and Mr Ballantine asked further questions about the excavation of the hole in which the body was found, to which Barnes replied that he had used the crowbar and then the shovel.

Barnes' companion on that day, PC James Burton from Southwark police, confirmed his colleague's evidence. He attested that he had visited Minver Place for the first time on 14 August, accompanied by PC Wright and the victim's acquaintances, where he had found twenty-eight or thirty pieces of linen: 'It was not new, but clean linen, piled up on shelves in a cupboard in the front kitchen, as if it had been washed.' He further mentioned finding the shovel in the back kitchen, which he indicated in court.

After the police officers, the first surgeon to arrive on the scene, Samuel Meggitt Lockwood, was examined by Mr Clerk for the prosecution. He relayed the details of his initial examination of the body after removing it from the hole, which included the extraction of the false teeth. He told the court how he had found a bullet, which he then produced, from the victim's skull, as well as sixteen pieces of bone. At the end of his testimony, he surmised that the wounds must have been made by a sharp instrument, such as the chisel that had been exhibited at the police court. The surgeon concluded that these injuries would have been sufficient to have caused death, even without the shooting with the firearm. Finally, he identified the set of false teeth, which were shown by the coroner's court officer, Charles Slow. The provenance of the dentures was further confirmed by William Comley, the dentist who had made them for the victim.

The jury's attention turned to Patrick O'Connor's final movements and his relationship with the Mannings. William Clarkson began by questioning the deceased's acquaintance, Pierce Walsh, who had last seen him alive on 8 August when they had visited Minver Place together. He mentioned that Patrick had told Maria that he was intending to pursue a bill from a grocer named Pitt. William Bodkin then called William Keating, who worked with Patrick at the customs office. He recounted his last sighting of the deceased on London Bridge on 9 August, stating that he had seen Maria's name on the letter that O'Connor had shown him. Her barrister objected and the attorney general clarified that the letter had not been found. His objection was upheld.

Keating told the jury about his visit to Minver Place on the Sunday after Patrick's disappearance, when he had discussed the matter with Maria Manning. Mr Ballantine asked the witness about his acquaintance with the Mannings, to which he answered that he had known Maria first, and he had seen her twice at the victim's lodgings. On further inquiry by Charles Wilkins, he said that Frederick and Patrick had 'always appeared on friendly terms'.

Another of O'Connor's colleagues, David Graham, deposed that he had been with William Keating when they encountered Patrick on the bridge. He corroborated the previous witness's statement about the visit to the Mannings' house. In response to questions from the defence, he confirmed that London Bridge was about half a mile from Minver Place and that he had often witnessed Patrick walking with Frederick Manning but had only seen Maria at his lodgings once. He did not know whether she was 'intimate' with him. The trial was paused for a 15-minute break.

The hearing resumed with the evidence of two more of O'Connor's acquaintances, James Jarvis Coleman and John Younghusband, both of whom had also seen him on 9 August on London Bridge. Their statements added further confirmation that Patrick was going to Minver Place the evening he disappeared. No further questions were asked. They were followed by the Mannings' neighbour, Sophia Payne, who lived next door.

Once again, she narrated the details of her meetings with Frederick, both on the night Patrick disappeared and the following Monday. Mr Wilkins asked her for further detail, to which she responded that when she had seen him on the evening of 9 August, it had still been light. Manning had been sitting on the wall with his legs dangling into his own garden, and he 'appeared as usual.' Mrs Payne explained that her house adjoined that of the Mannings and that they could hear them moving about when it was quiet until after tea, when she and her husband usually began their lithographic printing. She also clarified that the time she had seen Manning was about 7 pm, which she could remember as it was at that hour that her husband returned home after his day's work in the City.

The attorney general moved the sequence of events forwards and questioned customs officer William Flynn about the inquiries he undertook after Patrick went missing. The witness related his conversation with Maria Manning on Monday 13 August, during which she had turned pale at the mention of O'Connor's name. Mr Sergeant Wilkins and Mr Bodkin both asked about his visit to the deceased's lodgings the day before, and Flynn confirmed that the cash box had been empty.

The next two witnesses were sisters Ann and Emily Armes, Patrick O'Connor's landladies. Firstly, Ann confirmed her last sighting of their lodger on the morning of 9 August, after which she told the court about the several visits Maria Manning had made to his rooms with her husband and alone, including the time the prisoner had spent at their house after Patrick's disappearance. She also described the visits of his acquaintances during that period. In response to a question, Miss Armes stated that the deceased always kept his keys on his person. In addition, she said that her parlour was directly under Patrick's room, and she could hear any visitors walking up and down the stairs. She said that he was on good terms with the Mannings and their boarder, William Massey. William Ballantine, for the defence, asked her if Maria had told her where she had acquired her money for the purchase of shares, to which she replied that she assumed that she had saved it during her time in service. Ann Armes concluded by saying that she had heard O'Connor advising Mrs Manning on which shares to buy and also that some boxes had arrived at the premises in Greenwood Street addressed to Maria de Roux over a year before O'Connor had disappeared.

Emily Armes corroborated her sister's statement and added that Mrs Manning had looked 'very pale' when she had visited their confectioner's shop on 9 August. The prisoner had bought a biscuit on her way out after visiting O'Connor. Mr Ballantine suggested that his client could have passed through a private door, and not been in the shop at all. Miss Armes conceded that Maria could have unlocked the door and exited without her knowing, but that she had never left the shop that way. She also mentioned the boxes that had arrived in her unmarried name, adding that Maria had come with them and stayed for the night. Frederick had not joined her.

Following these testimonies and in keeping with the order of the events that led to Patrick O'Connor's murder, the prosecution next produced their principal witness, William Massey, whose evidence would be crucial, especially in convincing the jury that Frederick Manning had planned the victim's death.

Chapter 19

An 'extraordinary and painful scene'

The Mannings' former lodger was the only person who had first-hand knowledge of the couple's conversations and actions in the weeks leading up to Patrick O'Connor's death. His evidence was potentially damning. The attorney general led the examination.

The medical student repeated his statement from the previous hearings. After confirming the length of his stay at Minver Place, he stated that he had seen the deceased at the property several times. He also pointed out that Frederick Manning told him that his wife had seen O'Connor at the docks 'in a state of intoxication', which Massey explained was due to his fear of contracting cholera. Jervis then posed the key question as to whether Manning had spoken to William about stupefying drugs, to which he replied by recounting the conversations he had had with the prisoner about the effects of chloroform and laudanum. He directly quoted Frederick Manning as saying, in relation to Patrick's fear of the epidemic: 'You frighten him well about the cholera and persuade him to take brandy as a specific for it.' However, on this occasion, the witness did not mention Manning's plan to lace the alcohol with narcotics. The prosecutor asked about the accused's questions to the lodger regarding which part of the head would be most susceptible to injury. Massey added that his landlord had once asked him where the brain was located. The examination continued with reference to the airgun and, finally, to the discussion of the wax figure of James Blomfield Rush at Madame Tussaud's, which inspired a conversation about the fate of murderers after death. Charles Wilkins asked the witness whether they often talked about medical issues, due to his studying medicine, to which he answered, 'Yes'.

Having established the possibility that the murder of Patrick O'Connor had been a premeditated crime, the prosecution proceeded to present the evidence of the Mannings' preparation for carrying out the act. Mary Wells confirmed that Frederick Manning had purchased lime from her father and that their premises were just five minutes' walk from Minver Place. The errand boy, Richard Welsh, told the court that he had been present during the transaction, after which he had delivered the lime to the address given by the prisoner. He identified Maria Manning as the woman who had paid him when he returned to Minver Place a day later.

Following the purchase of the lime, the next witness, William Danby, gave his testimony about the order for the crowbar. Producing a similar one in court, he attested that the one he had sold to Frederick Manning was 5 inches longer. He described how he had taken the tool to Minver Place when he had met Manning, who had asked him to wrap it in brown paper. Again, it was Maria who had paid for it. William Ballantine asked the witness if the prisoner had said what he was intending to use the crowbar for – he had not. The surgeon, Samuel Lockwood, was recalled and the attorney general questioned him about whether a crowbar, such as the previous witness had described, could have caused the injuries sustained by the victim, to which he concurred that it could: 'The wounds might have been inflicted by a shorter one as well as by a longer instrument than that now produced.' The chief baron interjected to push the surgeon for more details about the nature of the wounds, after which Lockwood concluded that the injuries must have been inflicted about a week before the body was discovered, due to the state of decomposition, thus giving an approximate date of death.

Returning to the likely preparation for the crime, ironmonger's assistant William Cahill deposed that Maria Manning had bought a dust shovel, which he had delivered to Minver Place. PC William Sopp produced the shovel and said that he had acquired it from Mary Ann Bainbridge, the furniture dealer's wife. His colleague, PC Barnes, stated that he had not found a shovel at the Mannings' house.

The prosecution progressed to the events after the alleged murder of Patrick O'Connor, beginning with the testimony of Hannah Firman, who was engaged by Maria Manning to clean 3 Minver Place. The girl explained how she was unable to do the work on the Monday, due to her having to sell matches and laces on that day, so she had agreed to do some cleaning on the Saturday, which was 10 August. The child had cleaned the steps, the back kitchen and the basket which had held the lime. She told the court about seeing Frederick Manning stamp his foot but offered no context or explanation for his outcry. On further examination, Hannah revealed, to the amusement of the spectators, that she had stolen an egg, a razor, a purse and a pair of stockings; she had taken them from the larder and a drawer when 'their backs were turned'. Hannah's evidence was followed by a brief statement from the Mannings' landlord, James Coleman, who verified that the couple had been yearly tenants, but they had left abruptly on 14 August.

Next, Charles and Mary Ann Bainbridge took the stand. Firstly, Charles described the negotiations with the Mannings over the price for their furniture. This took place almost three weeks before O'Connor's disappearance. He disclosed the details of Frederick Manning's stay in Bermondsey Square after he had left Minver Place, during which he had asked the dealer to buy him some linen and a new hat, as he was intending to go into the countryside for two months. When Bainbridge removed the furniture from the Mannings' lodgings, he remembered that there had been some fire irons, but he could not recall having seen a shovel. Mr Sergeant Wilkins asked whether he had made a list of the items, and Bainbridge assured him that he had and that he would bring the inventory to the court the following day. In response to further questions, Charles stated that Manning had left the new hat with him, as well as a lightweight zephyr (a type of fabric) coat and a paletot (an overcoat). The furniture dealer had not seen any men's clothing, a pickaxe or a crowbar among the Mannings' possessions, which he had taken from Minver Place.

However, Bainbridge's wife told the court that there had been a shovel belonging to the Mannings, which had been brought to Bermondsey Square as part of the sale. She also stated that there had been four dresses, one of which was bloodstained. Mary Ann corroborated her husband's statement by saying that Frederick Manning had left their home after two days. She added that he had taken a carpet bag with him and that he said he was going sea-bathing. Mr Ballantine asked her for more information about the bloodstains, and she confirmed that she had only seen them on the cape, not on the dress, which had been scorched from ironing. She explained that it had looked as if the blood had been washed from the dress. The Bainbridges' servant, Matilda Weldon, had little to add to her employer's testimonies.

The next witnesses testified about the Mannings' flight from London. Neighbour Mary Ann Schofield recounted Maria's departure in a cab and Frederick Manning's subsequent visit to the property later that day. The two cab drivers, William Byford and William Kirk, deposed that they had taken Frederick and Maria respectively on separate days to the relevant railway stations. Porter William Day identified Maria as the passenger whose boxes he had carried into London Bridge station, where she had left them in the luggage office.

The final three witnesses on the first day of the trial were the police officers who arrested Maria in Edinburgh and Frederick in Jersey. The defence barristers questioned Superintendent Richard Moxey of the Edinburgh police, and elicited that Mrs Manning had not decided, when she left London, whether she would travel to Scotland, and that she had told him that the railway shares she had on her person, when she was arrested, were bought by Patrick O'Connor on her behalf.

Concerning the arrest of Frederick Manning, Detective Sergeant Edward Langley described his actions which led to the prisoner's apprehension in Jersey and their ensuing conversations on the way back to London. A juror asked him about Manning's shooting coat. The detective replied that he had found the gunpowder in the pocket of the garment when he had examined it at Scotland Yard and that he had not known the defendant to go shooting when he had lived in Taunton. Finally, Detective John Haynes, who had recently been transferred from Scotland Yard to Southwark Division and promoted to the rank of superintendent, told the court about his discovery of Maria Manning's boxes at London Bridge station and his subsequent journey to Southampton to accompany her husband back to the capital. He affirmed that he had read the murder charge to Frederick Manning, who had blamed his wife for O'Connor's death.

After Haynes' statement, Sir John Jervis intimated that he wished for a letter to be admitted to the evidence but, due to the late hour, he suggested that, instead, the trial be adjourned to the following day. The judges agreed and set the time for resuming the hearing at 10 am. The prisoners left the dock, again without looking at each other. Before she left, Mrs Manning curtsied to the bench before being led away by a female warder. The jurors filed out and were escorted to the London Coffeehouse, where they were to be accommodated overnight. As a judge's order required them to stay together, they were housed in a large room with twelve beds.

The second day of the Mannings' trial drew even more crowds than the first. People began to assemble early in the morning and the numbers increased throughout the day. Everyone was talking about the outcome and likely verdict. Between 8.30 and 10 am, cabs and other vehicles brought those lucky enough to have a ticket to the public galleries, which were completely full. The fashionably dressed spectators, both from home and overseas, had their opera glasses with them again, so that they could watch the defendants' faces closely.

Just before 10 am, the jurors arrived after their night at the London Coffeehouse. Five minutes later, the Lord Chief Baron and Mr Justice

Cresswell resumed their places on the bench, just before the entrance of the prisoners, who both looked paler than the day before. Mrs Manning had swapped her white headdress for a black one and had donned white kid gloves.

Continuing the witnesses for the prosecution, William Odling gave his deposition. Describing himself as a 'practical' chemist, he was the son of police surgeon George Odling, who had conducted the post-mortem examination on Patrick O'Connor's body. It was the first time that he had given evidence. Odling explained that he had analysed the blood spots on the dress belonging to Maria Manning. The 20-year-old confidently concluded: 'I have subjected it to the usual chemical tests and have arrived at the conclusion that the stains are blood.' William Ballantine, Maria's defence attorney, asked for further details. Odling said that he had been alone when undertaking the tests. He had cut out a piece of the dress and seeped it in cold distilled water. However, he conceded that, although in his opinion the stains on the dress were blood, he could not say whether the spots on the collar were also blood. Seemingly unsure about his statement, Mr Bodkin asked for Odling's credentials. The young man attested that he had been studying chemistry at Guy's Hospital for five years and had received several prizes for his work. He then defended the results of his analysis by saying that the stain on the collar could have been blood, as he had disproved the possibility of it being iron rust or any other substance. As for the portion of dress, he expounded on his experiment, claiming that when the pieces had been placed into the distilled water, they had imparted their smoky red colour into the solution. From this, he had obtained a precipitate including albumen, one of the blood's constituents, and subjected it to various chemicals in a process of elimination. He added that he had not used a microscope and admitted that: 'There is no direct chemical process which will identify blood stains.' (The first specific test for blood was developed in 1853, but it was not possible to differentiate between human and animal blood until 1901.)

Following William Odling's scientific testimony, several stockbrokers gave their statements relating to the railway shares bought by Patrick O'Connor. Francis Worrell Stevens had purchased the shares in the Sambre and Meuse Railway, which were found in Maria Manning's possession. She had come into his office to inquire about buying the same shares but had not returned. He added that his client had never mentioned her name to him. Alexander Lamond had also bought railway shares for the deceased, and a transfer from the Eastern Counties Railway was produced in court as evidence. Clerk John

Green produced the certificate of transfer for twenty shares with the value of £400, which had been signed by him and the railway company secretary. Mrs Manning had also paid Lamond a visit but, in contrast to the previous witness's statement, she had brought a letter of introduction from O'Connor. Finally, Mr Hayward, the treasury solicitor, showed the jury another transfer of stock, in the stead of the late John Bassett, who had died of cholera.

After further discussion of the shares, attorney Henry Webb Shillibeer confirmed that the signature on the back of one of the transfers purportedly belonging to Patrick O'Connor was actually the handwriting of Frederick Manning. The shares had been taken by John Bassett to Richard Hammond, who told the court that he had given the deceased broker a £100 Bank of England note: 'I saw him [Bassett] hand them across the table to Manning, who represented himself as O'Connor, in the private room.' Later, Hammond had gone to the Bank of England to try to stop the banknote from being cashed. George Nash Linthorne, who had been present during the transaction, confirmed that he too had seen Manning sign the document in the victim's name. Linthorne had been asked by Hammond and Bassett to witness the transfers. Archibald Griffith and Joseph Reece Adams, who were both clerks at the Bank of England, stated that Frederick Manning had brought the notes to the bank to be exchanged for cash, for which he was given 50 sovereigns and five £10 notes, which were later found with Maria Manning.

The final pieces of evidence for the prosecution were then submitted. Firstly, Patrick O'Connor's attorney, John Blatchford, further stated that the signature on the back of the transfer was not his client's. Next, PC Barnes proved that the distance between Patrick's lodgings in Greenwood Street and the Mannings' house was 42 minutes on foot, 35 minutes in an omnibus, and 25 in a cab. There was no explanation given for these measurements. Lastly, a customs officer and a messenger both told the court that they had received a letter for Patrick O'Connor on 10 August, which had been delivered to his lodgings. They did not open it but, presumably, it was the dinner invitation from Maria Manning which had been delayed in the post.

Following the prosecution's final witness, Mr Sergeant Wilkins rose to address the jury on Frederick Manning's behalf. After fulminating against the press, which he described as 'base and cruel', in that it judged without trial – he gave their treatment of the French revolution as his example – he urged the jury to banish any prejudices and to make their judgement solely from the evidence presented to them. Focusing on his client's defence, he stated that there was no doubt that Patrick O'Connor had been murdered but the question was, by whom?

Challenging the prosecution's contention that both Frederick and Maria were involved in O'Connor's death, he contended that the only evidence against his client was the purchase of the lime and the crowbar. He prefaced his examination of that evidence with a general statement, in which he claimed that women, as shown throughout history, 'soared higher in virtue and sank deeper in vice than man' and that, in this case, he hoped to demonstrate how a woman had duped her husband and sought to save herself by his 'destruction'. He then moved onto the facts of the case.

In relation to the lime, he suggested that there was no reason to believe that Manning had not made the purchase with the intention of killing slugs, as he had freely given his address to the shop assistant, and the use of lime was 'natural' for a garden such as that at Minver Place. Moreover, the two-day delay between the purchase and delivery did not elicit any impatience on his part. As for the crowbar, he postulated that his client could have bought such an instrument 'for a deadly purpose' at any marine store, yet he had chosen one of the most respectable shops in King William Street. Wilkins further suggested that Frederick's desire to cover the tool with paper could be accounted for by his 'very conceited and consequential person'. Regarding the use of a crowbar as a murder weapon, the defence lawyer advocated that a poker would have been 'a far more fitting instrument'. Thus, he concluded, that this evidence was not sufficient to inculpate his client, and he further propounded that the murder could have been committed solely by one person; the pistol would have been fired by one hand, and that same person could have buried the body after the act. The sergeant-at-law reminded the jury that PC Barnes had been able to lift the flagstone in the back kitchen single-handedly.

Charles Wilkins followed his theory of a single perpetrator with an examination of possible motive. He argued that Frederick Manning was not a jealous man, and he was 'too easy' in his treatment of his wife. The witnesses had agreed that Manning's relationship with the deceased was 'a perfect friendship'. Prior to the cashing of the £100 note, there was no evidence of his client having benefitted financially from their acquaintance.

After analysing the evidence, the tone of the defence began to shift towards Maria Manning. The barrister contended that she would have been strong enough to tie up Patrick's body. She had written the note inviting the victim to Minver Place on the evening he was likely to have died. Mrs Manning had lied to O'Connor's friends when they inquired about his whereabouts, and she had feigned shock at his apparent disappearance. And, most damningly, she was in possession of the victim's railway shares and money after his death. And it was Maria's clothing which was stained with blood – there was no evidence of such staining on her husband's.

Wilkins painted a picture of Maria Manning as a controlling and hypocritical woman who was capable of 'consummate wickedness', which she could easily conceal. Her husband, who still felt affection towards her, was unable to influence her, as she considered herself to be far superior to him. The defence barrister contended that his client's actions, as recounted by the witnesses, were innocent and that he was afraid of his wife. After commenting on all the testimonies, he expressed his regret and sorrow that, due to the prejudice shown towards Frederick, he had been compelled to incriminate Maria. At the conclusion of his address, the jury retired for refreshment.

On their return, Maria's lawyer, William Ballantine, appealed to the bar. He too assessed selected statements and discounted specific witnesses, such as the Misses Armes who, he stated, 'had no very friendly feeling towards Mrs Manning.' He then focused on the distance between Minver Place and Patrick O'Connor's lodgings, as measured by PC Barnes, concluding that if the murder had been committed between 5.30 and 8 pm, his client could not have been a participant due to the timing of her arrival and departure from Greenwood Street. His contention was that the deceased had arrived at the Mannings' home at about 5.30 pm, and was killed soon afterwards, during which time Maria was absent. This was further supported by the likelihood that only Frederick Manning had the strength to carry out the murderous attack. Moreover, Manning had never given any explanation of the multiple fractures sustained by the victim which, according to the medical experts, had been the cause of his death. Mr Ballantine concurred with the contention made by his learned colleague that the murder had been committed by one person, and that was Frederick Manning, who had tried to cast the blame onto his wife.

Mr Ballantine next discussed the facts of the case and argued that, when his client had bought an ordinary coal shovel, she 'could hardly have been contemplating a deed of darkness.' In relation to Frederick's purchase of the lime, there was no evidence of slugs in the Mannings' garden. He also raised the question as to why Manning had tried to conceal the chisel, when it was a commonplace domestic tool. Furthermore, the stains on Maria's cape could have been iron mould, and the blood on her dress could have arisen from 'natural causes'. Mrs Manning was not present during the conversations between her husband and William Massey regarding Patrick O'Connor's will and the use of stupefying drugs.

In reference to the night of the supposed murder, Maria's defence lawyer claimed that she had been induced to send the invitation to the deceased by her husband, and that she had been telling the truth when she told his friends that she did not know where he was. In fact, in his opinion, Mrs Manning had every reason to maintain her relationship with O'Connor. However, Mr Ballantine did not deny that his client had become acquainted with the murder, which had taken place during her absence, but that 'her conduct was consistent and reconcilable with her entire innocence.' In the light of this, he argued that she had taken the railway shares that she believed had belonged to her, as Patrick had bought them for her. She wanted to invest without her husband's knowledge, and she had intended to use them to flee from Frederick. Mr Ballantine concluded his address by appealing to the jury to view the property in Maria's possession, which had belonged to Patrick O'Connor, within the context of his client's innocence.

Exercising his right as the crown representative, the attorney general expressed his hope that the jury would base their decision on the evidence. He then summarised the aspects of the case on which the two defence counsels agreed; that Patrick O'Connor was murdered and that the act had been committed by one person, which in his view was 'highly improbable'. He believed that the murder was committed later in the evening, when both parties were present: 'It was impossible, then, not to come to the conclusion that both prisoners were concerned in this atrocious case.'

Finally, the Lord Chief Baron addressed the jury. After reminding them of their legal duties and the various possible outcomes of the trial, he summarised the details of the case once again. He exhorted the jurors to make their judgement on the facts and to take a 'broad, general, and comprehensive view' of the circumstances, rather than focusing on the minutiae as: 'There are crimes which, committed in darkness and secrecy, can only be traced out and brought to light by a comparison of circumstances.' After an expression of his confidence in the jury, he dismissed the men to consider their verdict.

The jurors retired at 6 pm, and, after 45 minutes, they returned to the courtroom. As they entered, both the prisoners looked at them anxiously with Maria exhibiting signs of emotion. Frederick, on the other hand, appeared to be unmoved and, resting his chin upon his right hand, he calmly waited for the result. The deputy clerk of arraigns asked the jury for their verdict, to which the foreman answered, 'Guilty', first for Frederick and then for Maria. Waving her hands violently, Mrs Manning exclaimed, 'I will not stand here – I have not had a fair trial!' Ignoring her, the clerk asked each prisoner if they had anything to say regarding the death sentence.

Maria Manning placed her hands on the bar and, overcome with intense emotion, she addressed the bench. In imperfect English, she complained about her unfair treatment: 'I have been treated most cruelly in this country. I am a foreigner and I have been denied justice.' She spoke of her affection for Patrick O'Connor and the long history of their relationship, saying that: 'I could not attempt the life of a man who was my most honoured friend on earth.' She concluded her speech by blaming her husband, whom she believed had committed the act out of jealousy. Frederick Manning, who had watched his wife intently during her address without moving, said nothing. When Mr Justice Cresswell attempted to continue his final statement, Maria interrupted, shouting in a loud voice, 'I shan't hear it – I won't stand here any longer.' And with that, she tried to leave the dock. The prison governor, who was sitting behind, took hold of her arm and brought her back to the front.

In the absence of any further comments from the prisoners, Mr Justice Cresswell put on the black silk cap and addressed the prisoners, admonishing them for their act: 'Your crime is of the deepest dye – as cold-blooded, calculating, and deliberate a murder as I ever read of.' He then passed the sentence of death on both Frederick and Maria Manning, who were to return to Horsemonger Lane Gaol to await their execution. Maria cried out: 'My lord, you consider you have done your duty, then, in sentencing me to death, as if I was one of your own country-women.' As she was shouting, she seized some sprigs of rue – a herb which was traditionally used to disguise the smell of unwashed prisoners suffering from gaol fever – from the front of the dock and cast them violently over the table occupied by the barristers, exclaiming, 'Base, shameful England!' She was removed from the courtroom. In contrast, Frederick Manning remained unperturbed, and he followed his wife out of the dock. The court rose at 7 pm and the condemned couple were transferred to Horsemonger Lane Gaol two hours later.

Chapter 20

'The last scene of this horrible tragedy'

When Maria and Frederick Manning arrived back at Horsemonger Lane Gaol, the governor, John Keene, and his deputy were waiting to receive them. Mrs Manning, who was described as reserved and looking sullen, was immediately taken to the infirmary, where she had been previously housed, accompanied by two female turnkeys. A male warder was placed outside her door. After shouting aggressively at the guards, she quietened down and retired at 10 pm. During the night, her sleep was disturbed several times and she rose from her bed before finally settling down at 3 am. Maria slept soundly until 8 am, after which she got dressed with her usual care and ate a hearty breakfast. She then received a visit from the prison chaplain, but refused to speak to him, claiming that she had been unjustly convicted.

Frederick Manning was placed back in the cell in which he had been accommodated before the trial. Although he seemed downhearted, he slept well. The following day, he sent for his solicitor, Thomas Binns, who was unavailable due to having left London on business.

In the days following their return to the prison, the Mannings both seemed to settle down. Maria became more subdued and, although she continued to complain about not having had recourse to a fair trial, she became less vociferous and aggressive. It was noted that she slept well in the condemned cell. She had eggs and toast for breakfast, and a pint of ale every day. She attended chapel daily and gave her guards little trouble. Maria paid close attention to what she wore and was optimistic that Lady Blantyre or Lady Blantyre's mother, the Duchess of Sutherland, would intercede for her and save her from the gallows. In addition, her solicitor had also begun preparing an appeal against her conviction. Frederick, on the other hand, seemed very depressed and hardly ate anything. Asserting strenuously that his wife was the one who shot Patrick O'Connor and therefore was mainly responsible for his death, he spent his time reading religious books and receiving instruction from the prison chaplain.

Frederick Manning had had little contact with his family for some time which, according to the press, was due to his siblings' ill feelings towards his wife. His brother, Edmund, was said to be deeply distressed by the whole affair, especially as he had always sided with Frederick during domestic quarrels. Edmund had also experienced violence at the hand of Maria Manning in Taunton, when she had attacked him with a quart pot, which he had managed to wrestle from her grip before she struck him. After the trial, Edmund wrote to Frederick asking permission to visit him, which his brother granted.

A week later, Edmund Manning had an interview with Frederick during the afternoon of Friday 2 November in the presence of the prison chaplain, Reverend Rowe; the governor; and his brother's solicitor, Thomas Binns. As reported in *Lloyd's Weekly*: 'The interview was a most painful and heartrending one.' When Edmund entered the cell, Frederick was sitting at a small table. The prisoner was so changed and downhearted that his brother barely recognised him. Edmund shook his hand, holding him in his grasp for some time. Both of them were so overcome with emotion that they could not speak. After a while, Edmund said, 'Surely, Frederick, you are not guilty of this horrible charge?' Manning replied: 'No, I am innocent.' He told his brother that he had made a full confession to Reverend Rowe. The chaplain nodded in assent. Manning explained: 'Edmund, she murdered him. I was upstairs, dressing myself, at the time she shot him. I did not know she was going to do so. I had no hand in the murder.'

Edmund asked if Frederick had written to Maria to encourage her to confess to the crime, to which he answered that he had asked her repeatedly to admit her part in the act. He showed his brother the letter he had written to his wife, which comprised three pages of endearments and entreaties. On receipt of the letter, Mrs Manning had asked for pen, ink and paper and had drafted a four-page reply, telling Frederick that she was innocent and had been wrongly convicted. She implored him to exonerate her and stated that she would not see him until he had done so. Maria concluded her letter by saying: 'You know that the party who went with you to Jersey committed the murder, and that I was from home when it was committed.'

After reading the correspondence, Edmund exclaimed: 'Frederick, she exculpates herself from the charge and accuses a third party – who does she mean?' His brother simply replied that her statement was false, adding that no one had accompanied him to the island. He ended their interview by saying: 'I know, Edmund, you will believe me when I assert that I am innocent, for you have always been my best friend, and I should never have married that woman if I had listened to your advice.' He asked his brother to take care of his documents and all his possessions after his death. Edmund urged Frederick to make his peace with God, after which he left, promising to return soon. Manning cried bitterly following his brother's departure.

Edmund Manning returned to Horsemonger Lane Gaol at 1 pm the following Tuesday. This time, he was accompanied by one of their sisters, who had arrived in London. Once again, the meeting, which was supervised by the same individuals, was very emotional. After the initial feelings had subsided, Edmund implored his brother to divulge everything he knew about the murder. After reiterating that Maria had shot Patrick, he further stated that O'Connor had noticed the hole being dug in the kitchen floor during his visits to Minver Place and that Maria had told him that they were making a drain. On the day of his death, Frederick had heard Patrick ask her: 'What, haven't you finished the drain yet?' These were his final words as Manning then heard a shot ring out and a heavy fall to the floor. Frederick confessed to his siblings that he had pledged a pair of pistols, one of which was used to shoot the victim, on the evening that Maria had left town, as he was penniless. He also revealed the whereabouts of O'Connor's watches and the crowbar that was used to finish the murderous act. Edmund took his leave, agreeing to return on Saturday, but their sister bid him a final farewell. Frederick had another brother and sister in London, the former having just returned after a long cruise to Mauritius, but they did not come to the prison. After the visits from his family, Frederick perked up a little and began to eat his meals more regularly. He was still anxious to see Maria, but she continued to refuse him a meeting. She also declined to speak with Edmund or his sister.

The hearing for Maria Manning's appeal was appointed for the following day. On Wednesday 7 November, just five days before the date set for her execution, judges Lord Chief Justice Wilde, Lord Chief Baron Pollock, Mr Justice Cresswell, Mr Justice Coleridge, Mr Baron Rolfe and Mr Baron Platt met at Westminster Hall to consider her petition. Mrs Manning's lawyer, William Ballantine, made the appeal on the same point he had raised at the beginning of the trial, in that she had been entitled to a separate trial by a jury, half of whom should be 'foreigners', due to her status as an 'alien'. He argued that although she was married to an English man, she should have retained her rights as a foreign national. After a lengthy debate on various parliamentary acts and relevant cases, the attorney general stated that he still believed that Maria had not been eligible for a separate trial before a jury of mixed nationality, after which the judges retired to make their decision.

Half an hour later, the justices returned to the chamber and Lord Chief Justice Wilde pronounced that, after considering the matter carefully, the panel had concluded that Maria was a naturalised British citizen, due to her marriage, at the time of the offence and was legally tried. Thus, her appeal was denied. The news of the judges' decision was sent immediately to Horsemonger Lane Gaol. Maria received the information in the company of the prison chaplain, who urged her to 'prepare to meet her Maker'. She seemed surprised at the outcome and exclaimed once again that she had been unjustly tried and that her husband could exculpate her if he confessed the truth. After her outburst, she put her hands to her face and cried bitterly. The chaplain exhorted her to spend her remaining time in prayer and repentance. When he again encouraged her to confess, she replied that she was not guilty of the murder. Later that day, the fate of the Mannings was finally sealed when Mr Keene received the official warrant for their execution at Horsemonger Lane Gaol on 13 November between 8 am and 2 pm.

After the damning warrant was delivered, the prison authorities were worried that Maria Manning might injure herself or worse, so they instructed a third woman to watch over her. Mary Ann Randall, the female searcher and police sergeant's wife from Southwark police station with whom Maria had seemed to form an attachment, was sent for to attend to the prisoner. When she entered the cell, Mrs Manning was very pleased to see her, and they chatted together about several subjects. The condemned woman continued to assert her innocence and began writing letters to her influential contacts, asking them to intervene on her behalf. On being reminded that her legal representatives had done all they could for her, she stamped her foot and exclaimed: 'Why, they have done nothing; they and everybody else in the court decided upon hanging me before I was tried.' In alluding to her husband, she said: 'Ah, he is a vagabond. I never said anything about him. He knows who murdered poor O'Connor and can tell all.' Enraged, Maria refused all religious instruction and ignored the chaplain. Still optimistic that she would be spared from the scaffold, she continued to eat and sleep well, and was happy to join in conversations with her warders.

After hearing about the warrant, Frederick Manning slumped further into depression and refused to eat. Now quite emaciated, he sent an urgent request to speak to his lawyer. On Friday morning, Thomas Binns visited his client for the last time. On his arrival in the condemned cell, Frederick seemed in better spirits. He shook hands with the solicitor and thanked him for his kindness. He said that he was prepared to meet his fate and that he could die happy if his wife told the truth. Manning informed Mr Binns that he had taken some railway shares with him to Jersey, which he had destroyed in a water closet before his arrest. He gave the lawyer a full description of them so that they might benefit the deceased's family. He also revealed the name of the railway station where he had disposed of the crowbar.

Finally, he directed his brief to dispose of all his property and, after paying his legal expenses, to give the remainder to his brother Edmund. He then gave Mr Binns his letters along with permission to publish them in the press. The solicitor bade him an emotional farewell and left. That evening, Frederick Manning made one final appeal to his wife, imploring her to see him 'to bring peace and comfort' to them both, but once again she denied him.

The next afternoon, the two brothers met for the very last time. In contrast to previous occasions, Frederick was cheerful and seemed resigned to his fate. He told Edmund: 'I am very well; I feel very happy and comfortable.' During the visit, which lasted for 30 minutes, he repeated his claims of innocence and produced a pencil drawing of the back kitchen of 3 Minver Place, on which he had marked the position of Patrick O'Connor's body when he first saw it, to prove to his brother that he had not been present at the death. After further discussion, Frederick asked Edmund to give his love and blessings to his relatives, especially to their sister who had visited him. The brothers then knelt together as the prison chaplain said a prayer, after which Edmund asked Frederick if he could see him one more time. But his brother replied that it was of no use and that he would rather he did not. As they separated, the condemned man remarked that he hoped they should meet before long 'in another and a better world'.

On the same day, Patrick O'Connor's brother arrived back in London from Ireland to undertake the administration of the deceased's property. He had an interview with Inspector Yates at Southwark police court, where he received an inventory of his possessions. Also, Thomas Adams, a pawnbroker from Bermondsey, attended the police court to request the return of the pistols used by Maria Manning to shoot Patrick O'Connor, which had been confiscated by the police. The applicant stated that a police constable had visited his shop in Bermondsey Street to inquire if anyone had pledged any pistols in the days before the murder. Mr Adams had told him that a man answering Frederick Manning's description had pawned a pair of pistols on 14 August. They were

163

quite new and only one of them had been used. However, the pawnbroker had later failed to identify Manning. The magistrate replied that Frederick had since confessed to the pledging of the pistols, but that he had no power to return them.

In the early hours of the next morning, Sunday 11 November, Maria Manning attempted to take her own life, as feared by the prison authorities. At about 3 am, when two of her watchers fell asleep, she took the opportunity to try to strangle herself by grasping her throat and digging her fingernails, which she had grown long for the purpose, into her windpipe. As she began to convulse, the third guard noticed and alerted the others. They jumped up and stopped her before she could do any permanent damage to herself. After that, they watched her more carefully. At 9 am, she attended the chapel service with her husband for the final time. Although the Mannings were separated in the chapel and unable to see each other, they tried to look over the partition but to no avail. Frederick looked pale and downhearted. As the service proceeded, both prisoners became distressed and cried during the sermon, especially when Reverend Rowe alluded to them. The chaplain prayed for strength and comfort on their part and beseeched them to ask for God's forgiveness. After the service, they left the chapel still seemingly affected by his words. Maria was quiet for the rest of the day; she refused to repent or to see her husband. That evening, the chaplain visited her in her cell and returned the letters which she had written to Queen Victoria via her former employer, the Duchess of Sutherland, and to the home secretary, Sir George Grey. It seemed that neither had reached their intended recipient and her intercessions were to no avail.

The preparations for the execution of the Mannings had begun on Saturday 10 November. The judges had applied to the Metropolitan police commissioners for 400 to 500 additional constables to manage the throngs of people expected to come to Horsemonger Lane Gaol to watch the spectacle. Local residents had erected viewing platforms made from planks of wood on poles outside their houses, with the intention of selling tickets, the building of which led to heated discussions with their neighbours whose view had been obscured. Some of the most vociferous debates were taken to the magistrate, Isaac Secker, who repeatedly told complainants that these were private matters over which he had no say. At the same time, the under-sheriffs were plagued by requests by individuals for admission into the prison, particularly to attend the chapel service but, as the home secretary had decreed that no one should be granted entry, their applications were denied.

In the early hours of Sunday morning, an immense crowd had assembled in front of the prison. People milled about, commenting on the murder and the perpetrators' imminent fate. When the public houses opened at 1 pm, they rushed in, and the bartenders were kept busy as the observers sought to relieve the tedium of waiting by downing several pints of ale. More spectators arrived in cabs and carts during the afternoon, including many well-dressed individuals, who amused themselves by gazing ostentatiously at the top of the prison, where the event was due to take place. The gathering was so large and chaotic that some people were trampled by horses and the police officers struggled to maintain control.

By midday the following day, some 10,000 people had congregated near the gaol. They watched eagerly as the black timbers of the scaffold were being constructed on the prison roof over the porch. At the same time, barricades were also being erected on the ground to ease the pressure of the masses and to keep the onlookers safe from accidents. Local residents continued to sell tickets for seats at increasingly exorbitant prices as the demand for a ringside view grew. There were even ladders on most houses for those who wished to watch from the rooftops, and sightseers also found places in windows overlooking the gallows.

The scaffold was completed at 4 pm. The windows of Maria Manning's cell had been covered so that she would not be able to see it, although the press speculated that she must have been able to hear the incessant hammering. Despite still refusing to see her husband, she asked about his health. The prison chaplain spoke with both the convicts during the day, who behaved as they had during previous meetings, with Frederick accepting spiritual instruction and Maria denying it. Instead, she wrote letters to several of her friends, telling them that she was about to be 'murdered'. At 8 pm, Reverend Rowe visited her once again and they spoke for more than two hours. Maria continued to deny any part in the murder and repeated that it had been an acquaintance of her husband in Jersey. After the chaplain left, she undressed and went to bed but slept badly. The priest then visited Frederick, who also seemed very unsettled. He managed to read from the Bible and then wrote some final messages to the prison officers, after which he threw himself on his bed. He remained wide awake for the whole night.

As the evening drew to a close, the excitement outside the prison increased. Spectators jostled for their places for the night so that they had a good view for the morning's proceedings. Almost 500 police officers were on duty keeping the roads clear and the eager observers at bay. The gin shops and taverns were full to bursting as landlords took full advantage of the unprecedented custom. Street stalls sold brandy, hot potatoes and pies. Itinerant salesmen touted biscuits and peppermints, all bearing the name of the condemned couple. Broadsides and ballads were also hawked, retelling the story of the heinous murder. In a festive mood, people drank, smoked and chatted. Later, small groups danced to keep themselves warm during the bitterly cold, damp night.

By daybreak, all routes to the prison were completely blocked and the mob continued to swell, pushing the constables' efforts to the limit. After the foggy night, it was a bright day, with a clear sky slightly tinged with red. At 7 am, even more people poured into the area, with several cabs arriving with visitors from out of town. One man tried to gain a better view by putting his leg through one of the barriers, which fractured the limb, and he had to be pulled painfully from the midst of the throng.

At the same hour, the prison chaplain visited Frederick who asked for forgiveness, which he granted. After he had left, Manning had a light breakfast of bread and butter and tea, after which he walked around the exercise yard. However, hearing the roar of the crowds outside the prison walls made him feel faint and he rushed back indoors. Meanwhile, Reverend Rowe went to see Maria, who seemed more depressed than ever. She said little to the chaplain, who left after a brief prayer.

A short time later, Maria Manning finally agreed to see her husband and the couple met at 8.20 am in the chapel with their respective chaperones. Frederick leaned towards her and said: 'I hope you are not going to depart this life with feelings of animosity towards me?' She answered that she would not. Overcome with emotion, he asked if he could kiss her, to which she agreed. They stood up, shook hands and kissed each other several times. By this time, the chaplain had entered to administer the sacrament. Afterwards, Manning embraced his wife again and they sobbed.

Following the brief service, Frederick Manning was taken into an adjoining room, where he was to be pinioned ready for the execution. He was wearing a plain black suit, with his shirt collar loosened to accommodate the noose. Executioner William Calcraft stepped forward and the prisoner asked him if hanging would be painful. The hangman answered that it would not be if he kept still. Once the preparations were completed, Frederick was moved to the chapel yard to wait for Maria's arrival. Wearing a fine black satin gown, she had undergone the same process in a different room and, on seeing the executioner, she had almost fainted and was given some brandy to revive her. After she had recovered, she took a small, black silk handkerchief from her pocket and asked that it might be placed over her eyes. The prison surgeon did as she requested and then put a black lace veil over her head and tied it under her chin. During this emotional scene, one of the female warders wept audibly and Maria said to her: 'Do not cry but pray for me.' She was led out to join her husband in the yard.

The prison governor led the procession through the passages of the prison towards the scaffold, along with the chief officer and the district high constable. The chaplain came next, followed by Frederick, who was supported by two warders, and then Maria, who was held by the prison surgeon and another official. As she was blindfolded, Maria cried out to her aides to make sure that she did not bump into anything, and she complained that the cords on her wrists were too tight. The prisoners made their way with hesitant steps, passing over the place where their graves had already been dug. The account in *Lloyd's Weekly* pointed out that a thin layer of lime had been placed in their graves, which was 'an instance of retributive justice for the crime for which they had been so righteously convicted'.

They ascended the narrow staircase to the gallows and, on reaching the top, Calcraft removed Frederick's neckerchief. As he climbed the final steps to the gallows, the condemned man stumbled. Below, between 30,000 and 50,000 people (contemporary accounts differ) stood silently as Frederick's pale and emaciated face appeared on the prison roof. At the top, he gazed out away from the crowds while Maria ascended to join him. After her more hesitant arrival, due to her still being blindfolded, the throng held their breath as the executioner placed the white caps over their heads and adjusted the ropes. Despite being pinioned, Frederick tried to lean over to whisper to her. While the final preparations were being made, the chaplain intoned the burial service. When he had finished, he asked Maria if she had anything to say. She replied, 'Nothing, except to thank you all for your kindness.' The hordes remained quiet as Calcraft adjusted the ropes. The drop fell and both prisoners died without a struggle. Their bodies hung on the gallows for an hour, before being removed.

Chapter 21

'The two miserable creatures'

As the excitement over the double 'hanging match' subsided and the crowds of spectators drifted away, the police began to clear the area around Horsemonger Lane Gaol. Hats, bonnets, shawls, shoes and other items of clothing, which had been discarded or lost in the seething mass of onlookers, were strewn about the site. At the corner of nearby Swan Street, men were found lying on the pavement, some in a state of intoxication and others who had been injured in the crush. Several people had been hurt as the crowd surged forward to take a closer look at the Mannings ascending the scaffold, such as the man who had fractured his thigh when pushed against the barriers. Worse still, 30-year-old Catherine Reid had fallen to the ground in a faint and been trampled underfoot. She died later in Guy's Hospital. Thomas Overall also fell to the floor and was taken to Guy's where he remained in a critical condition. Other individuals suffered injuries as they attempted to escape the crowds, including a number of women and a child who was passing by.

Over the following days, there were also court appearances connected with the execution. Just after Maria and Frederick had been 'launched into eternity', Elizabeth Howe, who was in the crowd, took a phial out of her pocket and placed it to her lips. Quick-thinking Sergeant Watkins from Southwark Division knocked it out of her hand before she could drink it. Elizabeth became violent, shouting that she was one of Manning's sisters and that she wished to die with her brother, who had been unjustly convicted. She was taken to the nearest police station, where the inspector on duty declared her to be insane. He later confirmed to the magistrate that Elizabeth was not a relative of Frederick Manning, and she was given into the care of her friends.

Observing the mayhem was Charles Dickens, on whom the spectacle had a profound effect. Nine years earlier, in 1840, the writer had attended the execution of François Courvoisier, the Swiss valet who was hanged for the murder of his employer, Lord William Russell. This had taken place at Newgate Prison, and the author had hired an upper room close to the gallows, from where he could view the event. He had told his friends: 'I should like to watch a scene like this and see the end of the Drama.' The following year, he published *Barnaby Rudge*, in which he described the observers watching the execution of rioters Hugh and Dennis: 'It was terrible to see … the world of eager eyes, all strained upon the scaffold and the beam.' In 1846, he wrote four letters to the editors of the *London Daily News* advocating the abolition of capital punishment due to the 'horrible fascination' and 'depraved excitement' of those in attendance, which he had witnessed at Courvoisier's hanging, and which he felt did not work as a deterrent.

The week before the scheduled execution of the Mannings, Dickens was in two minds about attending. He told his friend, the *Punch* illustrator John Leech:

> I give in, about the Mannings. The doleful weather, the beastly nature of the scene, the having no excuse for going [after seeing Courvoisier] and the constantly recurring desire to avoid another such horrible and odious impression, decide me to cry off.

However, despite his initial reluctance, he and his friends rented a spot on a roof in Bath Terrace for 10 guineas, from which they followed the proceedings. Later that day, the author wrote a letter to the editor of *The Times,* in which he revealed that he had not only witnessed the Mannings' execution, but that he had been present at the site during the previous night, with the intention of observing the crowd and their reaction to the event. With the caveat that he was not raising the question of capital punishment, he stated his wish to turn the 'dreadful experience' into further support for the home secretary's intimation that he might change the current system by ensuring that, in the future, executions should take place within the privacy of prison walls. Exhorting Sir George Grey to take steps towards legislative change in this regard, Dickens illustrated his opinion with a vivid description of the double hanging:

> I believe that such a sight so inconceivably awful as the wickedness and levity of the immense crowd collected at that execution this morning could be imagined by no man and could

be presented in no heathen land under the sun. The horrors of the gibbet and of the crime which brought the wretched murderers to it, faded in my mind, before the atrocious bearing, looks and language, of the assembled spectators.

When he had arrived at the site at midnight, he had been struck by the high pitch of the cries, which he presumed were from children waiting to attend the spectacle and which made his 'blood run cold'. During the night, he heard screams, laughter and the singing of ballads, of which the words had been changed to include the name of Maria Manning. As the day dawned, thieves, sex workers, 'ruffians and vagabonds' flocked to the site, and indulged in 'every variety of offensive and foul behaviour'. There were fights, people fainting, whistling, lurid jokes and 'tumultuous demonstrations of indecent delight when swooning women were dragged out of the crowd by the police with their dresses disordered'. Dickens described how the sun rose, gilding thousands of faces 'as inexpressibly odious in their brutal mirth or callousness'. When Frederick and Maria Manning 'were turned quivering in the air', the spectators showed no pity, emotion, restraint or thought 'that two immortal souls had gone to judgment'.

Despite his impassioned plea, *The Times* did not support Dickens's views, maintaining that it was important for the public to see that 'great offenders were really executed'. (Public executions would not be abolished until 1868.) The general public also clearly did not share the author's opinion as journalist Henry Mayhew estimated that the trial and execution of the Mannings resulted in sales of two and a half million broadsides, the same as had been sold for the Rush case. Also, author Robert Huish penned an 800-page fictionalised account of the life of Maria Manning and the murder of Patrick O'Connor. *The Progress of Crime or The Authentic Memoirs of Marie Manning* (the title uses her birth name of 'Marie' not 'Maria') was serialised at the time in weekly 'penny bloods' (later renamed 'penny dreadfuls'). He later combined them into one volume.

While Charles Dickens had been expressing his distaste about their very public execution, casts were taken of the Mannings' heads, after which their remains were buried side by side in the corridor leading to the prison chapel, their graves marked with simple plaques bearing only their initials. The requisite inquest into their deaths showed that Frederick seemed to have died instantly, but Maria's face showed signs of a struggle for breath, suggesting that it had taken longer for her to expire.

Despite the perpetrators' deaths, interest in the 'Bermondsey Horror' continued due to the publication of Frederick's alleged confession in the press in the days following the execution. According to the newspapers, Manning had confessed to the prison chaplain, in the presence of two other witnesses, over two consecutive days preceding his execution. Reverend Rowe released the details. The condemned man stated that he had spent three weeks in Guernsey in mid-March, while his wife had taken the tenancy at Minver Place, returning to London on 5 April. He confirmed that Patrick O'Connor had provided the reference for their landlord, James Coleman, and added that their friend had stayed at the property on the first night, after which he had promised to return with his belongings. However, he visited the couple a few days later to tell them that he could not move in with them, as he was concerned that he and Frederick would not get on, mainly due to Manning's tendency to come home drunk late at night. Maria accused Patrick of having broken his promises before and blamed him for influencing them in other decisions, such as taking the lease on the public house, the King John's Head, which had resulted in a loss of £100.

Three weeks later, according to Frederick, Maria made a claim on O'Connor for the lost rental income. The day before the county court summons, Patrick paid her 30 shillings to settle the debt and apologised. Frederick further accused him of defamation, saying that he had heard that O'Connor 'had spoken disrespectfully' of him. Apparently, this caused Patrick to burst into tears and he retorted that he had always spoken to Manning 'in the highest terms'. The two men shook hands and Frederick said, 'O'Connor, I owe you not the slightest animosity, and never did,' after which he left the house on good terms. After his departure, Frederick alleged that Maria said: 'That old villain has been the cause of my losing so much money, and I am determined, as I am a living woman in this room, to have my revenge upon him.' When her husband questioned her intentions, she replied: 'I will shoot him if I am hanged for it, as he has deceived me many times,' later adding, 'there would be no more harm in shooting him than in shooting a dog. He was a perfect brute.'

Frederick Manning alleged that he tried to convince his wife to relinquish her plans for vengeance. In response, she outlined her scheme, which consisted of seeing O'Connor frequently to find out how much money he was worth. Manning verified that this plan had been carried out and that Patrick had even made out his will in Maria's favour, bequeathing her £1,300. After this, she reportedly told her husband: 'Now, I shall begin to cook his goose.' However, at this time, Frederick was offered a position as a sales representative with a stationer's, with a salary of £2 per week. Due to the potential benefit of a regular income, he apparently implored Maria to relinquish her plans. She replied, 'You fool! You would never be able to save the amount which I shall get by murdering O'Connor.' She even withheld his hat and coat so that he could not take the position.

After reaffirming her intentions, Mrs Manning set about preparing for the murder. She purchased the shovel and began to dig the grave. This took two or three weeks to complete. When it was finished, she induced their lodger, William Massey, to write to O'Connor inviting him to dinner at Minver Place to meet his sister, who had travelled down from Derbyshire, on 26 July. However, when Patrick arrived at the house, she told him that William and his sister had gone out. She pleaded with Patrick to stay, but he left again and declined to return.

About ten days later, Maria sent the letter to Patrick which would bring him to Minver Place for the final time. When he arrived, the table was set for five, as Maria maintained the pretence that William Massey and his sister would be dining with them. No food was prepared. She told the visitor that the Masseys were upstairs dressing for dinner. Saying that Miss Massey was a very 'particular' young woman, she asked Patrick to go downstairs to wash his hands. At this time, Frederick was upstairs in his bedroom. A minute later, he heard a shot ring out. As he rushed down the stairs, he met Maria, who said: 'Thank God, I have made him all right at last.'

Frederick told the chaplain that he had found Patrick in the kitchen lying over the grave. He was moaning. Frederick stated: 'As I never liked him very well, I battered in his skull with the ripping chisel.' Maria took Patrick's keys and left the house, while Frederick went out into the garden and sat on the wall smoking a pipe. At this point in the confession, Manning drew another map of the house on which he marked the position of the body, and the chaplain showed it to the reporter. Maria later returned with the railway shares and some of Patrick's jewellery. Frederick also revealed that his wife had cut the clothes from the body and burned them in the fire. As well as the lime, they had poured a pint of vitriol over his remains, which they had bought from a local oil merchant.

Frederick Manning disclosed to Reverend Rowe the whereabouts of the missing crowbar which he used to bludgeon Patrick O'Connor to death. He revealed that he had wrapped it in brown paper and sent it to Lewes with a label bearing the name of 'Mrs Smith' – the same name as was written on the luggage boxes left by Maria Manning at London Bridge station. A Brighton railway clerk located the weapon at Lewes railway station just as Manning had described. The *London Daily News* reported that 'a considerable quantity of hair was adhering to it, and the murderous weapon was very much stained with blood.'

Although this final discovery was not made by the police, the officers involved in bringing the Mannings to justice were rewarded for their 'extraordinary exertion and skill in detecting'. Inspector Yates, who had led the investigation on the ground at Southwark Division, received the highest award of £20. John Haynes and Charles Field, the Scotland Yard senior detectives, received £15 each, with the former also being credited with the excellent organisation of the policing of the execution which, according to the newspapers, resulted in a notable absence of thieves. The other officers were awarded payments between £2 and £10. The highest amounts were given to Detectives Jonathan Whicher and Edward Langley, as well as PC Henry Barnes. PC James Burton received slightly less than his colleague, with a payment of £8. PC William Sopp, who recovered the shovel, was paid £2. The Edinburgh police were also rewarded, with Superintendent Richard Moxey receiving £30. (He died two years later from 'disease of the stomach'.)

It was the following summer that Charles Dickens and his colleagues invited the Scotland Yard detectives to the 'social conference'. As they sat round a table in the middle of the room, with glasses and cigars, he interrogated them about their investigative work, observing that: 'Every man of them, in a glance, immediately takes an inventory of the furniture and an accurate sketch of the editorial presence.' Having lit their cigars and filled their glasses, Dickens opened the discussion by asking about the 'swell mob' (respectable-looking criminals), to which Field replied, after removing his cigar from his lips and waving his hand, that Whicher had the most experience. Detective Whicher duly regaled the gathering with his knowledge 'very concisely and in well-chosen language'. The chat turned to other related topics, such as cracksmen (burglars, especially safe-breakers), fences (receivers of stolen goods), public house dancers and young people who go out 'gonophing' (pickpocketing). After this, the conversation switched to the 'most celebrated and horrible of the great crimes' of the previous two decades, which inevitably focused on the race to track down the Mannings. Detective Sergeant Thornton recounted his experiences of boarding the emigrant ship in the fruitless search for the fugitives.

After further lengthy tales of detective adventures, Dickens concluded his account of the meeting by describing the celebrated law enforcers:

> For ever on the watch, with their wits stretched to the utmost, these officers have, from day to day and year to year, to set themselves against every novelty of trickery and dexterity that the combined imaginations of all the lawless rascals in England can devise.

The 'curious and interesting party' ended at midnight and the detectives left. Dickens's final comment was to claim that 'the officer best acquainted with the swell mob', presumably Whicher, had his pocket picked on the way home.

A year later, Dickens accompanied Inspector Field in his patrols around London. Beginning at the British Museum, he described the detective's modus operandi:

> He is bringing his shrewd eye to bear on every corner of its solitary galleries ... Inspector Field, sagacious, vigilant, lamp in hand, throwing monstrous shadows on the walls and ceilings, passes through the spacious rooms. If a mummy trembled in an atom of its dusty covering, Inspector Field would say, 'Come out of that, Tom Green. I know you!'

On another night, they met at St Giles' police station, where Dickens encountered a lost boy, an intoxicated woman, a pickpocket and an elderly pauper in the cells. Afterwards, the detective and the writer walked together through the infamous rookeries of the surrounding area to Southwark on the south side of the Thames, before crossing the river again to the Ratcliffe Highway. They visited cellar dwellings, crowded outhouses, lodging houses and taverns. Dickens described Field as fearless, calm and at ease in the company of the suspicious characters of London's underworld. He was greeted by members of the criminal fraternity, who deferred to him and laughed at his jokes.

Although Dickens refuted it at the time, it is generally accepted that Charles Field was the inspiration for Inspector Bucket in *Bleak House*, which was first published in serialised form from 1852 to 1853. The author's description of the fictional detective is very similar to that of the real-life investigator: 'He [Inspector Bucket] is a stoutly built, steady-looking, sharp-eyed man in black, of about the middle-age.' Even more convincing are Dickens's frequent references to Bucket's 'fat forefinger', which is reminiscent of his description of Field in *Household Words*:

> When Mr. Bucket has a matter of this pressing interest under his consideration, the fat forefinger seems to rise, to the dignity of a familiar demon. He puts it to his ears, and it whispers information; he puts it to his lips, and it enjoins him to secrecy; he rubs it over his nose, and it sharpens his scent; he shakes it before a guilty man, and it charms him to his destruction.

Charles Frederick Field left the Metropolitan police in 1852 and worked as a private detective. He is famous for having investigated the case of the murderer William Palmer, known as the 'Rugeley poisoner', in 1856. Following Field's retirement, Stephen Thornton was promoted to inspector and took charge of the detective department at Scotland Yard. During his service, he visited America several times in pursuit of forgers and fraudulent bankrupts. Detective Thornton died suddenly of apoplexy while still in service in 1861. The *Morning Advertiser* reported that he was 'respected and esteemed by his superior officers and looked up to with reverence by those of a humbler rank.'

Frederick Shaw continued working as a detective at Scotland Yard until his retirement in 1856, at the age of 48, due to cerebral disease. In the same year, Detective Edward Langley was also discharged because of chronic rheumatism. John Haynes remained in post as superintendent of Southwark Division for seven years, until his discharge in 1856, due to an injury sustained to his legs when a horse suddenly jumped up and pushed him against a post while he was on duty. The 49-year-old was also suffering from rheumatism. At the time of his discharge, Haynes was living in Horsemonger Lane, close to the spot where the Mannings had been hanged. Jonathan Whicher remained at Scotland Yard until 1864, when he retired due to congestion of the brain. During his service, he was known for his involvement in the Road Hill House murder in 1860, which resulted in the conviction of Constance Kent for the murder of her young half-brother. Detective Whicher was the inspiration for Sergeant Cuff in *The Moonstone* by Wilkie Collins, published in 1868.

The efforts and expertise of the Scotland Yard detectives who brought the Mannings to justice remained in the public consciousness long after the event. This was also true for the notorious perpetrators, particularly Maria

Manning. In the months following the execution, the rumour was circulated that the dress worn by Mrs Manning during the trial and subsequent hanging led to the unpopularity of black satin, due to women being reluctant to wear this colour and fabric in revulsion towards her heinous crime. This belief persisted for over a century. In 1981, author Albert Borowitz conducted a study of fashion magazines and textile dealers' advertisements in the years following the Bermondsey murder. He found that there was no evidence that this style of dress had fallen out of fashion.

However, the legacy of the Mannings continued in other ways. Within three weeks of their execution, Madame Tussauds was advertising the exhibition of wax models of both Maria and Frederick in the Chamber of Horrors. They remained there for 122 years, until 1971. The initial display comprised a plaster cast of Patrick O'Connor and a model of the kitchen where he was murdered. In the catalogue for July 1854, the following items connected to the Mannings' case were also listed: the pistol and a letter about the weapon from the pawnbroker, the crowbar, Maria's death mask (which had been added by the proprietor's son, Joseph), framed engravings of the couple and a broadsheet recounting the details of the murder. The exhibits also included the original copy of Frederick's confession.

The Mannings were also represented in china figurines. Between 1840 and 1880, Staffordshire potters produced miniatures of celebrities. These included famous criminals such as the Mannings. At least two sets of the murderous couple were fashioned and they depict Maria with a round face and full, rosy cheeks. She is wearing a dress with a pink skirt with a dark blue day coat and a white bonnet, rather than the black satin dress, for which she had become renowned. Dressed in similar colours, Frederick's expression is more serious. Bareheaded and wearing a rather oversized top coat, he is leaning with his elbow on a pedestal with a document in his hand. They look more like a respectable middle-class married couple than convicted killers.

The memory of the Bermondsey murder also lingered in the mind of Charles Dickens and, three years after witnessing the execution, he was still haunted by the spectacle. In 1852, he published an article in *Household Words*, in which he shared that, as he struggled to sleep at night, the image of the Mannings hanging from the scaffold would invade his nocturnal thoughts:

> those two forms dangling on the top of the entrance gateway –
> the man's, a limp, loose suit of clothes as if the man had gone

out of them; the woman's, a fine shape, so elaborately corseted and artfully dressed, that it was quite unchanged in its trim appearance as it slowly swung from side to side. ('Lying Awake', *Household Words*, 30 October 1852)

He described how, during the weeks following the hanging, he had not been able to think of the prison without seeing 'the two figures still hanging in the morning air.' This continued until, one night, when he was strolling past the gloomy prison walls in the deserted street, he saw for himself that they were not still there and this helped him to push the sight from his thoughts: 'my fancy was persuaded, as it were, to take them down and bury them within the precincts of the jail, where they have lain ever since.'

However, when Dickens published *Bleak House*, his description of Lady Dedlock's French maid, Hortense, bore a striking resemblance to the woman who had invaded his dreams:

> My Lady's maid is a Frenchwoman of two and thirty, from somewhere in the southern country about Avignon and Marseilles, a large-eyed brown woman with black hair who would be handsome but for a certain feline mouth and general uncomfortable tightness of face, rendering the jaws too eager and the skull too prominent. There is something indefinably keen and wan about her anatomy, and she has a watchful way of looking out of the corners of her eyes without turning her head which could be pleasantly dispensed with, especially when she is in an ill humour and near knives.

The similarity between the fictional maid and the well-known female murderer was confirmed in 1890 by JP Donald Nicoll. He had participated in the Mannings' trial at the Old Bailey as a sheriff fifty years earlier and he wrote about his experience in his memoir. Nicoll revealed that Charles Dickens had been present in court during the proceedings and that he had depicted her accurately in the character of Hortense:

> Maria Manning's broken English, her impatient gestures, and her volubility are ... imitated in the novel 'Bleak House' with marvellous exactness; and in the frequent dramatic adaptations of the work of Dickens for the stage, the French lady's maid and

murderess described in 'Bleak House' is ever made the vehicle to demonstrate the dramatic power of the most talented of actresses.

One hundred and seventy-five years later, the Bermondsey murder is still a prominent and infamous historical homicide. Like the Scotland Yard detectives, such as Inspector Charles Field and his 'corpulent forefinger', the notorious Maria Manning has been immortalised by the pen of Charles Dickens.

Bibliography

Archival sources

The National Archives

CRIM 1/6/1
CRIM 6/7
CRIM 6/72
CRIM 12/9
CUST 40/30
DPP 4/2
HO 44/39/21
HO 44/39/22
HO 44/39/23
MEPO 3/54

Online printed primary sources

The British Library, www.bl.uk
The British Newspaper Archive, britishnewspaperarchive.co.uk
The Proceedings of the Old Bailey, 1674–1913, www.oldbaileyonline.org
The Wellcome Collection, wellcomecollection.org

Published primary sources

The Bell's New Weekly Messenger
John Bull
Caledonian Mercury

The Daily News
The Era
Evening Mail
The Express
The Globe
The Illustrated London News
The Jersey Times
John Bull
Lloyd's Weekly London Newspaper
The London Evening Standard
Morning Advertiser
The Morning Chronicle
The Morning Herald
The Morning Post
The Scotsman
The Standard
The Sun
The Times
The Tipperary Free Press
The Tipperary Vindicator

Furniss Harold, ed. *Famous Crimes Past and Present* 6, no. 70. London: Harold Furniss, 1901.

Huish, Robert. *The Progress of Crime or the Authentic Memoirs of Maria Manning*. London: Robert Huish, 1849.

The Bermondsey Murder: A Full Report of the Trial of Frederick George Manning and Maria Manning for the Murder of Patrick O'Connor. London: W.M. Clark, 1849.

Verbatim Report of the Trial of George and Maria Manning for the Murder of Patrick O'Connor. London: George Vickers, 1849.

Books

Ackroyd, Peter. *London: The Biography*. London: Vintage, 2001.

Ackroyd, Peter. *Dickens: Public Life and Private Passion*. London: BBC, 2002.

Alpert, Michael. *London 1849: A Victorian Murder Story*. Harlow: Pearson, 2004.

Altick, Richard D. *Victorian Studies in Scarlet*. London: J.M. Dent & Sons Ltd., 1970.

Baxter, Carol. *The Peculiar Case of the Electric Constable: A True Tale of Passion, Poison & Pursuit.* London: Oneworld, 2013.

Boast, Mary. *The Story of Bermondsey*, 3rd ed. London: London Borough of Southwark, 1998.

Borowitz, Albert. *The Woman Who Murdered Black Satin.* Columbus: Ohio State University Press, 1981.

Byrne, Richard. *Prisons and Punishments of London.* London: Harrap, 1989.

Cobb, Belton. *The First Detectives.* London: Faber, 1957.

Collins, Philip. *Dickens and Crime.* London: Macmillan, 1962.

Dickens, Charles. *Bleak House.* London: Bradbury & Evans, 1853.

Flanders, Judith. *The Invention of Murder: How the Victorians Revelled in Death and Detection and Created Modern Crime.* London: HarperPress, 2011.

Guy, W.A., D. Ferrier and W.A. Smith. *Victorian CSI.* Stroud: The History Press, 2009.

Humphrey, Stephen. *Southwark, Bermondsey and Rotherhithe in Old Photographs.* Stroud: Sutton Publishing, 1995.

Humphrey, Stephen. *Bermondsey & Rotherhithe Remembered.* Stroud: Tempus, 2004.

Lane, Brian. *The Murder Club.* London: Harrap, 1988.

Lock, Joan. *Dreadful Deeds and Awful Murders: Scotland Yard's First Detectives 1829–1878.* Taunton: Barn Owl Books, 1990.

Nicoll, Donald. *Man's Revenge : Anecdotes and Causes Célèbres.* London: King, Sell & Railton Ltd., 1890.

Stratmann, Linda. *Trial of the Mannings.* London: Mango Books, 2021.

Summerscale, Kate. *The Suspicions of Mr Whicher: Or the Murder at Road Hill House.* London: Bloomsbury, 2008.

Tomalin, Claire. *Charles Dickens: A Life.* London: Penguin, 2011.

Wilson, Patrick. *Murderess: A Study of the Women Executed in Britain since 1843.* London: Michael Joseph, 1971.

Journal articles

Dickens, Charles. 'Detective Police' in *Household Words*, 27 July and 10 August 1850.

Dickens, Charles. 'Lying Awake' in *Household Words*, 30 October 1852.

Dickens, Charles. 'On Duty with Inspector Field' in *Household Words*, 14 June 1851.

Acknowledgements

Firstly, I would like to thank the staff at The National Archives for their help during my research. It really is my favourite place to work as it is a veritable treasure trove, and you never know what you might discover. Thank you to the British Library too, where the service is always friendly and efficient. Also, it has been wonderful to have another chance to collaborate with Pen and Sword Books and thank you to everyone who has supported this project, especially to commissioning editor, Harriet Fielding, and to Michelle Higgs for her insightful and invaluable editing.

One of the joys of researching and writing historical true crime is meeting and chatting to interested, and interesting, people along the way. I have been thrilled to have the opportunity to share my work-in-progress with others at talks, through interviews and on social media. Many thanks to all those who have joined me in my exploration of this historical case so far. I would like to give special thanks to Stewart Evans, who kindly shared with me a unique collection of images and articles relating to the Bermondsey murder, which had been originally amassed by William Courthope Forman. In 1922, Mr Forman approached a publisher with a proposal to use the material for a book on the Mannings, but it never came to fruition. I feel immensely privileged to be able to publish some of his work now, a century later. I would like to thank Lindsay Siviter for generously sharing some of her historical artefacts relating to this case. Also, thanks to Geoff Fairbairn for sending me information and images of Bermondsey, for which I am very grateful.

Finally, I would like to thank my family – Warren, Ella and Ethan – who joined me enthusiastically in the exploration of the Bermondsey streets where their ancestors lived, and where this crime took place.

Index